ALSO BY JULIE GILBERT

Opposite Attraction:
The Lives of Erich Maria Remarque and Paulette Goddard

Ferber:
A Biography of Edna Ferber and Her Circle

Umbrella Steps (a novel)

GIANT LOVE

GIANT LOVE

Edna Ferber, Her Best-Selling Novel of Texas,
and the Making of a Classic American Film

JULIE GILBERT

PANTHEON

NEW YORK

Published in the United States by Pantheon Books,
a division of Penguin Random House LLC, New York,
and distributed in Canada by
Penguin Random House Canada Limited, Toronto.

Pantheon Books and colophon are registered
trademarks of Penguin Random House LLC.

Library of Congress Cataloging-in-Publication Data
Names: Gilbert, Julie Goldsmith, author.
Title: Giant love : Edna Ferber, her best-selling novel of Texas, and the making of a classic
American film / Julie Gilbert.
Description: First edition. | New York : Pantheon, 2024. | Includes bibliographical
references and index.
Identifiers: LCCN 2024012851 | ISBN 9781524748432 (hardcover) |
ISBN 9781524748449 (ebook)
Subjects: LCSH: Ferber, Edna, 1887–1968. Giant. | Ferber, Edna, 1887–1968—Criticism
and interpretation. | American fiction—20th century. | Ferber, Edna, 1887–1968 Giant—
Film adaptations. | Giant (Motion picture) | Stevens, George, 1904–1975—Criticism and
interpretation. | Motion pictures—United States—History—20th century.
Classification: LCC PS3511.E46 Z674 2024 | DDC 813/.52—dc23/eng/20240729
LC record available at https://lccn.loc.gov/2024012851

www.pantheonbooks.com

Jacket photographs: (bottom) James Dean by Floyd McCarty/mptvimages.com;
(inset) Portrait of Edna Ferber, c. 1935. Private collection. Courtesy of Julie Gilbert.
Jacket design by Jenny Carrow

Printed in the United States of America
First Edition

2 4 6 8 9 7 5 3 1

This book is for Bob Holof, my own personal giant.

Contents

GIANT LOVE

Preface

My great-aunt Edna Ferber would periodically say to my mother, "Someday I'll tell you everything." Maybe she meant to, but she never got around to it. In the years preceding Ferber's death, the "everything" got increasingly larger in our imaginations until it became giant—as enormous as the state of Texas.

In the late 1970s, as a young biographer on the trail of Ferber's life, I was able to surmise that at least a couple of secrets harbored had to do with four men. One of them was an early beau of Ferber's named Bert Boyden, a newspaperman out of Chicago; another was her collaborator George S. Kaufman; then there was the director George Stevens, who perhaps borrowed her heart along with her novel *Giant*; and the fourth—and most wrenching—was the young actor, soon to be star, James Dean.

As Ferber tended her secrets, her fame became increasingly public and never really subsided until shortly before her death in 1968 at the age of eighty-three.

There were two more books of hers published after the phenomenal success of *Giant* in 1952: *Ice Palace* in 1958 and *A Kind of Magic* in 1963. *A Kind of Magic,* her last book, was the conclusion of her first autobiography, *A Peculiar Treasure*, published in 1939. Ferber was nothing if not thorough. She ended her active life with published words.

Ironically, her last spoken words, expressed while fending off death in her own bed in her Park Avenue apartment, were numbers. She was constantly, ritualistically counting down from one hundred. After decades of rigorous practice, she had trained herself to be only practical. Counting would keep her mind on the task at hand. Uttering the name of some long-lost dream of love would not.

I have devoted a good deal of my professional life and personal thoughts to my great-aunt, whom I loved and admired without question. She was the one who left "average" in the dust, catapulting way-over-normal expectations for a woman born at the approach of the twentieth century. In Kalamazoo, Michigan, in 1885, the standards for a girl were comely, calm, neat, frugal, and, perhaps, musical. She would soon learn the domestic arts of sewing, cooking, and housekeeping. She could be clever enough, but without an intellectual bent. If she knew sums, it would be all the more meritorious later on, when at marriageable age she would already know how to manage a household.

Ferber took early stock of her role in her Immigrant American Dream family. Her mother, Julia Neumann, was a dominant, high-spirited, intelligent beauty, born in Milwaukee of Jewish German heritage. Her father, Jacob Ferber, was a gentle, hardworking, patient man who had emigrated from Hungary with his parents when he was seventeen years old. Her older sister, Fannie—"the pretty one"—was graced with domestic virtues: seamstress, cook, decorator. No one was particularly passionate about the arts; all were average readers. So, because there was ample room, Ferber became the Sarah Bernhardt of the family. Not only did she have a flair for and love of the theater, but she was a voracious reader and an energetic writer. Stocky, with blunt features and unruly hair, she had a gift for people, language, and communication. Her overwhelming vitality served as a magnet; people flocked around her. She figured out early that although she would never be a prom queen, she could have something more lasting. Her looks seemed relatively immaterial to her—and to others—as her inner life became increasingly more colorful, her curiosity more rewarding, and her strivings more applauded. She was one of the most popular girls at Ryan High School in Appleton, Wisconsin; she was editor in chief of the school newspaper and yearbook. At seventeen, she was already experiencing a keen sense of herself.

But her young life had a downside. Ever since she was born, her family had been nomadic. Dry goods was the Ferber trade, and they moved the location of their store several times, always touching luck yet always with the wind at their backs. Although a good deal of the Ferber/Neumann clan had settled in Chicago when they left Hungary and Germany, Julia and Jacob had set down a stake in Kalamazoo when Julia became pregnant with her second child. She had counted on having a boy and had already chosen "Edward Victor" as his name. She was convinced that a boy would complete her family. After the delivery, "Ed" was reluctantly changed to "Edna."

Sisters: baby Edna (left) and Fannie, 1885

After six years of their store being solvent in Kalamazoo, Jacob had a vision of relocating to Chicago and opening a store in the limelight of the World's Fair. The venture went flat and the family migrated to Ottumwa, Iowa, where supposedly they would flourish once more. Contrary to an open-armed midwestern friendliness, this was where Ferber came upon raw anti-Semitism. Every day as she walked to school through the cornfields, she would encounter a little golden-haired girl sitting atop a fence to one of the farms, who would bray at her, "Sheeny, sheeny, sheeny!" This happened every school day for what seemed like years. Adult males as well rained verbal abuse upon her and her family, even spitting on them and yelling taunts in a mock-Yiddish accent. Although at the time Ferber had no defense, no retorts, she was able to build up an arsenal of outrage against any and every kind of prejudice. It became a battleground within her. She had to consistently expose, examine, and attempt to disarm the scourge of racism.

The family's fortunes flagged in Ottumwa, and so in 1895 they were on the road again. Years later, in retrospect, Ferber sounded wise about her family's diaspora:

> If this did not make for assurance it definitely did give variety and tang to existence. In these ever-shifting scenes there were elements of excitement, of drama. As the English saying goes, what you lose on the swings, you gain on the turnabout.

The Ferbers' family business, circa 1890

All this shifting geography meant that constantly I was leaving childhood playmates, girlhood friends, having to form new human contacts, make fresh adjustments, fitting the viewpoint to the new view. With this the child and the girl and the young woman frequently knew loneliness and sometimes fear and a nameless depression. But just as frequently it was challenging, and tough and educational. All this uprooting and readjustment may have been frightful for my psyche but it was fine for my later life as a writer.

The next stop was a fortuitous one. In Appleton, Wisconsin, it all fell into place for a while. The dry-goods business, called My Store, flourished, as did the girls. Fannie was, as ever, pretty and handy, and Edna earned the "smart and popular" title in the traditionally challenging high-school years. She treated being editor of her school paper and the yearbook with an easy, sunny competency, and right after high school she took courses at a junior college, acing a job as a cub reporter

In Appleton, Wisconsin: Edna (third from left), the Ryan High
School graduate, class of 1902

for the *Appleton Daily Crescent*. This helped the family financially when
Jacob Ferber's eyesight began to fail. When funds became scarcer, Julia
Ferber alchemized into a rather shrewd businesswoman, somewhat
reversing their dwindling finances. While Fannie took on the household chores, Edna took on the wide world of Milwaukee, obtaining a
job as a reporter on the *Milwaukee Journal*. The family experienced four
productive, occasionally fun years until again came the all-too-familiar
sickening swerve.

Edna was working in her fourth year in Milwaukee when she was
summoned home to Appleton. Her father's optic nerves had progres-
sively shrunk to blindness, and her mother needed her help running the
business. "Edna's head is good" was Julia's most glowing compliment.

Edna's promising career in journalism was cut off by her family's
woes. Her love for her gentle father was ringed with resentment as she
fought against perceiving him as weak and useless. Her proud, indomitable mother became her scourge, and her spirited sister, an irritant.

When Jacob died a short time later, in September of 1909 after four
days of an undisclosed illness, Edna had what today would be recognized as a nervous breakdown, but at the time was termed "anemia."

First novel: *Dawn O'Hara: The Girl Who Laughed*. The manuscript was saved from the trash bin by Edna's mother, Julia Ferber.

She drew inward and became listless, which was unlike her, and she lost weight, which was most uncharacteristic. While recovering, she began to write a novel. As she grew stronger, it took shape as *Dawn O'Hara: The Girl Who Laughed*; but once she read the finished product, she judged it a failure and tossed it into the trash. Fate directed Julia Ferber to find it there, dust it off, and send it to a leading New York publisher, the Frederick A. Stokes Company, which published it in 1911.

And this is where the ascent of Edna Ferber began. The novel was met with welcoming reviews, and she was steadily gaining a reputation for her quintessentially midwestern short stories collectively known as "the Emma McChesney stories," which traced the picaresque adventures of a traveling saleswoman, a divorcée with a young son in tow. President Theodore Roosevelt, a big fan of the series, called her "the best woman writer of her day in America." Her newfound fame eventually led her and her family to the welcoming arms of success in New York City and a Broadway production called *Our Mrs. McChesney* (1915), which she wrote with George V. Hobart and which starred the "divine" Ethel Barrymore as Emma.

Prior to the family's move, they became accustomed to Ferber's growing celebrity—from Appleton's darling to the tyro of Milwaukee journalism, back to Appleton as a first novelist, and then on to Chicago, where they returned so many years later to Ferber's fame as a short-story writer and novelist. In her next novel, *Fanny Herself*, published in 1917, the characteristics of her heroine supposedly resembled those of her sister, Fannie, who felt it was a mixed tribute. However, when Ferber reminisced, the thrust was somewhat different:

Edna with colleagues at the Republican-and-Democratic
Conventions of 1912 in Chicago, as a reporter for the
Milwaukee Journal

I started *Fanny Herself*, the story of a Jewish family in a small
Wisconsin town, which I called Winnebago, Wisconsin. A good
deal of it was imaginary, a good deal of it was real. Certainly
my mother, idealized, went to make up Molly Brandeis. Bits
and pieces of myself crept into the character of Fanny Brandeis.
Appleton undoubtably was the book's background . . . The first
half is good. I recall having written it with zest and even enjoyment. The second half is weak and floundering. The trouble
was that in the middle of the book I killed Molly Brandeis
because she was walking off with the story under the heroine's
very eyes. When Molly Brandeis died, the story died with her.
She was too sustaining and vital to dismiss . . . Book characters
must have their way or they take a terrible revenge.

Then, in 1921, came *The Girls*, which simultaneously lauded and
skewered the trajectory of the midwestern matron. It was her first

Collected short stories, published in 1914

novel to explore multiple generations, establishing a recurrent theme in her work. It is the story of the Thrift women: a great-aunt, a niece, and a great-niece, living on Chicago's South Side, and determined to climb the rungs of society. The novel recounts six decades of middle-class history and intergenerational squabbles. Ferber puts her firm insignia of the sexes on this novel: strong women, weak men. "*The Girls* was a mature novel," Ferber claimed. "I felt it marked a definite advance and that it was by a large margin the best piece of writing I had done."

If one had asked Ferber and her boosters if she had any female writer rivals at that time, the answer most likely would have been no. However, there was another Jewish woman novelist who grew up in the Midwest: Fannie Hurst, born October 1889, four years Ferber's junior, whose short stories and novels became highly popular after World War I. Her specialty was writing about commonplace characters, often women, who were nonetheless vital, plaintive, and quite progressive in their romantic and social needs. Her characters were coping with assimilation from midwestern life to big-city demands. She depicted, like Ferber, aspects of race relations (*Back Street, Imitation of Life*) and women's acceleration in society (*Four Daughters*). She, too, saw many of her novels translated into successful movies. Her personal life detoured from Ferber's in that she married early—in 1915—and remained married until the death of her husband in 1952, whereupon she continued writing weekly letters to him until her own death in 1968.

Considerably more experimental than Ferber, although married, Hurst took a lover, an Arctic explorer named Vilhjalmur Stefansson with whom she had a long affair. In 1958, Hurst published her autobiography, called *Anatomy of Me*, in which she describes some of her famous

Edna (left) and Julia after their move to
Chicago, circa 1915

associations, such as with Eleanor Roosevelt. In their "six degrees of
separation," she never mentions Ferber, who also had a close association
with Mrs. Roosevelt.

Since I have written Ferber's biography, *Ferber: A Biography of Edna
Ferber and Her Circle* (Doubleday/Applause Books), I will be brief here
and provide only a sketch of her dazzling achievements leading up to
Giant, which, for all intents and purposes, seems the most vast.

Ferber and George S. Kaufman always designed large casts in their
plays, while in real life Ferber's circle was compact and close-knit. There
was Julia, her mother; Fannie, her sister; Fannie's husband, Jack Fox;
and their two girls, Janet—my mother—and Mina. Later, Janet became
an actress and Mina a journalist. Jack Fox died in early middle age, quietly, during one of his wife's card games; and in 1929 Fannie, Janet, and
Mina moved from Chicago to New York City, where Edna was already
a literary lioness, to form a four-woman tribe.

George S. Kaufman, Ferber's
favorite collaborator, circa
1927

Earlier, once in New York, circa 1919, Ferber was embraced by her successful peers and invited to join their small circle for lunches at the Algonquin Hotel on West Forty-Fourth Street. Sitting at the Round Table, she was flanked by Kaufman, Alexander Woollcott, Marc Connelly, Dorothy Parker, Heywood Hale Broun, Robert Benchley, Franklin P. Adams, Harold Ross, Neysa McMein, and occasionally Harpo Marx and Helen Hayes. There are variations on who was there, who were the regulars, who dispensed the most pungent quotes. Edna Ferber was one of the first and foremost in the mix. What she wasn't, however, was a devout regular. She was too busy turning out novels and collaborating on plays with Kaufman, who had requested her hand in playwriting after he had taken her measure of salty, amusing retorts in those early days around the table. To his "Satire is what closes on Saturday night" was her "If American politics

Edna, age thirty or thirty-one, a successful midwestern writer, circa 1916

are too dirty for women to take part in, there's something wrong with American politics." They formed their collaboration at the doorway of their flourishing careers. She was a well-regarded short-story writer and novelist who would win a Pulitzer Prize for the novel *So Big*. Kaufman, already a successful drama critic for *The New York Times*, would go on to write the hit plays *Merton of the Movies* and *Beggar on Horseback* with Marc Connelly and *The Cocoanuts*, which was wackily graced by the Marx Brothers. Both Ferber and Kaufman were popular nonconformists. Theirs was a relationship as complicated as it was successful, yielding *The Royal Family*, *Dinner at Eight*, *Stage Door*, and the lesser-known *Minick*, *The Land Is Bright*, and *Bravo!*

Kaufman's friend and biographer, Howard Teichmann, wrote of their pairing:

> In many ways she was very much like Kaufman: middle-western birthplace, same German-Jewish background, same training as a newspaper reporter, same discipline toward work. In other ways she was the direct opposite of Kaufman. She was small in physical stature, and a great believer in exercise. She had great personal courage, an overwhelming desire to travel, to seek new people, new places, new ideas. She did not have Kaufman's wit, but she did have the ability to write rich, deep love scenes.

Love scenes written but not lived? I once dared to ask Aunt Edna if she was ever lonely. Her face was like stone for a moment, and then a spark of something— mischief, maybe—in her sherry-colored brown eyes: "Oh, no. Never," she said emphatically. "The characters in my books are my friends. They provide sustenance." That was it. Door closed.

William Allen White, editor of *The Emporia Gazette*, and Edna, circa 1923

Barbara Stanwyck as Selina and
Dickie Moore as a young Dirk in the
1932 film of Ferber's Pulitzer Prize–
winning 1924 novel, *So Big*

Ferber's next novel, *So Big*, published in 1924, was a major achievement and earned her the Pulitzer Prize in 1925. Of *So Big* Ferber said:

I had thought *The Girls* would be a success. I never dreamed that *So Big* would be. I wrote it against my judgement; I wanted to write it. It was the story of a middle-aged woman living on a truck farm just outside of Chicago. Nothing ever really happened in the book. It had no plot at all, as book plots go. It had a theme, but you had to read it for yourself between the lines. It was the story of the triumph of failure. There was in it practi-

Samuel Goldwyn and Edna in Hollywood, circa 1926

cally no action. The book's high point came when Selina drove to town with a load of cabbages, turnips and beets . . . I knew literally nothing about farming or truck gardening. The entire background was farm. The South Water Street night market chapter was written purely out of my imagination. I meant to visit the market . . . but never did. I wanted to write the book more than anything else in the world.

Then Ferber makes a statement that is probably the most revealing about her abilities as a novelist: "I can project myself into any age, environment, condition, situation, character or emotion that interests me deeply. I need never have experienced it, or seen it or, to my knowledge, heard or read about it." This sounds magical. Harry Houdini, under his original name of Ehrich Weiss, had also lived in Appleton, Wisconsin, when Ferber was a girl. Perhaps some of his illusions and escapes had rubbed off on her.

The well-known journalist and editor William Allen White was a

The 1936 movie *Show Boat*, directed by James Whale. Ferber was a big admirer of the picture, which starred Irene Dunne and Allan Jones, with Paul Robeson as Joe. She was less than taken with the 1951 MGM remake directed by George Sidney, feeling it was too lavish and not in keeping with her story.

friend and champion of Ferber's. As a Pulitzer Prize voter, he was able to successfully exercise his zeal for *So Big*, enabling Ferber to come out on top.

Three and a half movies were made from the novel. The first adaptation was a 1924 silent film, directed by Charles Brabin and starring Colleen Moore. A smaller version of the story was made into a short film in 1930 with Helen Jerome Eddy. The next version, in 1932, was pre-Code. It was produced by Warner Bros., directed by William A. Wellman, and starred Barbara Stanwyck, one of Ferber's favorite actresses in one of her favorite creations, the character of Selina Peake. The *New York Daily Mirror* called her performance "exquisite and magnificent." The exotic note was Bette Davis in the good-girl role of Dallas O'Mara. It was the second of eleven movies that Davis would make for Jack L. Warner.

The final version of the classic was made in 1953, again with Warner Bros. producing. It was directed by Robert Wise and featured Jane Wyman, Sterling Hayden, Nancy Olson, and Steve Forrest. In this last, the story was deemed "dated" by *New York Times* critic Bosley Crowther, and "loaded with some typical Hollywood flaws." However, Crowther tips his cap to the first Mrs. Ronald Reagan: "For the better part of the picture, we are largely indebted to Jane Wyman . . . who holds up right through to the end, and the character she sets throughout the first part stands firm amid the flow of glycerin tears."

In 1926 came Ferber's groundbreaking novel *Show Boat*. Two years earlier, her first collaboration with George S. Kaufman had resulted in the play called *Minick*, whose tryout in New London spelled disaster. A postmortem was held in the hotel room of the producer, Winthrop Ames, whom Ferber recalled saying, "Never mind, boys and girls! Next time I'll tell you what we'll do. We won't bother with tryouts. We'll all charter a show boat and we'll all just drift down the rivers, playing the towns as we come to them, and we'll never get off the boat. It'll be wonderful!" Ferber's response: "What's a show boat?"

As was her stock-in-trade, the novel chronicles three generations of a family: performers on a floating theater called the *Cotton Blossom*, presenting plays for small towns all along the Mississippi River from the 1880s to the 1920s. It combined an irresistible story of a bygone day along with a tough depiction of racial issues. *New York Times* critic Louis Kronenberger wrote in his review: "Miss Ferber . . . establishes herself as one of those reviving first-rate story-telling."

Opening back-to-back on Broadway in December 1927 came the productions of Kaufman and Ferber's *The Royal Family*, on the 28th, and, a day earlier, the musical version of *Show Boat*, with its book and lyrics by Oscar Hammerstein II and score by Jerome Kern. On both opening nights Ferber took her dinner on a tray at home. She reflected some years later: "I am now somewhat ashamed to confess that I never saw the opening performance of *Show Boat* or the opening performance of *The Royal Family*. I don't know why. I deeply regret it. They were spectacular, they were enormously exciting events. I couldn't bring myself to go. It must have been a psychological quirk which I was powerless to overcome. I suppose I cared too deeply."

There were three film versions of *Show Boat*. The first, in 1929, was conceived as a silent and initially reflected the novel more than it did the stage musical; later, scenes with sound were added that incorporated two of the songs. It was released by Universal in two editions: one of them wholly silent, for theaters not yet equipped for sound, and one with the added sound and music. The producer was Carl Laemmle and the director was Harry A. Pollard; and leading the cast were Laura La Plante as Magnolia, Joseph Schildkraut as Gaylord Ravenal, Otis Harlan as Cap'n Andy, and Alma Rubens as Julie. The two songs from the musical—both "sung" by La Plante (dubbed by the uncredited Eva Olivetti)—were "Ol' Man River" and "Can't Help Lovin' Dat Man." La Plante lip-synched two other songs in this version, one of them a "coon song" from the early 1900s titled, cringingly, "Coon, Coon, Coon."

The second version, in 1936, was the full-blown Kern-Hammerstein musical. This one was produced by Universal Pictures and Carl Laemmle Jr., directed by James Whale, and written by Hammerstein. It starred Irene Dunne (Magnolia), Allan Jones (Gaylord), Charles Winninger (Cap'n Andy), Paul Robeson (Joe), Helen Morgan (Julie), Hattie McDaniel (Queenie), and Helen Westley (Parthy). This has been, for *Show Boat* purists, the favorite. History was written all over it. Robeson, for whom the role was originally written, had already appeared in the London production in 1928 and then in the Broadway revival of 1932. He and his performance of "Ol' Man River" were so legendary that he actually got away with changing some of the lyrics to make the language less offensive to contemporary audiences. Irene Dunne had been brought into the original Broadway production to replace Norma Terris, and then gone out in the touring company in 1929. Director James Whale expended every effort to honor the original production.

And then there was the 1951 MGM extravaganza, directed by George Sidney. Kathryn Grayson was Magnolia; Howard Keel, Gaylord; Joe E. Brown, Cap'n Andy; Agnes Moorehead, Parthy; Ava Gardner, Julie; William Warfield, Joe; with Marge and Gower Champion as Ellie and Frank. It was shot in Technicolor, so that the material feels as broad as the screen. There is nothing intimate about this high-gloss version, which was the most financially successful of all the film adaptations, and the second-highest-grossing film of that year.

Ferber's next best-selling novel was *Cimarron* in 1929, depicting the development of Oklahoma following the Land Rush of 1889. A sense of geographical bliss was hers while writing it as the house guest of Louis Bromfield, an extremely popular writer of the day, all but forgotten now. His splendid chateau in Saint-Jean-de-Luz in the French Basque country served as inspiration for Ferber: "If *Cimarron* had bounce and vitality it was because I, stuffed with sunshine and the Spanish one's [the Bromfields' Spanish cook's] food that summer, had too. The writing of *Cimarron* went steadily on in this gay but secluded environment. Nothing could have been farther from Oklahoma, not only geographically but in spirit, background and feeling. That was good, that was what I liked. Here there was nothing so real as to make an impact that would jar the reality of the Oklahoma in which I was really living."

Cimarron, completed ten days after the stock market crashed, was a combination of elation and disappointment for Ferber. It sold more than two hundred thousand copies, and was, in Ferber's words, "made into a superb motion picture, the finest motion picture that has ever been made of any book of mine." Conversely, she was bitterly disappointed. The critics judged it as a colorful, romantic, Western American novel. Ferber did not see it that way. She felt the novel had been written with "a hard and ruthless purpose. It was, and is, a malevolent picture of what is known as American womanhood and American sentimentality. It contains paragraphs and even chapters of satire and, I am afraid, bitterness, but I doubt that more than a dozen people ever knew this."

Eerily, Oklahoma's reception of *Cimarron* was a harbinger of Texas

Cayuse Kate

The Cayuse was a member of a once nomadic indigenous tribe, located primarily in eastern Oregon and Washington.

and *Giant* years later. In the words of local Oklahoma historian Angie Debo, the novel was "rooted in nowhere." By Ferber's account:

> Oklahoma read the book and stood up on its hind legs and howled. By now I had realized that an American regional novel always is resented by the people of its locale, unless, of course, all descriptions and background are sweetness and light. Oklahoma had all the self-consciousness and inferiority feeling of the new and unsure. A flood of letters poured in upon me. They ranged from remonstrance to vilification. Oklahoma newspapers published editorials from the mildest from which I can select a plum or two: "This Ferber woman is the most unpleasant personality that has ever come into Oklahoma . . . Why doesn't she stay in the ghetto where she came from?"

The first of the two movie versions of *Cimarron* was made by RKO Pictures in 1931 as a pre-Code mega-Western. Directed by Wesley Ruggles, it starred Irene Dunne and Richard Dix as Sabra and Yancey Cravat. It was the studio's most costly production to date; its budget of $1.5 million ($25 million today) said a lot for filming in the middle of the Great Depression. The Land Rush scene is still extraordinary today, featuring more than five thousand costumed extras driving covered wagons, surreys, and buckboards. RKO bought eighty-nine acres in Encino, California, to construct this race for a grubstake. The movie won three Academy Awards, for Best Picture, Best Adapted Screenplay, and Best Art Direction.

The next version was produced in 1960 by MGM and directed by Anthony Mann, who was better known for his noir pictures and an uncredited Charles Walters, who took over from Mann during the middle of the filming. It starred Glenn Ford, Maria Schell, Anne Baxter, and Harry Morgan. MGM, less impressively, brought in only a thousand extras for the Land Rush scene, which was filmed in Arizona. Also less impressive was the leading lady, the German-born Schell, who, according to Anne Baxter in her autobiography, *Intermission*, had a mad affair with Ford that didn't last. Toward the end of filming, Baxter writes, "he scarcely glanced or spoke in her direction, and she looked as if she were in shock." MGM would be in shock as well, from an overall loss of $3,618,000.

How could Ferber have known that this major investment in a work was preparation for the Texas oil wells ahead? At the time, she could not have been firmer about her parameters:

> I made up my mind that I definitely would never again write a novel of the regional type whose background required a long period of research, whose period embraced three or four generations, whose characters were varied and numerous. A book of that type was hideously difficult to write; one had to prepare with months of research; the characters, purely creative, had to appear real and dimensional; the writer, in order to accomplish an atmosphere of credibility and vitality, had to throw herself into the past. This was, for me, a physical, mental and emotional effort. I had lived every step of *Cimarron* and the journey had exhausted me.

She revived on a trip to Wading River on Long Island, to visit the American writer, reporter, and political commentator Walter Lippmann and his wife. She had seen a dark-haired, handsome fellow on a walk along the shore, commenting to Lippmann that his looks seemed too vivid for Long Island, to which Lippmann replied, "That's one of the Polish boys. Polish farmers own all of the land around here, a good deal of the North Shore, too. Truck gardens."

And there it was—the dive into her next novel: "So then here I was, deep in another background . . . I was trying to draw a circle . . . as I saw the pattern of the past two hundred years in Connecticut." She had sleuthed out where the Polish community had settled upon coming to America in the early twentieth century, and learned that there had been a massive influx into New England, specifically Connecticut, the setting for her next familial tale. Her main guidebook was called *The Polish Peasant in Europe and America*, which she said "was more absorbing and exciting than any fiction I'd read in years."

She did her solid background work for this novel but then went rogue, as was her custom: "I peopled the book out of my imagination, I invented the incidents, I made sure that my background and all factual matters were sound and authentic. Incidentally, I learned an awful lot about tobacco-growing."

Her description reveals her to be a combination of writer and Method actor: "For exactly three days I walked and drove about that section of Connecticut's tobacco country. The pores or antennae or whatever the means through which I am capable of absorbing in vast quantities every detail of that which I see and hear were working beautifully. I was able to recede into another period, I lost sight of myself . . . I became a human being quite outside myself, I was a New Englander in the Connecticut of the eighteenth century."

American Beauty was published in 1931 with this rubric: "The novel relates the decline of a staid old Connecticut family and their property, along with their tense relations with Polish immigrants." Its publication brought a torrent of abuse. Seasoned as Ferber was becoming

Edna at age forty-three, having had her nose bobbed, circa 1929

toward the public's reaction, her defense mechanisms kicked in nonetheless: "I had fought against writing it. I was tired . . . But the urge to write the New England novel was stronger than the desire to smother it . . . Perhaps I should have been stern about practicing birth control on *American Beauty*. Conceived in careless love I hadn't meant to have it . . . Connecticut was hopping roaring mad . . . Even staid Boston papers called me nasty names . . . What right (one newspaper actually demanded) had a Jew to come into New England and write about it! . . . Then, my Polish readers raised objections." In its initial quarter, the book sold short of one hundred thousand dollars. There were only 150 copies of the first edition signed by Ferber. A low for a Ferber novel. But then came a letter to Nelson Doubleday from Rudyard Kipling, reviving her drooping spirits—especially his last line: "I don't think her own people realize her value as a historical painter—yet. They will later."

In 1933, Ferber returned from an exotic trip sailing on the Swedish liner *Kungsholm* to Iceland, Finland, Sweden, Norway, Denmark, and Russia. The last four days of the trip were spent in the Kremlin ("Fascinating. And I make you a present of it") catapulted her back to embracing her midwestern roots. "I began to write a novel of Wisconsin and Michigan, whose background and people had been so large a part of my childhood and young girlhood." Her main reservation was that some of it she didn't know at all—the lumber camps and the whole vast woods life and industry. And then, so true to her nature: "December found me up in Ironwood, Michigan, trudging knee-deep in snow (and an incongruous mink coat), eating in lumber camps, watching the giant pines crashing to their death in the forest slaughter, talking to the paper-mill millionaires whose names had been so familiar to me since my Appleton days; breathing in the dry cold air, lifting my face to the feathery snowflakes; saddened by the sight of the cut-over land with its miles and miles of rotting stumps where once a glorious forest had stood."

Come and Get It, published in 1935, is a saga of life in the Northwoods of Wisconsin as lived by a family who run a lumber mill and papermaking operation. Thematically, it exposes the robber barons who ruthlessly plundered our vast, rich continent. In order to get her story, Ferber made a visit to the home of a German-born American lumber baron, who proceeded to announce at the dinner table that all bankers in the world were Jews, that Jews possessed all the money in the world, and that they were scheming to obtain control of the world. Ferber locked her bedroom door that night and put a chairback under the doorknob. In the morning her host did not speak to her and tried to prevent her from visiting a nearby lumber camp.

The prestigious 1936 MGM movie of *Come and Get It* was co-directed by William Wyler and Howard Hawks and starred Edward Arnold, Joel McCrea, Frances Farmer, and a memorable Walter Brennan. Goldwyn bought the rights from Ferber for $150,000 ($3.2 million today) with the understanding that it was to be "primarily a story of the rape of America . . . by the wholesale Robber Barons of that day." Coincidentally enough, Howard Hawks's grandfather had been the role model for the main character of Barney Glasgow. Goldwyn tried to borrow Spencer Tracy from MGM, but Louis B. Mayer refused to accommodate his rival.

There were many shenanigans attached to the picture that made it less Ferber and eventually more Wyler than Hawks. Critic Frank S. Nugent of *The New York Times* concluded: "You won't find *Come and Get It* a thoroughly Ferber work, but enough of her has been retained and enough good Goldwyn added to make it a genuinely satisfying picture."

Saratoga Trunk, published in 1941, came after a bit of a drought, as Ferber had written little between 1936 and 1938. She explained: "Deeply disturbed, emotionally and spiritually, writing seemed not only difficult but unimportant unless that which I wrote might be of some help, however slight, to someone or something."

The book that she began to draft in 1939 is basically a romance between an ambitious Creole woman and a gambling railroad man from Texas. This was Ferber's "fun" novel, with seemingly less social impact than the others. It reflects her first visit to New Orleans in 1940, of which she said, "It was enchanting. It was gay. It was hot and delicious and steaming." However, conversely, she noticed "shabby plantations and a lethargic way of life." A few months after the novel was published, she wrote to her editor at the time, Malcolm Johnson, "I've loathed every writing minute of it. Nothing will convince me that anyone will read this mass of blubber."

There was a 1945 movie, which Rotten Tomatoes has since evaluated as "melodramatic, mushy, and intriguing." It was produced by

Warner Bros., directed by Sam Wood, and starred Ingrid Bergman, Gary Cooper, and Flora Robson. The *New York Times* film review, by critic Bosley Crowther, matched Ferber's self-deprecating opinion of the book: "Warner's has taken the novel . . . a novel of high romantic polish and maddening emptiness underneath—and have given it visualization in the grand, flashy, empty Hollywood style."

She felt more sanguine about her next novel, *Great Son*, published in 1945. This one was championed by my father, publisher Henry Goldsmith. He thought that this saga exploring an American family dynasty over four generations in the Pacific Northwest, watching Seattle grow from village to skyscrapers, was rich, emotional, colorful, and deserving of a grand motion-picture production, which it never received. Producer Mike Todd did take a $400,000 ($6.6 million today) option on it, but the project was never realized before his untimely death in 1958 at forty-eight years old.

Ferber was verbal about her novels. She prided herself on citing their qualifications. In the case of *Great Son*'s Seattle:

> It seemed much farther away than Europe. There it was, that prodigious corner of the United States known as the Northwest. For years I'd tucked it away in my mind as a region fantastic, improbable and magnificent . . . The people and the background sounded high, wide and handsome. They sounded American. Fresh, vital, unspoiled and wondrously American. Also roses, they said, bloomed the year round, the salmon and rock-crab were a gourmet's dream, and the scenery would knock your eye out . . . It would be background for the Bearded Boys of America—the Bearded Boys of Seattle—all the way, perhaps, from 1851 to 1941. Adventurous, bold, nerveless, courageous . . . Fighting and dying for an intangible thing, a spiritual thing, a thing called freedom.

Although *Great Son* was critically deemed only fair Ferber, it was, as always, beautifully researched. Her notes are visceral:

> The saloons were the most imposing buildings in the towns. They looked like vultures on a huddle of tents, shacks. They

were the clubs, the home, they meant sociability, love, warmth, relaxation. Dark Indian faces, painted faces of women, bearded gaunt faces that had looked upon death and horror. They had heard the howling of the grey wolf-pack and the answering snarl of the malamutes.

A hamburger was $2 but caviar was $1. Oyster stew was $15. Eggs $1 each. Bread $1.50 a loaf baked by a woman who came in with the first (gold) rush. She sold tickets for the day's baking, the loaves came out of the oven hot and fragrant and the men stood sniffing in the doorway like hungry little boys.

The Marchons! of the French-Canadian sledgers became mush on! mush on!

An old thematic haunt was usually a good bet for Ferber. She admitted as much:

> I think I went back to Texas because I thought this strange commonwealth exemplified the qualities which must not be permitted to infect the other forty-seven states if the whole of the United States as a great nation was to remain a whole country and a great nation. This is pompous-sounding but not, in addition, naïve.
>
> Back I went to Texas then. This assignment I had given myself was as difficult as the state of Texas itself was enormous and diverse. It was as Spanish as Mexico; it was as American as ham-and-eggs; it was as Neiman-Marcus as Fifth Avenue; it was as Western as long-horns and cactus. Its people were outrageous and delightful; and hospitable and resentful; and arrogant and insecure; and flamboyant and deprecatory; simple and complicated. Geographically and economically nature had thrown two hazards at the Texans; unlimited pace, and seemingly unlimited wealth.

According to Ferber, many of her other novels had been "mere frittering compared to the labor of researching and authenticating this book in preparation."

Dimitri Tiomkin said of his heavily measured, sweeping score ushering in the new work, that in composing it for the subsequent movie "he wished to capture the feelings of the great land and state of Texas."

Giant was published in 1952 to stupendous fanfare and controversy. What follows is how Ferber's first inkling of the enormity of Texas eventually became 825,000 acres of the imagined ranch she called Reata.

PART ONE

Precognition

She was between writing *Come and Get It* and *Saratoga Trunk*, although she had already begun drafting the latter by 1939. Ferber was approaching age forty-four, which at the time was considered more than pushing middle age. She had led the life of a celebrity for a couple of decades, but conversely had lived as a rigidly disciplined writer, sitting every day for four hours with her back to the view. Having earned a great deal of money, enjoying her amusing and overachieving friends, traveling most of the world, seeing many of her novels and plays turned into successful movies, she referred to herself as "a stage struck, Jewish nun." Although austere in her work habits, she had a wild, investigative heart. And so, it was time to meet another mysterious geographical stranger.

Her cherished, not quite fatherly friend William Allen White, editor in chief of *The Emporia (Kansas) Gazette*, had suggested a seemingly improbable connection for her: a Texan, an authentic American tycoon named Glenn McCarthy, who had nicknames such as "Diamond Glenn" and "King of the Wildcatters." An oil prospector and entrepreneur, he owned many businesses in various sectors of the economy. White suggested that she pay a visit to the Lone Star State, take in its vast measure, and maybe look up McCarthy.

Ferber took her first trip to Texas in 1939. She was ambivalent. She had been busy exploring a notion of writing about Saratoga Springs,

New York, which turned into fussing about whether the form would be a novel or a play. She had introduced her playwriting collaborator George S. Kaufman to this latest notion, coercing him into a terrible trip: "Up to Saratoga Springs then, at the wrong time of year. Born in Michigan, inured in my childhood and girlhood to the rigors of Iowa, Wisconsin and Illinois winters, certainly Saratoga in December held no terrors for me."

It was cold, damp, and empty of life. Everything appeared closed down and waiting for another season. Ferber coerced a cranky caretaker to open up and show them around the United States Hotel. Ferber wrote later of this woebegone visit in search of creative inspiration:

> I have visited the crypts of St. Peter's. The Roman Catacombs. Point Barrow Alaska on the Arctic Ocean in January. A theater on the closing night of a play that is a failure. Any of these would seem cosy—even tropical—compared to the mortuary atmosphere which engulfed us as the waiting caretaker opened the door with a clanking and squeaking of chains and bolts and we stepped into the charnel marble halls of erstwhile gay Saratoga . . . George turned up his own coat collar over the muffler and thrust his gloved hands into his coat pockets. Our breath froze on the indoor air.
>
> A sound emerged between the caretaker's cap and his collar. "D'you want to see the whole place?" He carried a flashlight.
>
> "NO," George Kaufman said distinctly. That was all. That was it. George took the late afternoon train back to New York . . . Practical. That's the thing. Be practical. You have been thinking about *Saratoga* as a play. That is ended unless you do it alone, and you're scared. Why not first as a novel? But it doesn't seem to take that form. Then leave it. Go away somewhere, see something you haven't seen before.
>
> And then it came: The classic writer's insemination.
>
> You've been hearing a lot about a mythical place called Texas. Why not go to the Southwest, you haven't seen anything of it since Oklahoma and *Cimarron*.

She put the play *Saratoga* aside temporarily; it emerged later, in 1941, as the novel *Saratoga Trunk*.

Ferber was a woman who kept the promises she made to herself. Often, following painful deliberations, she was able to steady herself and be loyal to her decisions. There is jauntiness in her description of what—unbeknown to her—would become her future: "Even in that day . . . it was slightly eccentric to take a train for a journey as long and as potentially tedious as this jaunt to Texas. To fly was considered THE THING, but in 1940 it was not taken for granted as it is today—just a routine form of locomotion. Flying was thought to be definitely adventurous, though chic. As a general thing I flew, but for this journey I wanted no sudden whirl into another region of the United States—another civilization altogether, I had been told—this Texas which I had never seen."

Whenever she planned a journey, it was meticulous and lavish. She had a shrewd feel for money and yet lived within an echelon that had opulent expectations. One could trace her preoccupation with spending on the "right things" to her childhood, as she laid out in a fraught letter to her family: Julia, sister Fannie, and nieces Janet and Mina.

> I'm really disappointed to learn that you, Mama, and the girls are not combining to give me half a dozen knives. I'm about the last person in the world to want you to spend money on me, God knows. But it does seem fantastic to know exactly what I want, to be told that I'd rather have you all combine to give me half a dozen of anything in that set than any other collection of what-nots, and have you say you won't do it. In fact, if you would give them to me after Christmas, and take back what you may have ordered, I'd rather have them. Six knives, costing, I suppose, somewhere in the neighborhood of fifty or sixty dollars (though maybe I'm wrong. As I know absolutely nothing about those things) would please me more than a lot of God knows what. Of course I can't work up any feeling about Christmas, I'm sorry to say. I think it's lovely getting flowers, and candy and such things, for grownups. But the My Store soured me forever for any big emotional urge toward this store-keeper's orgy, and if I could I would run away and hide until it was over.

As she planned to spend a "time-proportioned" Christmas with her family around when she was arranging her Texas trip, she reveals herself in her stylishly jaunty way: "It's God's mercy I never married. If I'm not alone for just so many hours a day I get as haggard as though I had had typhoid. I have always thought that was a little cuckoo, but it's true."

The personal themes that surfaced throughout her adult life were work, food, money, social consciousness, and her mother. Most of the trips that she planned included her mother, but not the working ones. When she researched, she needed tremendous mobility, which her mother would not emotionally afford her. Julia required almost constant attention. She liked to shop, she liked to "schmooze," she liked to play cards, she liked to be lively. Ferber never stopped rewarding her for rescuing that first novel from the trash so long ago. The state of Texas during that first trip did not seem vast enough to house the loaded relationship of Julia and Edna Ferber. Too much time spent with each other and a combustion was not only likely but promised— and it could be more deadly than fiery. Terrible statements were flung, followed by long, sullen silences.

So, in late February 1940 Edna Ferber was alone for more than a thousand miles on a Texas-bound train which was "hot, stuffy and an hour late. The journey began to seem interminable and I thought of the old joke about the Englishman who, on his first long trip across the United States, said, 'I wonder why such a fuss was made about Columbus discovering America. I don't see how he could have avoided it' . . . Because of the difference in East-West time our arrival in Dallas was inconvenient. Arrivals are almost always inconvenient to hotels; and morning arrivals always. This was morning, and early morning."

This next description is quintessential Ferber. Although she certainly knows and elevates the bigger picture, there is a lively peevishness about the small one:

Though you've made the reservation and verified it, and, as a final precaution, reaffirmed the reservation, it's all a surprise to the room clerk. After two nights spent on a train there is almost nothing more revolting than to walk into a hotel bedroom to find the bed unmade, a mass of soggy towels strewn on the bathroom floor, empty whiskey bottles, dregs in glasses, cigarette stubs, grimy soaps, wads of paper, drifts of newspapers.

I went for a walk. It was late March. Dallas, to my astonishment, was like a Northern town. An unexpectedly worldly city, geographically flat but pleasantly lively. A drive around town, a saunter through that fabulous bazaar which is the institution known as Neiman-Marcus. One had heard of it, of course; crammed with porcelains and linens and laces and silks and furs and jewels for the delectation of the multimillionaire oil men's wives. Here on the desertlike plains of Texas, was lavish luxury rivaling anything in New York or Paris. It seemed an anachronism; or a mirage. Back at the hotel there was awaiting me a young man who introduced himself as Joe Linz of the *Dallas Journal*. He turned out to be full of charm and New York conversation, having lived there for some time before his college years.

Although Ferber could not have foreseen the outcome, this young man was to become a fixture in her life. Ferber was so taken with him that she attempted to make a romantic match. So, she introduced Joe Linz to my mother as soon as possible. Her instinct told her that he would make my mother, Janet Fox—who was a young, talented, fancy-free actress on Broadway—a wonderful husband. My mother was a serious actress as well as being glamorous and amusing. She had made her debut in Kaufman and Ferber's *Dinner at Eight* in 1932 and had gone on to play in many other Broadway shows, including Arthur Kober's *Having Wonderful Time*, *The Man Who Came to Dinner*, *They Knew What They Wanted*, and Kaufman and Ferber's *Stage Door*. She was relatively accomplished by the time she met Joe Linz in 1941. As our family lore has it, he fell very much in love with my mother. Here is an example of his ardency, which feels so genuine and having nothing to do with who her aunt was: "Janet, dear, sometimes I feel so presumptuous. I suppose you think I've taken an awful lot for granted. I haven't, really. I take for granted only the fact that I love you . . . You didn't ask me to feel that way, did you? And I know it only too darn well. Only sometimes I feel a little encouraged and then at other times terribly discouraged. The hell with all that. You're the girl for me and I'm going to get you."

My mother tried to return the sentiment but fell short. This was mainly because she had been fixed up by Vivian Vance (known for playing Lucille Ball's best friend on the TV series *I Love Lucy*) and her husband, actor Philip Ober, with a dashing young lieutenant on leave named Henry Goldsmith, whom she married after eight dates. All this, however, happened several years after Ferber's initial trip to Texas in 1940.

Linz was to become more important to Ferber than to my mother. Theirs was an indefinable bond. It was a kindred one, as in "two lost souls on a highway of life," which lasted until her death. They both seemed to be searching for a deeper emotional connection than they were used to having available to them. Perhaps his loving and losing my mother strengthened it. Ferber decided that his name didn't suit him, that he wasn't just a guy named Joe, and so she renamed him David. On the small side and mentally swift, he reminded her of the David who slew Goliath. This was the salutation every time she wrote to him, and the way he signed his letters to her. This one from 1940 could almost be considered a love letter of sorts:

Edna Dear,

. . . The Linz family hasn't been the same since your visit. You're the only glamorous thing that's happened to us since Grandaddy Sanger met Lawrence Barrett the night the Dallas Grand Opera House opened in 1883.

Seriously I loved you the moment I discovered you on a Baker Hotel banquette, having your quiet lunch. And to think I almost went away when Molyneaux [another reporter] appeared frightens me. Nobody will ever frighten me away from you again . . .

I'm afraid that last night in San Antonio must have bored you. [After a dinner with his family, Linz took Ferber around to some of the local hot spots.] I kept wishing we hadn't had the Vice Squad along. I knew I wouldn't see you again and I was duller than usual because I was actually sad. THAT is no lie. Even Red, the vice-ridden escort said as we drove away from the St. Anthony, "Damn, that's the most wonderful woman I've ever met!"

Now. Where do you want the crayfish bisque and the fritos sent? To the hotel or to Connecticut? . . . I'm still blushing because you know what was canned. But you won't have to tell your fine friends.

. . . For the joyousness of knowing you I am very humble.
Life goes along and then suddenly—wham!

Please don't forget your ever loving,

"David"

Linz's memory of his time with her never dimmed; in fact, it seemed
to have been enhanced with age. He wrote to me some thirty-five years
later about the effect on him of that first meeting and subsequent visit:

Although with age the memory is apt to dim, my memories of
Edna are as vivid, exciting, heartwarming and fresh as though
I had talked with her yesterday. I suppose that feeling is shared
by many. She was that kind of person; once her "kind of magic"
had touched you, you were ever after somewhat bewitched.

Our first meeting was in February 1940. I was the film and
drama critic of the old *Dallas Journal*, and when I was tipped
off that she was in town I beat it over to the Baker Hotel for an
interview. She was having a solitary lunch in the dining room
and one of her first remarks was: "How in God's name could
anyone perpetrate a windowless, murky place like this in the
land of wide open spaces and perpetual sunshine?" I thought
it a good question. I had just finished *A Peculiar Treasure*, and
although I was a long-time Ferber fan, it was that book which
made me know she was a great, great woman quite aside from
being a fine writer. The two don't always go together.

Edna took a moment to complain about the indifferent fare
on her plate, and, since my mother at that time had a superb
cook, I invited her to our home the following day for lunch
to ease the monotony of her cross-country eating. She got on
famously with my family and they of course were enchanted
with her. In my interview I had stated that she had a "strong
face." She never let me forget it and teased me about it for
years afterward. "Who," she asked, "wants a strong face?" I still
believe, however, there was great strength and determination
apparent in her features, particularly if something displeased
her and her scorn showed in the set of her jaw.

Joe Linz continued to court her in what turned out to be a some-what peculiar and amusing way:

> I took a couple of days off—it wasn't difficult since my father published the paper—to show her around San Antonio. One of my father's close friends was mayor of that city, and when I suggested that she see some of the town's seamier night life he insisted on sending along as escort the Chief of the Vice Squad. It delighted Edna and gave me a sense of security, since I felt I had a very precious "charge" in tow. I guess the high spot of the evening was our ending up in a bordello—a famous one—managed by a lady named Hattie Baxter. Edna said, "Hattie Baxter! What a perfect name for a Madame." I wager no one else had the audacity to show your impeccably chic, totally ele-gant aunt a whorehouse. We had a couple of beers in the parlor and chatted at length with a couple of the girls who weren't occupied. I think Edna loved it.
>
> That first visit to Texas probably planted the seed for *Giant*, even though it didn't become a stripling until about ten years later.

Following her initial meeting and interview with Joe Linz, Ferber recalled, "this pleasant effect was cancelled by a dinner interval with three Texans whose talk was dull and dirty. Perhaps they were sadis-tically interested in the possible reaction of a spinster novelist whose work was unknown to them. They were like nothing so much as a trio of boys who have tied a firecracker to a cat's tail, lighted it, and were waiting for the explosion." Things improved the next day when she met a young member of the Neiman Marcus firm.

> A warm, sunny Friday this was, and as we walked along the teeming streets, I said, partly in curiosity concerning Texas lei-sure hours, "After all this rush and bustle I suppose you're going away for the weekend." I had envisioned a cool, green oasis not too distant . . .
>
> "No," he said, "we're not going anywhere. There's no place to go."

This shocked me. A week or ten days later I could verify the startling statement. There were ranches and comfortable ranch houses outside the busy towns and cities; there were country clubs; but these sat starkly on the desertlike plain with here and there a mesquite grove or even a painstakingly planted Northern tree, imported and as unsuited to the climate as the Paris gown of the ranch-owner's wife.

Ferber traveled alone when researching, but because she was a considerable celebrity there were always people stationed wherever she went to guide, help, and pamper her. She was rarely totally alone anywhere in the world. She went to Houston next.

That's the big one, I told myself, that's the brash one, that's the one about which the Luce magazines are always publishing incredible articles of improbable people named Glenn McCarthy and Jesse Jones and Ima Hogg.

It was March. I had left New York in late February, deep in snow and hard winter cold. I now began to feel rather odd. Perhaps it was the effect of that rocket streamliner from Dallas, very hot and with a side-to-side motion that now made your early Dallas breakfast a cause for apprehension and regret. I did not admit to myself, but already I had begun to reject this region as a background for any creative work of my own.

Although Ferber was not yet ready to commit to the Lone Star State in late 1940, she was attempting to grasp it all with bravado.

Twenty-five years ago the Shamrock Hotel had not yet risen to stare blankly at a thousand miles of flat Texas range land. The Rice Hotel, slambang in the center of the city, was the place. This was before the day of air-conditioning. The hot hotel lobby was milling with men all of whom appeared to be seven feet tall. [Ferber was five foot one, but her gaze was an elevator X-ray, zooming up to stare them, I'm sure, right in the eye.] They wore sand-colored clothes and big creamy Stetson hats and their faces were sherry brown or Burgundy red from

Edna (third from left) with Oscar Hammerstein II (second from left), Richard Rodgers (fourth from left), Dorothy Hammerstein (second from right), Dorothy Rodgers (right), and others at Hammerstein's Highland Farm in Doylestown, Bucks County, Pennsylvania, circa 1938

the smiting sun and dust-laden winds of the Southwest plains. Their voices were strangely gentle and even musical emerging from those giant bodies; their eyes had the far look of seamen's eyes, the eyes of men who daily gaze across endless empty spaces; somewhat hard, those eyes, yet strangely childlike, too, like those of tough big boys. They stood in little groups, talking quietly except for an occasional volley of Homeric laughter; or they sprawled silent, like collapsed behemoths, in the lobby's huge leather chairs.

In my bedroom that seemed unimaginably hot, a huge fan contrivance attached to the ceiling above the bed was equipped with four long lazy arms like oars and these revolved slowly, with a nightmarish dreaminess, shoving the heat from one corner of the room to the other.

Unpack the necessities; get a car for an hour or two and have a first quick over-all look at this hot noisy rich town sprawling fungus-like on the plain, almost as unbelievable a manifestation as the mythical, heroic but actual giant Sam Houston for whom the city was named. Into the car at noonday, up one section and down another; into the Mexican quarter, then along streets of fine houses where grounds, open to the street, were ablaze with azalea blossoms in feathery masses of pink and white and orchid and yellow and orange and purple. But by now I was feeling odder and odder, my face burning, my clothes a burden, my head a conflagration. You had to come to Texas, I thought acidly. New York and Connecticut in February weren't good enough, h'm?

Ferber had never lived domestically small. In her childhood she grew used to midwestern farmland; long, dusty country road walks; the sprawl of Chicago with its bracingly freezing, invigorating jaunts along the North Shore. When in New York City, she would think nothing of hiking from the Forties to the Seventies, Eighties, or Nineties. Her city real estate was always capacious. She inhabited many gracious rooms of balconied apartments equipped with liveried elevator operators and doormen. Her residential life was luxurious and first-class in every way. And yet she dreamed of a country manse with a view of endless green from every room, of long walks on her wooded acreage, wearing tweeds and oxfords in the fall, parkas while cross-country skiing the property in the winter, slacks and cashmere pullovers in the spring, and sundresses and large gardening hats in the summer. She was being courted by manifest destiny.

Many of her friends had lovely country houses where she was as frequent a visitor as she allowed. When she was deeply imbedded in creating a novel, she led a sparse social life. She was a good guest when she let herself go a bit, and loved a glass of wine or a cocktail, sitting on the custom cushioned porch furniture of her favorite colleagues. She sounded like an enthusiastic and knowing realtor in describing their luck and bounty:

A number of my friends had found and bought handsome old stone farmhouses built a century or more ago by the Quaker settlers in Pennsylvania and New Jersey. These houses, together

with the land, were incredibly low in price considering the
increasing desirability of that lovely, rural countryside and the
charm and solidity of the houses. George Kaufman and his wife
Beatrice had bought there; Moss Hart and Kitty; the Howard
Lindsays; Oscar and Dorothy Hammerstein; Alan Campbell
and Dorothy Parker. The countryside was rolling, green, fertile;
the stone dwellings spacious and dignified.

It had been a couple of years before Ferber finally made her move.
As she put it, "The agonizing pangs of the imminent World War II were
wrenching the vitals of Europe," her subconscious broke through.

Uneasily I worked and played in the Park Avenue penthouse,
so unreal, so artificially remote, so typical of the lunatic period.
And now the whole lovely mad eyrie with its view of the Hudson River and the East River and Central Park and the brilliant
towers and pinnacles to the south seemed almost perceptively to
quiver and sway with the first warning winds of the approaching world-wide hurricane.
    A little, nagging inner voice that represented the fragments
of my Midwest experience and wisdom now cautioned me,
"Get out of here. A piece of land and a house in the country,
that's the thing. Get out. There is no security here. Who can
write in a climate of chaos? Writing is your job. Get out! . . .
But my northern Wisconsin past nudged me, whispering that
when I again settled in a green spot it must be up, up from New
York, not down into Pennsylvania or New Jersey. My longing
was the cool, Connecticut landscape with the Berkshire foothills undulating gently against the horizon; the salt breeze from
the Sound so soothing yet so tonic; the Sound itself glinting in
the distance. An hour-and-a-half from the center of New York,
just a whirl up the new Merritt Parkway. That was the thing
for me. The vine-wreathed dream cottage must be so mild of
maintenance that I might be able to keep the New York apartment for winters and use the Connecticut retreat for intensive
writing and occasional collapses . . .
    One year later the little vine-wreathed dream cottage turned

out to be an enormous fourteen-room American Georgian stone house on one hundred and sixteen acres of rocky land, embellished with fields, woodland, swimming pool, orchard, walled flower-garden, vast vegetable garden, farmer-caretaker's house barns. Poultry house, tool house, croquet court, pool house, terraces, driveways and no mortgage. Stone by stone, shovel by shovel, day by day, month by month, with the most exhilarating anticipation, it was built for me. My family and my friends said, you're crazy, and how right they were.

This was in retrospect what might be considered an ill-fated love affair. However, not unlike the beginning of researching a novel, Ferber liked the cologne of the "mysterious stranger." She says so herself:

I had fallen hopelessly, inextricably in love with a gloriously handsome spendthrift stranger.

My meeting with the fascinating and irresistible stranger had come about by chance, as these fatal encounters often do. I was spending an early spring weekend with Theresa Helburn and her husband at their country place in Weston, Connecticut. Terry [no one ever called her Theresa] was a friend of long standing, dating from her days as one of the founders of the Washington Square Players . . . emerging from this early start to become one of the directors of the renowned New York Theatre Guild. At dinner Saturday evening she said, with misleading guilelessness that gave no hint of giant purpose—unless you really knew Terry,

"You've been looking at places all over Connecticut for years. I hear agents hide behind desks when they see you coming. I've found the ideal place for you."

Sourly I said, It's always somebody else's ideal, not mine.

"Will you look at it? I'll drive you up tomorrow before lunch."

After what I've seen I can look at anything. I suppose it's up on the Canadian border.

"It's actually about seven miles from here."

Living room with vaulted ceiling made from a barn; wormy

Edna's first autobiography, published in 1938. As Hitler rose to power she felt obliged to examine her life to date as an American Jew.

old oak beams, used to be a hayloft.

"No ceiling. No house. No nothing. Just heavenly hill with a view."

I won't build a house. I'll remodel one if I have to. But build in these times! No, thanks.

"Wait till you see this. Perhaps you'll change your mind. It's about one hundred and sixteen acres, more or less—"

Ideal? I'm looking for two acres. I'll settle for one.

"A whole hill, the highest hill in Easton, with fields and woods and rocks and rills— especially rocks. It's owned by a sort of farmer. I don't think he actually can bear to part with it, though it's for sale. He's really in love with it. There isn't another view like that on the eastern seaboard."

One hundred and—why, I wouldn't take it if your lovesick farmer gave it to me with a brand-new house thrown in. An ideal white elephant.

I could hear Terry's mind clicking like a precision machine. "Just look at it. I've got a plan. Sumptuous."

Sumptuous isn't for hard-working writers.

"But you can look at it, can't you?"

As Terry's car covered those seven or eight miles it was plain that we were climbing almost every foot of the way, hill after hill, sometimes a steep grade to be followed by a gentle incline; my spirits lifted with every inch of the altitude. By nature and metabolism I'm a mountain dweller; the ocean depresses me. Given anywhere between five hundred and eight thousand feet, I'm likely to feel as most people do who have just had a very

With architect Phillip Sands Graham, conferring about the grounds of Treasure Hill, circa 1938

dry very cold martini; not gay, just exhilarated. To the right and left of the road was woodland with dense green foliage. Higher and higher, the sky seemed nearer and clearer. Houses became rarer, sometimes there was a mile of fields and woods between them. Now we were in almost open country of fields and pastures, grazing cattle and faded red barns. We flashed past the neat white steepled church on a knoll, so characteristic of New England. The whole had the look of Connecticut rural land unchanged for a century . . .

Top of the hill now. Out of the car. We stood on the plateau. We faced south. And there it was.

"See what I mean?" Terry flung a hand out in the general direction of valleys and hills and treetops and green and green and sky and sky. "Knock your eye out, wouldn't it?"

As I first saw it now, and kept it forever in my memory, it seemed to me the loveliest view on the eastern seaboard.

Not only would it knock your eyes out; it made your heart turn over . . . The unique beauty of this landscape was its rise and fall, its valleys, its hills beyond; the feathery green of the massed treetops below; the little cluster of white house and red barn and tiny shed in the far distance, perched absurdly on the side of just one hill. And there—just there—distant and shining like a sword in the sun, was the silver glint of Long Island Sound. It was at once as spectacular and friendly, as soft and grand, as the heaven in which we believe in our childhood . . . I shut my eyes and turned woodenly around and stumbled toward the car.

I had fallen in love. I had fallen in love at first sight with a good-for-nothing, a ne'er-do-well, a gorgeous profligate and wastrel who had made all the others I had ever seen appear commonplace, loutish, grubby.

Terry said, "Well, what do you think?"

I shook my head slowly, sadly, even as I walked away. "There must be an easier way to ruin one's life."

———

Acquiring the land and building the house became the kind of obsession that usually writing a book necessitated. At this point, in 1938, Ferber was toiling on her first autobiography, *A Peculiar Treasure*, but the pull of erecting the house was in stiff competition. Being tugged in two separate ways didn't seem to bother her—much—as she recalled in a later autobiography, *A Kind of Magic*:

> The blueprints of the house and the detailed outline of the book had been painstakingly planned and revised and improved during the autumn and winter in New York. Now both book and house were well on their way. They had started off neck-and-neck. Their finish was anybody's guess. The book was the expression of my life as I had lived it and of the times as they had unfurled over the years. The house was, I suppose, an expression of the life I hoped to live in the future.
>
> The spring and summer and autumn turned out to be one of

the most exhilarating periods I had even experienced, mentally and emotionally; and the most painful physically. Understandably, I had developed a quite splendid duodenal ulcer. I was working under intense pressure for I had, unwisely, arranged to have the book serialized in a magazine before publication . . .

This progress on the book, the progress on the house, this seemed excitement enough for anyone; certainly it was for me. By this time Treasure Hill had been given the nickname of Ferber's Folly. A book to finish, a house to build, a large acreage to clear and landscape, trees to plant. I had set my sights for autumn. This was, of course, madness, but like many mad plans, it worked out . . . I would simultaneously attempt to build the Taj Mahal and write *War and Peace*. Friends and family had sorrowfully but firmly washed their hands of the whole crazy business. They waited ready and, I thought a shade eager, to aid me when and if I should collapse. In this I failed them.

I was having a wonderful time, pressure or no pressure, ulcer or no ulcer, progress or no progress on the two big projects.

My mother, Janet Fox Goldsmith—then just Janet Fox—corroborated the memory that Ferber was quite giddy during this period—although my grandmother Fannie Ferber Fox recalled that "with Edna, agitation and exhilaration could go hand in hand." In retrospect, she was perhaps suggesting mood swings, which at that time were not formally recognized as such. However, there was also a bit of schadenfreude peeking out from the older sister toward the younger upon occasion. At any rate, despite the darkening political climate in America, Ferber was riding high.

There was the land under my feet; there was the enchanting view daily as I visited the Hill; there was the house slowly taking the form of a habitation; there in the place that temporarily housed me were the pages marching tidily out of the typewriter and into the editor's office. The gruesome world of the shrieking paranoiac Hitler in Europe, the mounting unemployment and apprehension in the United States, took on a kind of unreality. Only the house was real and the land was real and the book was real . . . Nothing unpleasant mattered if you had land of your own a house of your own a book to be published . . .

Then there was "the reverse Bick Benedict syndrome" in play. In the as-yet-unwritten novel *Giant*, Ferber's leading male character, Jordan Benedict, known as Bick, employed a vast number of Mexican Americans to perform the labors of running his ranch. They were paid low wages, housed meagerly, treated marginally. They were certainly not given much thought until Ferber's heroine, Leslie Lynnton Benedict, came on the scene, attempting to point out and correct the age-old injustice.

When Ferber was having Treasure Hill built, she reacted humanely, sensitively, and courteously to the workers, as her character Leslie would a decade later:

> There was another reason for my cozy state of nirvana. All over the Hill, about the growing house and the grounds there swarmed a blithe and heartwarming crew of workmen . . . These men represented American labor in a day and in a crisis that might have excused any number of resentments . . . Their backgrounds were Italian-American, Swedish-American, Norwegian-American, Polish, Czech, and native New England American. They were all citizens of the State of Connecticut, Fairfield County. None lived more than twelve miles distant from Treasure Hill. They came to work in rather ramshackle cars, for this was the day, not merely of unemployment but of low and lower wages, no matter how talented the craftsman. There was an added zest for me in the knowledge that this Connecticut house in which I was to become a citizen of Connecticut was being built, inch by inch, by Connecticut citizens only . . .
>
> All these men were careful craftsmen, they were glad of the work in these perilous times, they were interested. They were amused and mystified by the fact that a middle-aged woman was building, alone and with evidently no outside help or advice, a very large stone house on a very large tract of very high land in a very remote situation; all this for the purpose of living alone in this handsome house, and writing.

Contrary to some allegations about Ferber, as well as reports on her behavior in certain tough situations, she liked men very much—good ones. She responded to men—even in an occasionally flirtatious manner when they had brains, ingenuity, and humor. She found macho swagger, smug righteousness, or belligerent stupidity unbearable. But she certainly tolerated and sometimes appreciated a dry joke—even if she was the butt of it—from a clever man. This was probably why she was able to have such a long collaboration with George S. Kaufman, who indeed

Portrait of Edna prior to her theatrical debut in *The Royal Family* at the Maplewood Playhouse in Maplewood, New Jersey, 1940

poked regular fun at her. Some of the anecdotes regarding his Ferber ripostes are fabled—particularly this one: Ferber was preoccupied with America's encroaching entry into the horrors of World War II. She announced her consternation to Kaufman and wondered what she could possibly do to help. Kaufman searched for his answer, and then, with his dependably dry delivery said, "Well, Edna, you could be a tank."

And in fact, she *was* a tank when it came to important creative people defending American liberties. Nineteen forty was an election year. On Democratic Women's Day, First Lady Eleanor Roosevelt held a caucus presented by the Democratic National Committee and broadcast on the radio. Gathered together were what was called "a group of our country's most outstanding and famous writers and actresses": Ferber, Marc Connelly, Katharine Hepburn, Frank Kingdon, Alice Duer Miller, Elmer Rice, Robert Sherwood, Rex Stout, Frank Sullivan, Hendrik Willem van Loon, and Thornton Wilder. (Ferber was a big Eleanor fan, as well as liking Franklin just fine. She was often invited to be a guest at the White House, where she laughingly complained that the bed was hard.) The following is a section of the broadcast that Ferber held dear:

Mrs. F.D.R.: Good Evening. Last Sunday afternoon I asked a group of my friends to picnic with us at Hyde Park. As we sat about the open fire at Val-Kill Cottage broiling hamburgers and hot-dogs, we discussed the subject each and every one of us believes is of vital interest today. What my friends had to say seems to me so important, that I wanted you all to hear them, and so they have unselfishly joined me here tonight to bring us their message as we celebrate Democratic Women's Day.

Apparently, the playwright Robert Sherwood said something here, to which Ferber replied, "It's an interesting thing about the American people, Bob. In the long run they're always right." Here, Mrs. Roosevelt picks up:

Well, Edna Ferber, then you go right on and pick up where Mr. Sherwood left off. But first, Miss Ferber, tell me something—we have all loved your fine books and plays about our country—*Come and Get It, The Royal Family, Show Boat*—I've known and enjoyed them all. But didn't you say at the picnic that you've never before taken any part in political matters?

FERBER: That's just what I said, Mrs. Roosevelt.

MRS. F.D.R.: Then I think we all would like to know what you didn't have a chance to tell us at the picnic. Why are you giving your time and energy to this presidential campaign?

FERBER: Because it's not merely a political campaign. Today we are all—whether we like it or not—engaged in a death struggle for the life of democracy. Until now I, like most writers, have wanted only to be left alone to work in a small quiet room without a view. That was called living in an ivory tower. There are no small quiet rooms left in the world. They are filled with the turmoil of a bewildered and apprehensive people. Our ivory towers are shaking like a custard.

It is startling to note how close—according to this astute and esteemed gathering—the democratic world was to sliding toward the brink. Indeed, everything old is new again, including the clarion words of Edna Ferber.

Ferber was not a foreigner to giving speeches—both written and oral—and in fact, back in 1932, she delivered this rollicking yet moving one to my mother's graduating class of the American Academy of Dramatic Arts, which was held at the Lyceum Theatre on West Forty-Fifth Street in New York City. Her talk emphasizes her rigorous love for the theater as well as its concentric circle.

I want you to believe me when I say that you see before you a stage-struck heroine. And I want to tell you that this afternoon the ambition of a lifetime has been realized. I came into the stage door of the Lyceum Theatre, and the stage doorman said, "A dressing room, Miss Ferber, with a star on it." [*Laughter*]

When I was seventeen, I wanted to go on the stage, and when I was seventeen I was a good deal younger than I am now, and I still want to go on the stage. So I can tell you that I am jealous of every one of these young men and women who are here today. And it seems to me pretty ironic that I should find myself a little in the position of a girl who finds herself invited to pin the wedding-veil on her friend who is about to marry the man she herself is in love with. [*Laughter*]

I have not any advice to give, for one thing, and I have not any particular warning, either. And that is a great handicap for a speaker at graduation exercises. [*Laughter*]

I think some of you are going to succeed brilliantly, and I think some of you are going to do fairly well, and I think some of you are perhaps not going to do so well at all, and that is what we know is Life. And I think that your success, or your lack of it, on the stage, is going to depend a great deal on whether you enrolled in the American Academy of Dramatic Arts because you wanted to be an actor, or because you wanted to act. I get letters sometimes from people who talk to me about writing, and they almost never say, "I want to write,"—they say "I want to be a writer."

I think there is an awful lot of difference in those two ambitions. I think if you want to act, you will be an actor, but if you want to be an actor you won't act so very well.

Of course, we will all tell you that the motion picture is a thing that you have to contend with. They say that the motion picture is going to exterminate, is going to wipe out, the theater. Well, I know different. And this is why I know.

The first time I went to Paris, I went out to visit the cemetery, and asked the guard to show me to the grave of Rachel, the actress. Now, I am not an actress, and naturally I have never seen—not naturally, but I have never seen Rachel. She was before my day. And I visited her grave, and I stood there a while. I visited the grave of Rachel two or three times. She is buried there in perhaps the most famous cemetery in all France, along with great figures of France. Then I went to the museum in Paris, and I asked to see the case that held the mementos of Rachel. And there was a pair of shoes that she had worn, and the little funny watch that she had worn. These mementos were not put into the museum for me to visit, and she was not buried at that cemetery for me to visit, but because the great public of France thought that Rachel, ugly, curious, almost unpleasant in her manner of speaking and conducting herself, a Jewess, was considered great enough by the French nation to become what they called a monument.

There is one thing that it seems to me is very important for people who are about to go on the stage or for people who are about to do anything at all that makes for adults' civilized living. I think it is very important particularly for people who are about to go on the stage, that they be themselves. That sounds very trite, and a little crude. This is what I mean: I think that here in America we are rather more inclined to be rubber-stamps than in most other countries, perhaps because we are not quite sure of ourselves. And so, in order to avoid being laughed at or talked about, or pointed out, we try to conform a little too much. We try to be like somebody else. We are so afraid of being thought queer, we are so afraid of being thought odd, we are so afraid of what I think we call being "goofy." Well, I think that being goofy is very important. [*Laughter*] Now, I don't mean that I would advise you all to walk down Broadway in sandals and a Greek robe. I think that to see Lynn Fontanne and Alfred Lunt and Katharine Cornell and Leslie Howard—[is] very important. And I think it is very human to want to be like Lynn Fontanne and Alfred Lunt and Katharine Cornell and Leslie Howard and any one of a dozen other splendid actors and actresses I might mention. But I think it is much more important to be yourselves. I think that any garment which is cut to fit you is much more becoming, even if it is not so splendid as a garment which has been cut to fit somebody not of your stature. And until you can fit yourself a garment as splendid as theirs, I think it is just important to be yourself. I don't mean that you cannot learn enormously from those people, but I think you cannot learn to be any one of them successfully. . . .

　　And the moral of that is—in fact, I am afraid it is the moral of my whole talk, if it has one, rambling as it has been, I am going to give a great, big moral point to my talk now, because I feel that the time has come for me to stop talking, and also because I remember in the days of the old melodramas, which you don't know anything about, poor things [*laughter*]—how they used to give this as the message, and so it is my tip to you, and it has to do with the theater. And I say to you, "No matter how stormy the night may be, she is still your mother." [*Laughter and applause*]

There were a couple of good men helping Ferber build her house, and the role she would play in it. It definitely had a theatrical slant; it could be likened to designing and erecting an enormous set. In fact, there is a photo of her kneeling among rows of plantings, in gingham dress and large sunbonnet with the handwritten caption "Rebecca of Sunnybrook Farm." She trusted these "stagehands," and when Ferber trusted someone, they were hers for life. For instance, one of her contractors, named Lou Forsell—whom she had never met in person—was an expert on water. He was not afraid to speak his piece about what she should do for an endless water supply on her rocky terrain. He wrote her a strictly geological note that carries its own kind of power, prowess, and beauty:

I suggest that you try the following operation. Have the well rig moved to the spot which I have indicated on the geological map of your land. If you decide to retain the present three-gallon well it probably will supply water sufficient for your house only. The site of the second possible water source is about fifty feet distant and at the base of a slope as you will see. It is a small hollow surrounded by gentle slopes. Drill there not more than fifty feet. I have indicated the precise spot. This well should, at fifteen feet, yield a flow of twelve gallons per minute. It doubtless is not the flow you originally hoped to have but it should suffice for your needs. If, at fifteen feet, you do not get this flow abandon this second well immediately. It will be useless to drill further in this spot.

He finished with "Sincerely yours."

Ferber set up her well right in the spot he indicated. She reports that "the thump-bump sounded afresh over the hills and valleys. They went down fifteen feet. We got twelve gallons of water per minute. Not only was he sincerely mine; I have been sincerely his for these past twenty-five years. He is my notion of a hero and a knight in the shining armor of scientific knowledge. I'd rather meet him and speak to him than the first man to reach the moon. I don't need the moon. But water is necessary to my life."

There was another stalwart man on whom Ferber depended—Angelo, the stonemason. Ferber stood in awe of him and said, "To watch Angelo, the master stone mason, at his craft was to see an artist in action . . . It was a performance intricately craftsman-like yet simple-seeming; masterly, repetitious but infinitely varied. One watched it in utter fascination as the stone house—the gay stone house—went up inch by inch before my eyes."

Ferber had a thing about stone. She was particular about wanting variety. Slate-gray stone was prisonlike and to be avoided. Brownstone was ugly, tenement-like. Yellow stone belonged in Yellowstone Park—otherwise it looked suburban. The trick would be to find "warm" stones of different hues; stones that would glint when they caught the light. She wanted her house to look "gay," friendly, welcoming. She insisted that the stones were the secret ingredient to a successful house and that when just the right ones were located, she would love each of them. They would make all the difference to her and to the onlooker. She wanted people—either guests or drive-bys—to admire "her" handiwork.

Ferber's tasteful good friend Dorothy Rodgers, wife of Richard, was also witty and shrewd. She had a key to their friendship, which was to kid, to tease, to be playful. She was amused by Ferber and the house:

> When she built the house in the country, it was during the depression. One night, in 1939, we took her out to dinner at the World's Fair. She was building the house, or had just built it, and we never let her off the hook. For years we used to kid her about it because it was such a staggering thing for anybody to do in the middle of the depression—for anybody to be able to build that kind of house.
>
> Then one time she took me around the house and said, "Peg [Margaret Leech, also known as Margaret Pulitzer] gave me this, and the Lunts gave me that and Noel gave me this . . ." and I said "My God, didn't you buy anything? Did your friends furnish the whole house?" Well, you could do that with Edna, and she could be amused by it. But you never knew what moment you would hit the wrong button. That was what kept you on your toes.

Dorothy was aware of Ferber's vulnerable quality and that people—particularly those involved with this house—often would "hit and run" with her:

> You know, people took advantage of her because she expected them to. I mean people who worked for her. For instance, I remember during the war we kept chickens and so did Edna. One day Edna called me, and she said, "How many chickens do you have?" I said about one hundred. Then she asked how many eggs I got and I said, "I don't know exactly, Edna. I know that most of the year we have all the eggs we need and enough sometimes to 'put down in water glass,' and other times of the year we have to buy some." "Well," she said, "I have twenty-five chickens and I get sixteen eggs and I think the caretaker is holding out." I said to her, "Edna, I have a word of advice for you: Either stop counting or get rid of the chickens."

Then there is this sad tale Dorothy tells of the house that Edna built:

> She put every bloody tree in that place, and one day she was
> at a nursery looking at a tree that she needed to buy and she
> found it and she said to the man who owned the nursery, "Now
> I'll tell you how to find my house." And he said, "Oh, Miss Fer-
> ber, I know how to find your house. I've been there. When you
> had a tree to sell I went to look at it." Whereupon Edna said,
> "You've never been to my place. I have no trees to sell. You're
> thinking of someone else." She gave him the directions anyway,
> dismissing what he'd said as a mistake.
>
> When he arrived, she said, "Now, you've never been here
> before, have you?" "Yes," he said. "The tree that was for sale was
> just back of that barn."
>
> Well, her caretaker had been selling the trees as fast as she
> was putting them in. But she kept feeding that house good
> things.

The house was located in an elite section of Easton, Connecticut, called Stepney Depot. I loved its title of Treasure Hill. I was not more than three when I first saw it, and because I was so small, and the house so gigantic, I thought, if only temporarily, that my great-aunt must be a real queen. But I absolutely remember it. I mainly recall the greenest grass I had ever seen before or since, the abundant number of butterflies, the enormously lengthy swimming pool, the bony grasp of my great-grandmother Julia and the plump, protective arms of my grandmother Fannie. I have no recollection of being in the proximity of Ferber herself—except, strangely, I do have her lovely, velvety voice in my head saying, "Mother, don't let her go too far."

That house was more than a carefully planned edifice. It repre-sented the new wardrobe of the same old Edna. Although she had transformed, certainly, from a dumpy, plucky child to a streamlined international-celebrity writer, she still had the original dream in her DNA. She had dreamt early on of life's available largesse, and now she could have it, build it, own it, live in it. It clearly represented more to her than a splendid home to enjoy, to entertain in, to worry about in seasonally threatening weather. What I've come to feel so many years later is that Treasure Hill was her Reata, the ranch that Bick Benedict owns in *Giant*—his refuge against time and change, the evolution of the economy and its shifting values, the threat of a new race of immigrant Texans, the challenges of remaining in an insular fortress—except that he felt proudly defensive about owning a kingdom and she felt somewhat guilt-stricken.

Another Texan, although a self-denying one, recalls his first experience as a guest at Treasure Hill. Joe Linz, who seemed to be everywhere in Ferber's life at this time, appeared there in the late forties:

> Edna invited me to that glorious house on the hill in Connecticut. Farm indeed! She had an admirable French couple as houseman and cook, and I'll never forget the meal. He passed a gorgeous mile-high molded thing, chocked full of fresh lobster. Thinking what a great treat it was for a hot day, I piled my plate high, gobbled it down and generously helped myself to a second portion. My God, it was only the first course. In came a rack of baby lamb surrounded by sparkling vegetables from the garden and a salad. Noticing my amazement, Edna said, "I understand. If I beg them for just a chop and a baked potato, they sulk for days afterwards. They'll kill me yet."

Treasure Hill served as both political and psychological refuge, as Ferber explained in her second autobiography, *A Kind of Magic*, which was to be written in the distant future of 1963 and would be her last published book:

> By the time 1938 dealt the third financial blow in a period of ten years the country was numb to that brand of shock. Now, with stunned unbelief, it heard of the insane but highly effectual mass atrocities committed in Germany by that comic character Schicklgruber. He now operated with great success under the more imposing name of Hitler, and he wasn't so funny anymore.
>
> England will stop him. France will stop him. They always have. Those power-crazy nuts like the old German Kaiser and Napoleon and Alexander and, uh, Genghis Khan. After all, it's their continent over there, not ours. We can take care of ourselves.

But now in the United States of America, so smug behind its oceans, you saw the swastika flaunting its zigzag madness on walls and fences and shop windows and houses. In that section of New York's Manhattan called Yorkville whose citizens were so predominantly German-born and now incredibly infected with the overseas homeland sickness, a New York Jew was almost certain to encounter insult or even violence if he walked there.

Things look bad, people admitted. They didn't exactly specify what Things. Every Thing, probably; but Every Thing will turn out all right, it always has it always will. Right will win. Just don't look and don't get mixed up in it. If you don't look It will go away. This is one war we won't be pulled into. Not again. Help, yes. Mix in? No. We're not a warlike nation, we never have been we never will be. We hate war.

This was gibberish—but understandable gibberish. An amorphous monster was breathing down your neck, its horrid, horny hoofs were scraping its heels. The newspaper headlines and the radio commentators' voices were like daily hourly

Researching *Giant* in Texas, circa 1939

doses of poison whose names were Apprehension, Insecurity, Horror.

The Thing to Do was to Get Away from It All.

Ferber was candid about Treasure Hill stoking her psychological yearnings:

> Puzzled and often too deeply uncomfortable emotionally in these thoughts from time to time, it wasn't until some years later . . . that I realized my fundamental reason (this is pure conjecture) for my having bought this huge eroded hunk of rocky and sour land; built this large and handsome house; planted its acreage with grains and fruits and vegetables and trees and flowers in lavish profusion and converted it into a dream house, a dream garden, thriving pastures and fields and orchard—all this against the considered counsel of those who cared about me and wished to protect me.
>
> I realized, vaguely at first but more and more definitely as the years went on at Treasure Hill that this was only the fulfillment of a childhood dream.

She was not yet ready in 1940 to build something as large again, but the state of Texas toyed with her. However, when she realized she was, for the moment, safe from immediately dedicating herself to a book about it, her reportorial interest resumed. After all, she was just grazing.

> Houston days were spent in spade-work for a possible novel whose background had piqued my interest for years. I talked to many people; vulgar people, charming people; literate, ignorant, bigoted, liberal; white brown black; rich, poor. And I walked the stifling humid streets and drove to giant ranches squatting starkly on the plain; and accomplished some research in the library and spent a day in nearby Galveston on the naïve notion that, being a seaport, it would be cool . . . humidity destroys me. Here in Galveston the humidity was like a clammy hand being held over your face. Yet the city had a ghostly charm . . . Of what did this city remind me? Miss Havisham, of course. That was it. Miss Havisham the spectral bride in *Great Expectations*.

One can see as she continues with this initial trip that she couldn't help being in hot pursuit of possible stories. Her descriptions are such full-blown cues.

San Antonio next, all dressed up for tourists with the old town restored as La Villita; the festooned lagoons; the Governor's Palace, so-called; the relic of a long-gone period in San Antonio's history. It was a little like a movie set representing a Spanish town. But the Alamo was real enough; and the centuries-old missions, golden-brown and crumbling in the sun, were touching and historically fascinating though the winding high ancient stairways to the steeple crippled your leg muscles for a week.

In and out of Texas towns. Talking to scores of Texas people. Amazed by their viewpoint, their braggadocio, their seeming unawareness of the world outside their own vast commonwealth; beguiled by their easy charm, grateful for their spontaneous hospitality, touched by their lavish giving of time, energy, thought, to a tourist stranger. Appalled and fascinated by turn.

It was a superficial tour, certainly. But the years of trained observation and the natural ability to assimilate even the indi-

Edna (second from left) in the South of France with designer Gladys Calthrop (left), Noël Coward (second from right), and Louis Bromfield (right), 1940

gestible sights and sounds and personalities encountered served me here in this Texas which was at once so American and so unlike the rest of the United States.

The next passage in this diary-like reportage is interesting because I've come to believe that Ferber felt a Semitic vulnerability at times when in Texas. Here, she ponders just that—though through a historic lens: "What was it? What was it that made me feel so alien in this vast vital expanse of throbbing plain and range? Egypt, perhaps? An atavistic throwback to that blood-drenched desert land and the arrogant emperors and the young Jew Jesus so many centuries ago?"

What she writes next in this initial report of Texas was her last for a long while. Her impressions here resemble some early passages in the novel *Giant* as seen from the viewpoint of her heroine, Leslie. The passage articulates the simultaneous horror and attraction of both writer and protagonist.

Miles—hundreds—thousands of miles of flat roads, flat fields, flat plains, stretching away to the always distant horizon with nothing on which to rest the sun-weary eye. Vast herds of cattle, many of which were strangely humped and mythological creatures imported from India and bred to the local Herefords to produce the famous Santa Gertrudis stock; ranches that were kingdoms; towering men; shrill-voiced women; blazing sky; fried food; oil rigs; millions millions millions. A violent climate, an atmosphere potentially violent. A tropical climate that was ignored by the Texans. Any other land in the world, under this heat and glare, would have been shuttered, slow paced. Not here. They rode they drove at breakneck speed. They ate huge, hot platters of fat-drenched food. They moved swiftly, dressed in canvas and leather; drank alcohol prodigiously. Everything they did would seem to have brought swift sure death in any similar climate; but not here.

South to Brownsville on the Mexican border to Corpus Christi on the bouncing wind-driven bay that was an inlet of the Gulf of Mexico; to Austin, capital of the state of Texas; to Lubbock, thriving cow-town; Up. Down. Up again to Dallas.

It was larger than life. Too big. Too massively male. Too

ruthless and galvanic and overpaced. Too blatant. Too undi-
luted. Too rich. Too poor. Cattle and Mexicans and oil and
millionsmillionsmillions. Braceros laboring for twenty-five
cents an hour in Brownsville.

And now, right here, comes what I call the "Hey There" moment—the
one in the musical *The Pajama Game* when John Raitt sings an arguing,
contrapuntal duet with himself:

> This was no book for me. Work is work, I told myself, and
> fun is fun, and you thrive on both these, and sometimes they
> seem almost interchangeable—not often but sometimes; but
> this novel of Texas life is not a book for a woman to write. It
> would kill you. This is a novel for a man to write—a man who
> is a combination of Hemingway and Faulkner and Thomas
> Wolfe and Sinclair Lewis. Let that Proteus write it. Go on
> home.

Ferber's protective instinct about herself and about others was
extrasensory. This was and is a family trait on my maternal side. From
Julia Neumann Ferber through me, there is a "get out now" gene. I used
to discuss it with my mother, who completely recognized the symptom.
I asked her if it related to the fight-or-flight syndrome, and her reply
was, " 'Flight' is the operative word. We flee before trouble breaks out."
And so, in 1940 Ferber deserted Texas:

> The fact was that neither the Texas novel nor the Saratoga novel
> was ready for writing. Often, I reminded myself, a novel or a
> short story idea had lain dormant in my mind for years before
> the actual task of writing was possible. Like wine, they must be
> stored away in a dim cool cave of the brain to mellow, to ripen,
> until they are palatable.

At the moment of this rather elaborate decision a truncated telegram
arrived:

JULIA SAYS YOU TEXAS HOW ABOUT MEETING ME
NEW ORLEANS. LOUIS

It was from Ferber's close chum Louis Bromfield. They seemed to mirror each other in terms of their careers. His first novel, in 1924—when Ferber's *So Big* had come out—was *The Green Bay Tree*. In 1925, Ferber won a Pulitzer Prize for *So Big*. In 1927, Bromfield won the Pulitzer for his 1926 novel *Early Autumn*. Among his many other novels are *Pleasant Valley, Mrs. Parkington, The Rains Came, Night in Bombay, The Farm, Possession,* and *A Good Woman*.

In 1928, in the midst of the first draft of her Oklahoma novel, *Cimarron*, Ferber had decided to bail for a summer of French fun at the home of Bromfield and his wife, Mary, in Socoa, near the ocean in Basses-Pyrénées in the Basque country. She wrote in *A Peculiar Treasure*:

> In that summer, I learned really to know and love the Brom-fields . . . For the acid-test of friendship there is nothing better than being thrown together for company on an isolated cliff in a foreign country for three months. Louis, Mary and I saw the best and worst of each other. We came through with flying colors. I never have encountered anyone with Louis Bromfield's capacity for enjoying life and his gift for communicating that enjoyment to others. Humor, amazing vitality, sympathy, and a limitless zest for life all are his.

Bromfield's memory, however, has lingered primarily as the forefather of the conservation movement. In 1939, he created the Malabar Farm in Pleasant Valley of Richland County, Ohio, which represented the essence of sustainable agriculture. He was an early zealot of organic farming and eating healthily off the fat of the land. Aside from a rich crème brûlée, Ferber loved nothing better than her greens. She visited Bromfield's farm often in the ensuing years, always eager to graze his lovely gardens and partake of his nutritious larder.

A high old time was always shared with Louis, who loved and understood both Ferber and her mother. They both thought he had "bonny good looks," as Ferber said, "not to mention every other important asset." They both were tickled pink at how he could plant three hundred and fifty varieties of flowers on his Malabar Farm. So, Ferber did not hesitate to join him and leave Texas behind in the dust of its sweeping plains. Bromfield, who obviously found Ferber as stimulating as she did him, wrote a rare profile of her around this time, which she pasted in one of her small black note-scribbling books, dedicating the piece to her mother: "For Julia Ferber who comes off best in the Louis Bromfield article." Bromfield, who loved Ferber but was not family and had some objectivity, had a keen grasp of her essence.

> She was one of the personalities of our time and in order to know her you must be her friend, because toward strangers she has a manner which is at once a mixture of shyness and hostility and because she shuns publicity as much as most novelists court it. She is difficult to write about, not only because I am very fond of her but also because she is a curious and complicated mixture of tastes, of impulses and emotions. The truth is, I think when America gained a fine chronicle novelist, and excellent playwright, and a writer of short stories of the first order, it lost a great actress.
>
> If, as one sometimes does in playing parlor games, one was to give Edna Ferber mythical parents, I should at once choose Sarah Bernhardt as her mother and the Prophet Jeremiah as her father. This strange parentage is one of the elements that makes her character difficult and sometimes a little confusing.
>
> We have one bond at least in common and that is our strange and unbalanced passion for and detestation of travel. She hates traveling and is uncomfortable and grumbling most of the time she is on her way. None the less she is one of the most restless souls I know. I have seen her planning trips which she does not in the least want to take. I have seen her departures and arrivals and can testify that she is likely to be ill-humored both before and after the event. And I think I know the reasons for this strange dementia. If she has escaped the New York disease, she had no such luck with what I call the Middle Western fever.
>
> What she likes best is America, and by that I do not mean the America of the crowded cities or even the small stuffy towns but the America of the Rocky Mountains and the desert of Arizona and New Mexico.
>
> The superficial biographical details of her life are, I should think, well known to practically everyone in the United States

who is literate . . . She came before she was twenty-one to know in detail the life of two or three small towns, each one a laboratory in which to study American life and she made the most of her opportunities. She has worked for her living and knows how to make one dollar go as far as five, if that were still necessary. She has known a large share of the clever and distinguished people of the world and as many of the worldly ones as she chose . . . She prefers to write about those solid, sometimes humble people who are the very essence of American life and she knows profoundly the difference between what is American and what is imitation European. She will never be one of those American writers who espouse the cause of the Left Wing or one of those who are influenced by the decadence of Europe. About everything she writes there is an atmosphere, a treatment, a penetration which is profoundly authentic and American.

Miss Ferber is an incorrigible romantic in the good nineteenth century sense . . . It is born of the profound belief, never abandoned in the face of the most disillusioning experiences, that people, especially one's friends, should always be nobler, finer, more virtuous, more glamorous, and more beautiful than it is possible for any poor mortal to be.

And then there is Miss Ferber's sainted mother, Julia Ferber, who has had a magnificent life, and I might add is still having one, for she is one of the fortunate who never lose their zest, and out of her life she has learned (if she did not always have them) wisdom, truth and taste. Much that appears in her daughter's books and plays and stories has been learned from her; much of it is reality. Both mother and daughter have the blessed gifts of vitality and friendliness. Known simply as Julia to her friends of all ages, she is ageless, indefatigable, handsome, entertaining and the best company in the world. And she has character. She is always as young as the youngest person in the room. She loves good food and the best food in New York (and I say this as one whose only vanities in life are gardening and food) is to be had at her flat and that of her daughter Edna. In Miss Ferber's flat the food is concocted by a fabulous and handsome colored woman called Rebecca Henry.

Ingrid Bergman and Gary Cooper in *Saratoga Trunk*, the
1945 Warner Bros. film of Ferber's 1941 novel

This last may seem a strange way to end a love paean, but it is
helpful for purposes of Ferber's transition from Texas surveyor to home
and hearth. She was more than ready for Rebecca Henry's popovers
and tart lemon meringue pie and to be done with the overblown state
of Texas, its fatty food, and its charming yet confounding denizens:
"Goodbye Texas. Goodbye forever. Some tougher sturdier writer will
have to undertake the feat of bulldozing you. Little (as they used to say
in the old-time novels) little did I dream that, in the next twelve years,
Texas was to have a staggering effect on my life—my health, finances,
emotions, work; or that weeks—months—of my time would be spent
in Texas."

The Varmint

The right time for *Giant* came out of a failure. Not unlike the writing of *Show Boat*, which emerged from the defeat of *Minick*—the first play she wrote with George S. Kaufman—the decision to start *Giant* was because of the failure in 1948 of another Kaufman-Ferber play, called *Bravo!* By the way, the reason Kaufman's name usually went before Ferber's was an understanding between them that whoever had the initial concept for the piece got first billing. Only on *Stage Door* does Ferber get first placement.

Bravo! was a heartfelt political play emerging from the spoils of the war. It was based on the plight of Hungarian playwright Ferenc Molnár (who wrote *Liliom*, on which the musical *Carousel* was based) and his stage-star wife, Lili Darvas. Both acclaimed in their country—and later, acclamation for him in the United States—they were forced to flee the Holocaust, and along with them came many of their theater colleagues. Once technically safe in America, they faced the problem of earning a living. They were heavily accented and, however talented they were, there were scant parts or places for them in the American theater. Kaufman and Ferber explore this dilemma with humor and poignancy, but the somewhat sardonic tone was not the victorious one that American audiences wanted to see right on the heels of World War II. Its limp reception was all the harder for Ferber, for two reasons. First, her

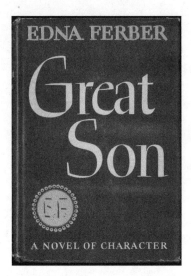

Great Son, published in 1945

niece Janet Fox—my mother—played the eye-catching role of a balle-
rina. The second reason was that *Bravo!* was the last play she ever wrote
with Kaufman, ending their collaboration, and the last play she wrote,
period. But out of the ashes: "Now, in 1948, the flavor of failure, usually
so bitter on the tongue," she recalled, "acted as a spicy appetizer, like a
helping of big, grey caviar bullets, or smoked salmon sharpened by the
piquant juice of lemon." Failure, perversely enough, seemed to impart
zest for the meal ahead: her Texas novel, *Giant.*

I think it was mysterious to her why she hadn't been ready to tackle
this work for so long. It seemed to stick in her craw as to how and why
it escaped her grasp. Her best defense was to analyze, solve, and cure:

> My rejection of Texas on that initial visit had not been on the
> grounds of pre-formed opinion or inexplicable emotion. On
> the contrary, I had been vastly interested, astounded; confused
> and startled; repelled and attracted. I had found it as virile as
> it was vast. I had found it incredible that a whole people could
> possess such energy, such self-complacency, such lack of inter-
> est in the rest of the United States and such enthusiasm for
> living in the midst of this hurly-burly heat, dust, glare, great

distances and seeming discomfort. Deep deep down, I think I went back to Texas because I thought this strange commonwealth exemplified the qualities which must not be permitted to infect the other forty-seven states of the whole of the United States if a great nation was to remain a whole country and a great nation. This is pompous-sounding but not, in addition, naïve.

Back I went to Texas then . . . Although the preliminary research for other novels—*Show Boat, Cimarron, Saratoga Trunk, American Beauty, Come and Get It*—and others—had been arduous and time-consuming, they now seemed in retrospect to have been mere frittering compared to the labor of researching and authenticating this book in preparation.

During the past decade she had hardly been idle. The fifth play she wrote with Kaufman, *The Land Is Bright*—relatively unknown—was produced in 1941. This time World War II was the centerpiece, raging through Europe shortly before America's entry. It is a long three acts covering three generations of the Kincaid family: infamous robber barons during the nineteenth century (first act) who work their way up into respectable high society (second act) and then learn the nature of patriotic sacrifice in order to embrace true American ideals (third act). It was the collaborators' only hard-hitting drama and never gained traction, opening on Broadway in late October 1941 and closing in early January 1942.

There were consistent patterns of interest in Ferber's work. She prized the weave and warts of familial cycles; she emphasized how geographical locale dictates economy, i.e., fortunes, social pecking order, and behavior; shining a harsh light on socioeconomic injustice; any suggestion of racism; and finally, industrial revolutions and their results. She was never cautious about writing and speaking out.

A play produced on Broadway and the publication of a novel were the output for 1941. The *New York Times* review of the book began: "The most cautious reviewer can predict skyrocket success for *Saratoga Trunk*—and not feel that he is getting out on a limb, either. Few of Edna Ferber's vastly popular novels of the past decade have arrived on the books counters with more fanfare." The book was sold to Warner Bros. and produced by Hal B. Wallis in 1945. The movie starred Ingrid

Bergman, Gary Cooper, and Flora Robson. Bergman played a fourth-generation Creole in light orange makeup and Robson played a West Indian in dark orange makeup. Gary Cooper, somewhat long in the tooth for the romantic, ironic Texan, was terrific in spite of it.

Ferber had begun her next novel, *Great Son*, soon after publication of *Saratoga Trunk*. This novel tells the tale of another family dynasty, this time in Seattle. The Melendys are an enterprising family who are nostalgic for the glorious geographical past and yet have helped to build a fantastic industrial future. In one of the most discerning of critical reviews, *Kirkus* began by not liking *Great Son*, saying, "Not a particularly distinguished addition to her reputation," but then held back from dismissal, throwing in a backhanded compliment: "This rather old-fashioned three-decker with plush trim makes for good reading and supplies a plausible cross-section of the elements of pioneer America which went into the makings of such families . . ."

Ferber wrote this footnote to her own novel from Treasure Hill in 1944:

> This may be an inadequate excuse for a slim book on a gargantuan subject. Here, in capsule form, is that which should have been a lavish and prodigious feast.
>
> Back and forth, in and out weave the people in this book, appearing, disappearing, vanishing into the mists of Mt. Rainier, or never really taking on human dimensions. This, then, is not so much a novel as a character outline of what will, someday, at other hands, be a stupendous and dazzling piece of Americana.
>
> The people in this book are no more unlikely than Seattle itself. But Seattle actually exists. They never have existed outside these pages.

The producer Mike Todd was partial to it. Todd, who was chronically up and down in luck, came forward in the spring of 1945.

> Mike was in the middle of a losing streak on stage, at the parimutuel windows and at the Friars Club. He played gin rummy at ten dollars a point and lost fifty-three thousand at one sitting. He was making only twenty-thousand dollars a week but

he was not discouraged. He was confident things would get better.

A position as an executive producer at a fabulous salary, even at Hollywood standards, plus a percentage of the profits of all pictures he made, awaited him at Universal-International Studios on the Coast. He needed a property, and the one he liked, Edna Ferber's *Great Son*, was priced at two-hundred thousand dollars.

He was tapped out on Broadway. He thought a moment and called Henry Crown in Chicago. After much negotiation Crown lent him the money to take an option on Miss Ferber's novel.

The best footnote to this endorsement of her novel by a producer was that Ferber returned the favor by taking a shine to Todd. She thought him a charming diamond in the not-so-rough, calling him "the dashing masher," and writing a posthumous sketch of him as vivid as he seemed to have been: "This ebullient man's memory probably will vanish after his Jovian death in the skies . . . But no one who knew him will forget him in a lifetime. Restless, dynamic, improbable and highly amusing, preposterous and handsome. A disarming showman. Vitality, but somehow exhausting, too, like being in the company of a ten million volt electric wire." However, in spite of all this energy, Todd never did film *Great Son*. What he did do was marry Elizabeth Taylor, who embodied Ferber's heroine, Leslie, in the movie of *Giant*. Todd died shortly afterward, in 1958, when his private plane crashed. The name of the plane was *Lucky Liz*.

Ferber had begun to feel at a disadvantage as a writer during the years the Texas book lay dormant. She had been psychologically preoccupied with the horrors of World War II and aesthetically and domestically preoccupied with her new Connecticut residence. Although her work shoulder was never far from the wheel, she became increasingly restless and irritable with the results. She made *Great Son* into her personal waterloo, using it as a gauge of her relationship with Doubleday & Co. It is interesting to note how powerful she was—or felt she was—in her campaign to withdraw herself from their celebrity-authors roster. Feeling that she was not receiving the attention she required—that there was a paucity of staff—as well as hinting that their accounting acuity had slipped, she decided to decamp. She rebukes Nelson Doubleday in this "Dear John" correspondence of August 1945:

> In the past eight or ten years, dear Nelson, I've done so much muttering that I'm certain this letter will not particularly surprise you. We differ so widely, your firm and I, on what constitutes book-publishing that I'm uncomfortable and perhaps you are, too. So I'm writing to say that we're parting as publisher and author.
>
> My thanks to you for the many pleasant things that have resulted from our long publishing relationship. I do hope I shall see you and Ellen during this autumn or winter before you are off to the plantation again.
>
> My affectionate greetings to you both, and every good wish in the world.

Doubleday was appalled, expressing such abject dismay that one feels not only his tremendous loss but the panic of trying to recoup it:

> Dearest Edna,
>
> Of course your letter was a great shock to me as I wired you, and I started digging around to find out what had happened to provoke the attitude of mind such as you indicated in your letter. It didn't take me very long to find out, and to say that I'm horrified beyond words puts it mildly. [In fact, Doubleday investigated the Ferber file of the previous year to view her complaints, which had been distributed.] I don't want to make excuses but I'm sure you realize the essential truths of the following statements. Our best boys, our most diplomatic, most careful-thinking people went to war. They are beginning to dribble back now, thank God. In the meantime we have had to make do.
>
> Personally, I have been flooded with so many difficulties—paper, manufacture, complete disruption through war energies of our whole manufacturing and business facilities that I am sad to relate I have neglected a great many publishing operations that under normalcy

I would have been able to spend more time on. It was not until your letter came in that I realized how damned foolish I had been not to keep a more careful hand on the editorial operations of the company.

You and our company have prospered together over many years (twenty-one years) and can prosper still further. The importance in the continuity of publishing is quite important to my mind. However, I realize that our organization has spilt milk which to me at the present moment is plenty sour. I should like to ask if you will let me do a reconstruction job, not on the milk that has been spilt but on re-creation. I don't want to reduce royalties. I care only about the increased values of properties. There are a lot of things I should like to have you think about, because after all, your older books are still in our hands and our job is, regardless of whether or not you leave us on new books you create, to do important publishing on those books you have trusted us with for lo these many years. I do think you ought to give some consideration to the development of the property as a whole.

I know that your indictment will be that I should have done this months ago. I accept the indictment and should like to make amends. Furthermore, I think that because of my love and affection for you, if you decide to go elsewhere I might be able to give you some advice that would have a bearing on the continuity in publishing your property, that I know you desire to be a monument to the world of literature.

Now that gas rationing is off, I do wish you would let me come to Easton and sit down with you for a couple of hours and talk about this whole matter. I promise to spend my time on constructive publishing and not shedding tears about this situation enough to fill your swimming pool, which I could easily do.

He signs his abject apologia, "Ever devotedly, Nelson."

The epistolary saga, far from over, left her with the final word to an open door, as she suggests in her following day's letter. But first, a good deal of finger-wagging:

Stage Door: the play (1936) and the movie (RKO Pictures, 1937)

Dear Nelson:

I am horrified to learn from your letter that you think my dissatisfaction is based on a matter of royalties. Nothing could be farther from the truth. You must have gotten this mistaken impression from someone other than myself.

Royalties and money (important though I think they are) never have been subjects of dispute between you and me. I myself have, on occasion, offered to cut royalties, as you know.

Your letter was a fine one, and it touched me deeply. I feel, though, that our conditions have had little to do with the points which have for years so irked me in connection with your publishing business. A book isn't just black marks on white paper with a colored jacket. A book should be thought, it should be life, it should be civilization.

In your organization there has been, for years, no one to whom one could talk as writer to editor. But that is an important part of book publishing. Important! It is book publishing.

Great Son is a faulty book. Intelligent editorship could have helped to overcome some of its most glaring faults. I sensed its weakness but I was too close to it, and, too disturbed by the war and the world, to right these faults. Your outfit wasn't even equipped to catch the book's mechanical boners. A thousand people have written me, calling attention to an error that I (or any sixteen-year-old reader) should have caught.

I'm not a word-machine. I'm a writer. Your list is too long, your presses too hungry, to make it possible for you to waste time and money and thought on any one book. You don't have to.

But I do.

I'd love to see you, of course, and I hope to . . .

Yours, E.F.

This exchange reveals the warrior Ferber: brave, arrogant, righteous on the verge of irritating, unvanquished.

Civility still presided over hotly cantankerous and staunchly justified issues. It is interesting that Ferber points to slipshod editing although she was certainly a homegrown writer whose imaginative grammar tracks through all her work. Her prose is what makes her work so readable, so devourable. Even a lesser-known—and perhaps a lesser-written—Ferber novel always reads better than a meticulously curated tome.

The Ferber-Doubleday correspondence also brings out an unusual form of courtship, perhaps evoking a subliminal need on her part. As seemingly straight-shooting as she appeared to be, there are also hints of emotional negotiation. Perhaps in her substantial need to win she fought harder than most to do so. However, her lifelong sense of fairness allowed her negotiating skills an element of seduction. She always left room for reentry.

I don't know exactly when Nelson Doubleday traveled from his home in Oyster Bay, New York, to pay his visit to Ferber in Easton, Connecticut. The result, however, is known. Ferber continued to be a Doubleday author for the rest of her life, with *Giant* considered her greatest seller as well as one of theirs.

———

Katharine Hepburn was a good friend of Ferber's. Although they did not spend substantial time together, they shared a deep understanding. They had met in 1936 when the Broadway production of Ferber and Kaufman's *Stage Door* was in the planning stages. At that time, Hepburn was the girlfriend of the appointed director, Jed Harris. It was thought that Hepburn would play the leading role of Terry Randall, until she and Harris parted ways over his infidelity with the actress and budding movie star Margaret Sullavan, who then inherited and debuted the role. Ironically, Hepburn later won the lead in the movie version, directed by Gregory La Cava in 1937.

Ferber and Hepburn immediately recognized a trait in each other. Hepburn had a term for it: "We were both unicorn women," she once told me. It is a phrase that at the time I interpreted as well as I could: they both remained single and dominant in a world of romantically paired people, where women were more often than not still subsidiary or recessive. Ferber and Hepburn strode proudly one-horned through their entire lives. Both were intolerant of injustice, laziness, stupidity, and arrogance, speaking their minds with passionate eloquence. They lived their lives—public and private—as they saw fit.

Later, I would reexamine what Katharine Hepburn had said. In 1975, while working on my biography of Ferber, I was summoned by Hepburn for a visit one midwinter day. Thinking more interview than visit, I lugged my cumbersome tape recorder from Philadelphia, where I then lived, to her town house in the Turtle Bay area of New York City. Her assistant, Phyllis, nicely but firmly removed the machine from my hands after taking my coat, putting both in the front closet. It was a wordless procedure that I found strangely charming, along with her offer of a bowl of Yankee bean soup.

The whole afternoon visit—from two to five—was magic among the lilacs, as Hepburn had just received a vast floral shipment the day before. Generally, in winter lilacs are out of season, but not when it came to Hepburn. She talked mainly about men and women, about Spencer, and about opportunities seized and missed. After winning an Oscar for *Morning Glory* in 1933 she had a slump. Studios didn't know quite how to slot her and audiences didn't know what to make of her upper-crust speech and manner. Although her dance card continued to be full of movie roles, she finally went home to Connecticut to recover and reassure herself. When she did return with full confidence to "the business," it was on Broadway, playing in Philip M. Barry's enormous hit *The Philadelphia Story*. She also talked about Ferber, mainly asking me questions—hard ones: Was she happy, fulfilled? Did she have any regrets or remorse? What did she consider her greatest achievement?

At the end of my visit, after winding up cross-legged on the floor, playing a Chinese checkers game Ferber had given her, I asked her what she thought a one-word summation of Ferber might be. "Giant," she said solemnly. "She was a giant individual."

It was in 1948, almost three decades before my visit with Hepburn, that Ferber got real about writing her *Giant*. Later it would be promulgated that it took her eight years to write when it actually took more like thirteen, what with the avoiding, the processing, the committing, and the vast research. She had told a few trusted people about her plans—maybe more than a few, because suddenly helping hands appeared from all over. Perhaps it is difficult to fathom now what a major name she was back then, but before the popular rise of television, the general public's main forms of entertainment were listening to the radio, reading newspapers and magazines, going to the movies, and poring over volumes of books, both classic and popular. So, the name Edna Ferber for book readers was a household one. And when it became clear that her newest fictional aim was the state of Texas, there were competitors lining up to offer the "best" help.

Because Ferber rarely left anything unsaid, she set down—in recollection—her aims for tackling the gargantuan project in a few little-known pages that clearly sell the book to herself:

> *Giant*, the novel, was the result of a haunt. Like any other specter it had to be exorcised by the customary mumbo-jumbo before its victim could be free of it. There is only one method by which a writer can be rid of a haunting subject, no matter how stubbornly resistant. The ghostly nuisance must be trapped and firmly pinned down on paper so that its wails and moans concerning neglect are forever stilled, its clammy touch on the consciousness banished. Many a woman has married an importunate childhood sweetheart in her later years just to be rid of his beguiling memory.
>
> *Giant*, in the guise of Texas, haunted me for a decade or more. I shrank from it, I shuddered to contemplate the grim task of wrestling with this vast subject. Finally I wrote it to be rid of it.
>
> Texas of the 1930s and 1940s was constantly leaping out at one from the pages of books, plays, magazines, newspapers. Motion pictures of Texas background were all cowboys and bang-bang. Texas oil, Texas jokes, Texas money billowed out of that enormous southwest commonwealth. The rest of the United States regarded it with a sort of fond consternation. It was the overgrown spoiled brat, it was Peck's Bad Boy of today, it was the crude uncle who had struck it rich. In a brief interval of semi-idleness and mental vacuity that occurs now and

then in the life of all writers I decided to go down and have a look at this southwest phenomenon as one might travel to gaze upon the Grand Canyon. This Texas represented a convulsion of nature, strange, dramatic, stupefying.

That first visit was in April, and it was accomplished by train, not air travel. Unbelievably now, air travel at that time was not casual as it is today. The journey from New York on the Atlantic seaboard to Houston so near the Gulf of Mexico was arduous and tedious even for a traveler who used to enjoy watching America slide past a train window. The temperature in Houston was in the high nineties, the old Rice Hotel was a mass of gigantic beef-fed men in ten-gallon hats and high-heeled boots and dun-colored clothes. In the residence section of the oil-rich there were the most glorious azalea gardens; and in practically every city and town one encountered the worst food to be found anywhere in the United States. Tough beef and fried everything. Houston, Dallas, San Antonio, all interesting, somewhat improbable; brash, overwhelming, hospitable, larger than life. No visitor, casual though he might be, could fail to feel the almost fierce vitality that rocked the whole vast region. Here was something that was being built and enjoyed at the same time; here was arrogance and hard work and almost stupefying riches spurting out of the earth in the form of oil, cattle, crops.

But I'll have nothing to do with all this, I said to myself. No, thank you. Nothing could ever induce me to try to pin this giant down on paper. This Gulliver would require a whole army of Lilliputians, this Goliath needs a David. I want none of it.

Years passed. I wrote an autobiography, three or four novels, two plays. I could not put Texas out of my mind. Improbable events, incredible people, fantastic incidents boiled up out of Texas. The effluvia penetrated every corner of the United States. The inner urge to try to pin down on paper this incredible form of civilization called Texas became irresistible. Ten years after my first visit I returned to Texas, this time by air. Brownsville on the Mexican border; Dallas, the north Texas fashion center; the Panhandle; little cow-towns; colonies of wetbacks living in wretchedness. Oil wells, ranches, palaces, shacks; fiestas, frijoles, champagne, tequila; the college professor, the grease-monkey, the rancher, the storied old city of San Antonio; the overnight oil town just rearing its frowsy head above the desert. Texas. Exhilarating, violent, charming, horrible, fascinating, shocking. Texas alive. A giant.

One of Ferber's literary assets was her rapacious research, which alchemized into vivid geographical portrayals. One of the helping hands toward her investigation was an old acquaintance, an American journalist named Holland McCombs. A bureau chief for *Time* and *Life* magazines in, among other places, Mexico City and Dallas, he knew about the pecking order of ranches and where literary oil was buried. Helping Ferber became a special project of his, as is evidenced in excerpts from this charming 1948 letter addressed to her at her Treasure Hill estate:

Dear Edna Ferber:

Dan Longwell [her editor at Doubleday at that time] tells
me that your interest in Texas has been revived and that you
would like to come down and spend some time at a ranch or
two . . . Why don't you write me and tell me specifically in
what way I can help with your project. As you know I will
do my best to perform in any way that will help such a fond
friend. And as you know, ranchers as a breed are a bit gruff-
like and, in these days, Texas ranchers and other Texans have
had their feelings somewhat bruised by what they consider the
enmity, antipathy and lack of understanding on the part of
Northern and Eastern writers . . . but I can tell them that you
are a personal friend and I believe that will make considerable
difference. However, it will help both me and them if you
can give me some idea as to what sort of material you are
interested in. As I say, the Texas ranch folks have become
pretty skittish of being written about—where they used to
just love it, as you know.
    There is, however, one ranch to which you are not only
welcome regardless of what you write but one to which

you will just have to come whether you think it will do you any professional good or not. And that is the McCombs' ranch at Cyprus Mill, Texas, 'way up in the blue hills of the Pederanales [*sic*] country . . . My wife and I have bought a cattle, goat and sheep ranch . . . Here, too, we can possibly give you some inkling as to what it is like on a hill country ranch, and we can introduce you to some of our neighbors. We have both kinds—good and colorful ones, and mean and sneaky ones. That's sort of the way it is in the world, isn't it? Anyway, we are very excited and pleased about the prospects of your visit . . .

People were beginning to beseech her to allow them to guide her toward the most valuable destinations. There was a Mr. W. G. Swenson from the SMS Ranches, who wrote to Margaret Cousins on Ferber's behalf. Cousins was the managing editor of *Good Housekeeping* magazine, who often serialized Ferber's novels. In her bid to being the chosen one to serialize the upcoming *Giant*, she had contacted rancher Swenson, who replied:

I am glad to learn that Edna Ferber plans to come to Texas to collect background material for a book on Texas ranch life. We shall be very glad to have her visit us and will be glad to show her around and show her how our ranches are operated. Hence, please tell her that she will be more than welcome at any time . . . I think probably you met the foreman of our Flat Top Ranch, Scandalous John Selmon, when you were here, and I think Miss Ferber will enjoy visiting this ranch and talking with John . . . I also hope you can both come to the Cowboy Reunion next summer . . .

One of the prize sweet-tongued correspondents, who I'm sure gave Ferber a chuckle—and she loved a good chuckle—was a woman who lived in San Angelo, Texas. Ferber obviously had previously visited her, and when it came time to draft the novel, a good deal of Vashti Snythe, the newly filthy-rich, good ole girl, was based on her. One can almost hear Jane Withers, who played Vashti in the movie, deliver these words:

I judge by now you have received my package mailed out via parcel post to you last week. It was sent like the cowpokes always do—not much on looks but hell for stout—. The sax [sacks] are all of different material and bear in mind they all contained salt and were picked up on the range or brought in from the range. I included two "spritzes." The little cake you may not want or relish but if you will keep in mind I've made over five tons of it you will at least appreciate this fact. I must admit they are not up to my standard. When I roamed the range and was monarch of all I surveyed I had ample wild plum jelly and all the luscious country butter I needed. These two ingredients made a world of difference in the flavor. Every few months we get Honey from Hell as we charge the bee man nothing for pasturage for his bees. I couldn't resist sending you some of that. It has a different tang from other honey due to the flowers the bees gather the honey from. Anyhow—I sent it all with my very best wishes and hope you take time out of your very busy full life to take a peek and taste of it all.

I cannot resist taking enuff time to tell you what a nice guest you were. Really—the pokes all say you give strong evidence that you will "belly right up to the lick log [meaning salt lick]." This in cow terms suggesting to "stand firm" is quite a compliment to a new comer.

My children liked you. My grandees liked you. My cowboys liked you. My husband liked you. My good friend Ruby liked you—and I liked you. Do feel at liberty to come down to a big branding and eat food really cooked out in the wide open spaces. These occasions happen twice a year in the spring and in the fall. Welcome anytime you can get away.

You will forgive my husband for making you eat the last nite you were here. These ranchmen live to eat only and he did I am sure annoy you by taking you to the airport but that is West Texas way of doing things. I repeat—no better people live on the earth—you will find them only in Heaven that excel us in any way.

May I say again you were a perfect guest, a grand sport [Ferber was apparently inducted into their indigenous ways] and took the wild and wooly west like a vet. We did appreciate this and appreciate you. I hope you come again sometime.

Ferber had a wide range of caring friends. Access was often a by-product of the famous, and she knew many of the high and mighty, but she could not abide phonies or those who put on airs. She had a no-fail midwestern barometer. One of her favorite friends was a Pulitzer Prize–winning cartoonist named Jay "Ding" Darling, who was Michigan-born but lived in Des Moines, Iowa. He was also the founder of the National Wildlife Federation. Although Ferber never had a domestic pet, she kept and grazed livestock on Treasure Hill. These two shared many of the same sensibilities. He was instrumental in leading her to where she eventually went. He wrote in 1949: "Dick Kleberg of King Ranch is in a most receptive mood I hear. If you didn't contact him on your last trip let me know and I'll engineer a friendly meeting."

A woman named Beatrice Griffith also had a keen nose for steering Ferber. She had published a book in 1948 called *American Me*. It was a look at Mexican American youths living and attempting to learn in Los Angeles in the 1940s. To quote a review from *Kirkus*, it was a "particularly eloquent presentation of a minority, the Mexican in California, and is often ingenuously appealing material as alternate chapters tell of incidents in the words of the children. Here is the tragedy of the Mexican in America . . . American me, American inside but Mexican on top . . . The inadequacies of housing, health, prejudice in schools and courts, exploitation of cheap labor; the old people, humble, helpless, confused; the hindrances to integration . . ."

The content in this book is what Ferber wanted in her novel: the indigenous lowdown on the Mexican situation. Griffith was more than happy to oblige in a 1949 letter: "I shall do my best to put you in touch with the right people in Texas. I think it is very important . . . On the other hand, the feel and flavor of the Mexicans is particularly theirs, and you should experience that too."

So, she did. She steeped herself in detective work on the Mexican side of life. Coming so soon out of a war against atrocious prejudice, injustice, and genocide, she felt a responsibility to represent the Mexican Americans vs. the state of Texas. Her written impressions alone could be compiled into a valuable tract. In some visceral remnants, one can see the hard-driving reporter in Ferber, collecting the evidence that would eventually deliver her case:

THE STREETS. White hot. Wind blown. The white buildings, the white walks, the white-blue sky seared the eyeballs. No one walked. If you saw moving people on the streets they were Mexicans. Squatting on their heels on the street corners.

Mexican settlement. Houses on crude stilts. Rather pretty with their white plaster walls and the oleander trees, the courtyard and the balconies. Inside you saw there were no toilets, they used the crude outhouse as a community; no running water, no electricity. As crude as the huts in which their Mexican ancestors had lived. Rotten floor. Rats shipped in at night.

In that vast kingdom the negroes had taken on an acceptance of their fate. They encountered little of the searing disrespect that the deep south gave their race. This was the southwest, there was a freer air for them. Besides, the Texans had another whipping boy, the Texans had the Mexicans. Here was a people of dark skins, here was their enemy to be kept in his place.

And then Ferber goes into uppercase, as if tracking activity in a screenplay:

SAN ANTONIO. ALAMO. A MEXICAN WITH HIS WIFE AND THREE SMALL CHILDREN TRAILING WIDE-EYED AND SILENT THROUGH THE ALAMO. THE MUSEUM WAS PRESIDED OVER BY A DUSTY DRY AND SPECTACLED DAUGHTER OF TEXAS. ABOUT HER THERE WAS THE AIR OF A SCHOOL TEACHER TOO WATCHFUL OF HER PUPILS. THE MEXICANS GAZED UP AT THE VIVID BAD PAINTINGS THAT ALMOST COVERED THE GRAY STONE WALLS. THEY DEPICTED THE BRAVE WHITE AMERICANS TRIUMPHING OVER THE SAVAGE DARK SKINNED MEXICANS. YOU WONDERED HOW THEY LIKED THIS, HOW THEY FELT AS AMERICAN CITIZENS AS THEY REGARDED THEMSELVES IN THIS LIGHT. THEY

SAID NOTHING. THE WOMAN QUIETED THE BABY
IN HER ARMS, THE MAN HELD THE HANDS OF THE
RESTLESS WIDE-EYED SMALL CHILDREN.

1835. ALAMO MUSEUM. THE LONG RIFLE. BRASS
TRIMMED. SIX FEET LONG, DECORATED WITH THE
BRASS EAGLE, USED IN DEFENSE OF THE ALAMO.
THESE MEN IN LEATHER BUCKSKIN WERE FROM
MASSACHUSETTS. HERE WAS THE ALCALDE OF
THE DISTRICT.

TEXAS BORDER TOWNS DIDN'T THINK OF
MEXICANS AS PEOPLE AT ALL. THEY WERE OF THE
HUMAN SPECIES, THEY WALKED ON TWO LEGS,
THEY WERE ON ANOTHER PLANE, THEY INHAB-
ITED A KIND OF LIMBO DOWN AT WHICH YOU
COULD LOOK.

Ferber made sure that her Mexican characters had appropriately
curated names. She researched first names and surnames, typing them
in her ledger under MEXICAN NAMES: "LUZ and POLO RIVAS,
CATERINA and ROSENDO VALDEZ, ADELICIA and RENALDO
SANDOVAL, ANGELINA and AMADOR MEZO, JUVENTINA
and FIDEL QUIROZ, LUPE and MAXIMO RODRIGUEZ, JUANA
and ARCADIO GUTIERREZ, PETRA and TOMAS QUINTAN-
ULA, DELUVINA and EUSEBIO SALAZAR."

More men's names followed. Like many fiction writers, she relished
homing in on a character's name. A Ferber specialty was in digging for
regional authenticity. It is clear from her research notes that she wanted
to properly represent the Mexican American population. She was clear-
eyed and without attitude in reporting the conditions, some repre-
hensible: "Mexicans in valley. Migrant workers. The valley vegetable
and cotton crop pickers. Subnormal living conditions. Mexican con-
sul in Hermosa refused service in a filling station barbeque sandwich
shop."

And then some of her scenarios were bursts of color, joy, and ritual
as the one titled "Mexican Wedding":

BODA wedding feast. Ceremony of showing the trousseau at
wedding reception. The bridegroom furnished the trousseau,

the brides dresses, etc. Her marriage success is gauged by the clothes he gives her.

BARBEQUE—Barbequed meat and beans. The Caque (one of the American words twisted to the Spanish tongue) Color de rosa. It was a favorite—pink dough sometimes colored with pink vegetable coloring, and sometimes simply colored with red crepe paper soaked in water, the water mixed with the caque dough, very tasty.

The table was spread out of doors. Not only the barbequed meat and the color de rosa but Pan de polvo, little round cakes with a hole in the middle, shaped with the hand and sugary and grainy, like sand cakes. Then Bunuelo, rolled paper thin, and big as the big frying pan in which they were fried in deep fat. Covered with cinnamon and sugar they were delicious with coffee. Beer, tequila, mescal.

The bride's dress was of white satin, with pearls, wax orange blossoms, wreaths. The dress was hung then in the best room, never again worn.

The bride appeared in her seven dresses, walking along the platform that had been built for her. The girls eyed her with envy.

And now, among the notes, she suddenly goes into story, as if she had already mapped out the framework of *Giant*.

JORDAN'S SON DIDN'T GO TO THE WAR, BUT THE MEXICAN BOY, SON OF HIS OVERSEER BROUGHT HOME AND THE LOCAL UNDERTAKER WOULDN'T BURY HIM. HE WAS BURIED AT ARLINGTON, WITH HONORS. HE LAY WITH LINCOLN, WASHINGTON, THE GREAT OF THE UNITED STATES OF AMERICA. BOXES CAME HOME, YOU TRIED NOT TO THINK OF WHAT WAS WITHIN THEM. BROKEN LUMPS AND BITS OF BONE AND MAYBE CLOTH.

The plot is straightforward, although the technique is not. The novel is a generational saga about a ranching scion who travels from

Texas to Virginia to buy a prize horse to add to his impressive stock. The daughter of the horse owner captures his eye along with the horse. He acquires the horse and marries the daughter, bringing them both back to Texas. We follow their marital, environmental, and theoretical ebbs and flows over the next twenty-five years as they raise a family and constantly cope with each other. There are other ingredients in the story—a jealous, possessive sister, a charismatic villain, several headstrong children, and many oppressed Mexican Americans. And there is Texas itself, ever itself, ever changing. The novel does not unfold in linear fashion, but begins at the end, works back, and then goes forward to meet the beginning. It is about class; about new Texas money and old; about oil barons and longtime cattle ranchers and the clash of both.

The formal first name of the leading male character, Bick Benedict, is Jordan. No one ever calls him that except for Leslie, who calls him nothing else. She is a fearless and unselfconscious heroine, constantly breaking from Texas convention and traditions. She is the heart of the novel and its engine for change. Bick is a towering figure but not the hero/protagonist of the story. Seldom, if ever, is a male character the hero in a Ferber novel or short story. He is the foil for the heroine. Somewhat of an exception is the character of Clint Maroon in *Saratoga Trunk*, who becomes heroic through the course of the story by fighting for the outsider against the powerful and corrupt without ever losing his devilish gleam. But Bick has the Aristotelian "fatal flaw" in heroine Leslie's eyes, which is also Ferber's unforgiving lens.

Their two children, Jordy and Luz (Luzita), resemble the mixed bag of offspring today, revealing more of Ferber's prescience. Jordy is considered soft and pacifistic and Luz is a bronco girl, hell-bent for anything in front of her. "IF HE'S A BOY," Ferber writes in her notes, presumably in Bick's voice, in the uppercase declarative,

I'M GOING TO HAVE THE BRINGING UP OF THAT ONE. AND HE WAS. AT FIVE HE BOUGHT HIM A ROPE, A HAT, BOOTS, CHAPS, GUN. HE THEN TAUGHT HIM TO LASSOO EVERYTHING FROM A FENCE POST TO THE DOG. AT ROUND UP TIME HE TAUGHT HIM TO CUT OUT THE STEERS, YOU SAW HIM HANDLE HIS HORSE WITH THE MOST

EXQUISITE DEXTERITY. "GET THAT WHITE-FACED ONE . . . THAT RUNTY RED . . ." GRUDGINGLY HE SAID, DRYLY, "YOU DID THAT PRETTY WELL." "THANKS, PAPA." THE BOY HATED IT. FROM THE FIRST SHE WAS HER FATHER'S DAUGHTER. RIDING. HANGING AROUND THE BUNKHOUSE. NEVER WORE SKIRTS.

And then there is Angel Obregon, the Mexican boy they grow up with, who embodies all that Bick believes in, who willingly goes to war for his country, and is the one given the hero's burial. It seems obvious that Ferber had already figured this out in her book plan.

She had mapped out the information that she needed to dispense from her sprawling yet illuminating notes. They read like a rather well-organized stream of consciousness. Her facts become impressionistic, as she keys herself for fiction, setting up the Anglo-Saxon world of the Texan. She always titles her notes—presumably easier to file.

THE RANCH. COWBOYS. CHARACTER STUFF. TECHNICAL. DESCRIPTIVE.

In round-up a man is posted East, South, and West.

You heard the click of high heels on wood or stone or cement. Like the sound of a woman's heels, but sharper, harder, quicker.

The Texas cowhands (white) had the most beautiful manners in the world. Quiet, soft-spoken, gentle. Their voices quite unlike the voices of the women.

They had the free mien and the spacious good nature, and the gentle voice (the men that is) of those who are uncrowded. They had space to spare. They breathed miles of air, each one. The gaze was straight and fearless, the eye did not slide round to the corner. They wore their freedom as a garment—they wore life like a flowing cloak about their shoulders, swinging free, billowing out life a sail behind them.

CHARACTER—TEXAS TOWNS—CITIES—HOTELS

Men in wide brimmed Texas hats (Stetsons) and blue jeans and cowboy boots lolled in the vast leather chairs amidst the

Roman columns—marble columns—of the Driscoll Hotel in Corpus Christi, or The Cactus in San Angelo, or the Rice Hotel in Houston, or The Shamrock.

WAITRESSES AT THE DRISCOLL HOTEL, CORPUS CHRISTI

You entered the vast and absurd room. The white hot sun never penetrated here. Everything was air conditioned. The Saracen Room, the Moorish room. There a band brayed brassily. You entered. In from June until November if you were a man and wore a suit coat you were immediately branded as an easterner.

At the door stood the head waitress and her second, hearty girls and hard working. As the prospective diner peered into the noisy gloom of the Moorish room these approached in welcome. Their hair was blonde, their skin bloomed even in that dimness, they wore evening dresses with valiantly flashing Woolworth gems and paillettes and flowers pinned in their hair. They were as guileless as milk, they mothered the dining room patrons.

"Hello there!" they said in airy greeting as they approached, menu in hand. "Hi!" When you left they called after you cheerfully, in parting, "Come back quick!"

Men and women came in, stood doubtfully at the entrance. The men were in shirt sleeves or often in denim pants. Not smart blue slacks but work pants with plaid shirts or blue. This was not sportswear or the garb of the Hollywood type. These were everyday clothes of the field and the prairie and somehow a shock in the Moorish room of the big modern hotel.

Judging by her notes, she devoted much time to understanding the Mexican situation in Texas. Alongside the beleaguered Mexican, there was, surprisingly, the rich oil Mexican, particularly someone named Lobo-Wolf, who

built a house in the midst of San Rafael. Spanish. The front hall was tiled in the design of a Mexican rug. The deep freeze was vast as a mausoleum. Through the glass door you saw it stuffed to bursting with food. All sorts of food. Meat. Vegetables. Gallons of ice cream—strawberry, peach, raspberry. There were six bathrooms in the colors of the rainbow—orchid bath, orchid toilet, orchid washstand. Rose bath. Rose toilet. Rose washstand.

In the front room the eye met objects which the mind rejected as trompe l'oeil. A floor lamp stopped halfway to become a clock. Gold-framed mirrors were female forms (draped) clutching cornucopias of bloated fruits. Overall an indefinable air of mustiness and bad housekeeping. The sun and the gulf damp were peeling the paint and warping the wood. Not a book of any kind in the house.

Ferber was intrigued by contrasts, which she could turn into irony and, even further, into satire. In fact, later, when reviewers got a hold of the novel, some lambasted her for making fun of the great Lone Star state. After studying her notes, it is clear that she was "painting" what she saw—the good, the bad, and the ugly. As she continues with her notes on the Mexicans, again she dips into story by subtitling this batch "New Look Benedict," meaning perhaps that time elevated the Mexicans who were, or had been, employed on the Benedict ranch, which was increasingly influenced by the humanitarian, forward-thinking Leslie.

The Town of San Diego. Ten or twenty miles to the east and twenty to the west lay the prosperous towns of Burdock and the town of Elsie and they flourished. Neat streets and store windows glittering with white enamel washing machines and deep-freezers. Self-service store and two movie houses and a white stucco hotel with purple over the veranda posts, and an air-conditioned coffee shop.

The women in their open-toed shoes (sandals) and their good cotton or crepe dresses, and their hair done every week at the Beauty Shoppe.

But Nopal was another sort of town. The houses were like whitened bones in the desert, gray-white, bleached and pitted by the wind and the rain and the sun and the fog. The walks were broken, the weeds choked the bedraggled flowers, flies droned at the doors of the shabby shops that said the tortilla factory.

El Nuevo Mundo was the dry goods store. The New World. A broken down shack, leaning crazily, its balcony slipping overhead at angle of ninety. Houses ghostly, bitten by the sand, the damp, the sun, the fierce northers.

"Oil leases" said a sign over hovel. The C.O.D. café. Pena's Place.

In Quintanilla's store window were printed signs. They advertised Lady Windermere sheets. "Advertised in LIFE," the tag on them read. The black-garbed women with five children tugging at their skirts and a baby in their arms—the young women old at twenty-five.

Her reactions to the racial disparity were rage and disgust. She made note of the racial pecking order of Blacks vs. Mexicans. Ferber came upon some hard evidence of how deep the rift was between Mexican Americans and Texans when she was told about the Blackwell School in Marfa. This was one of the leading components that fueled her outrage, increasing her appetite to tell a story large enough to encompass an ongoing civil conflict.

The Blackwell School of Marfa dates from 1885 (Ferber's birth year), when the doors were open to all children. Then in 1892, a sparkling new elementary school, called the Marfa Ward School, was built for only Anglo children. In 1909, the school board designated funds for a new adobe school building to be constructed and restricted to Hispanic children.

At first referred to only as the Mexican School, after 1940 both the adobe building and Marfa Ward were together renamed the Blackwell School in honor of its founder and longtime principal, Jesse Blackwell. The school's purpose was to teach children only up until the ninth grade. Blackwell closed in 1965, eventually reopening to integration.

Ferber learned that while the law mandated separate schools for African Americans during the Jim Crow era, the decision of whether to segregate Hispanics was up to individual districts in Texas. Many of the schools opted to do this, and by the 1940s segregated schools for Hispanics occupied more than 120 towns across the state. In 1936, Alpine built a segregated facility and named it the Centennial School to honor the one hundredth anniversary of Texas's independence from Mexico. I can see Ferber's quirky, sweet-and-sour smile conveying the irony of this.

Although cordoned off, the Blackwell School was known for its comprehensively upbeat education and achieving kids. One Lionel Salgado, who attended Blackwell in the forties, gave it high marks: "Our teachers were really good and kind, and a lot of those kids were bright kids. They'd get up to Marfa High School and be valedictorian or salutatorian. We carried ourselves pretty good."

Despite the students' successes and the reputation of Blackwell in consolidating Marfa's Mexican American students, it is no surprise that they suffered multiple indignities.

"Marfa is where I learned about racism," said Jesusita Williams Silva, who had started at Blackwell in 1956. She goes on to provide examples: "Seeing my mother pushed away at a store because she was Hispanic. Seeing my father work and not get paid enough because he was Hispanic. Seeing people humiliate my parents in front of their children. All that hurt. It still hurts."

Another child was in fourth grade when one day her teacher instructed the class to write down, "I will not speak Spanish in school or on the playground." The teacher gathered the notes and placed them in a cigar box. The class then gathered outside to witness the cigar box being lowered into a hole pre-dug at the base of the flagpole. In effect it was a funeral they had unwittingly attended, watching their liberties being buried. This memory was mentally recorded and spoken of years later: "They wanted us to speak English only. I told my friends, 'Nadie me va quitar que hable el español.' No one will take Spanish from me. A teacher heard me, walked me to the office and I got whupped hard with a big paddle. I ran home and didn't go back until my dad made me. I was black-and-blue." Yet another child bore witness to the scene around the flagpole: "You know what happened from that? I developed a habit of staying low. Don't speak out, don't speak up. I was intimidated."

One student was forced to bathe a classmate who was assumed to be dirty because her complexion was so dark. Blackwell boys of the fifties who were skilled enough to play on a combined football team with Anglos weren't allowed to use the locker room.

Even though the high schools were eventually integrated, they weren't really. During meetings in the auditorium, Anglos were directed to sit on one side, Hispanics on the other. The Palace movie theater in downtown Marfa was definitely segregated. And after dark, Hispanics had better be on their side of the tracks or safely tucked in bed.

One particular girl, who played high-school basketball with both Anglo and Hispanic girls, remembers an evening after a game in Alpine when the team stopped with their coach for burgers at a café. "The sign on the door said, 'No Dogs, No Mexicans.' So I said, "Watch and see." The girl, who had a light complexion, slid between her Anglo teammates, entered the café, ordered for her friends, then ran out to the bus with the food, to the cheers of the team. "I did it. I showed them," she crowed.

The nature of prejudice doesn't stop, and it didn't. This is what shook and inflamed Ferber when she was doing her research.

There is an exhilarating postscript that Ferber would have celebrated. Former Blackwell students are now the older generation. Many still live in Marfa. Some are teachers, one rising to become principal of a high school in Austin. Others made the law bar or worked in health care. Many served in the military. A few ran for elected office and won, breaking the all-Anglo, good-ole-boy lock. In increments, Marfa's political climate began reflecting the community's Hispanic majority. Most of Blackwell's buildings were torn down to build public housing; some inhabitants were descendants of the formerly segregated students. The school district still owned the school building but used it as deep storage. In 2006, a group of alumni calling themselves the Blackwell School Alliance transformed their former segregated school into an all-inclusive community center with a ninety-nine-year lease on the building and a historical marker erected outside. At the inauguration ceremony a woman pulled a Spanish dictionary from a small plywood coffin that had been symbolically buried for the ceremony. Holding it high, she cried "¡Yo tengo el español!"

The former student Lionel Salgado, now an elder statesman, shook hands with everyone there. "You treat people the way you want to be treated," he said. "It pays off. I don't have resentment. When I look out, I don't see Anglo or Hispanic. I see nothing but Marfans. I see only Marfa."

Had Ferber known the future of this school, the way things turned out so democratically, her spirits would have shot sky-high. As she always maintained, "The novels I wrote were novels of protest. Loving protest, but protest nonetheless. However, they had vitality, they told a story and they were not symbolic. In theme background plot characterization dialogue, they were written in the idiom of their day, clearly and purposefully."

This was where she put her faith: in writing novels of protest. I feel that after all her experience of cause and effect in her work, she anticipated a backlash coming toward this latest book. Perhaps she even welcomed it as an indication that her mission was accomplished. One of her favorite quotes was from Charles Dickens in his original preface to *Nicholas Nickleby*: "It is remarkable that what we call the world, which is so very credulous in what professes to be true, is most incredulous in what professes to be imaginary." After which her two cents were: "One can add little to that except to plead, somewhat plaintively, with reader and reviewer to believe that a writer of fiction, even today, may have an imagination."

———

Marfa was eventually where director George Stevens decided to film a good portion of the pivotal scenes in his movie of *Giant*. Marfa is a small town, about one mile wide and one mile deep, surrounded by ranchland in high desert of Far West Texas. It is sixty miles north of the Mexican town of Ojinaga. Today Marfa is known as home to many nonprofit organizations, the most illustrious being the Chinati Foundation, the creation of minimalist artist Donald Judd. A lively art community resides beside venerable ranching families, Mexican Americans who have been there for generations, and border patrol workers and their families. Marfa continues to be rediscovered by people seeking an off-the-beaten-path experience. Currently the topography nestling an artsy community, as well as *Giant* tales and artifacts, are the attractions. However, for at least a decade following the release of the movie, the only draw was the aura of *Giant*'s stars and lore.

There was a bit of lore connected to Marfa, and therefore to *Giant* and James Dean. This was known as the Mystery Ghost Lights of Marfa. These Marfa night lights, which physicists speculated were caused by a finite amount of mass and energy, were already infamous in the area. Some said they were lanternlike shapes, leading and lighting the way among the foothills of the Chinati Mountains, returning after sunset each evening. Dean was transfixed by this lighted path, rushing out to watch it night after night. After his death, the glow of these lights seemed to be stronger, and a myth grew up that they were the headlights of his long-lost Spyder racing car.

In America at that time, Texas was still mythical. Western novels (books by Zane Grey, *The Ox-Bow Incident*); early television (Gene Autry, Roy Rogers); movies (called "oaters," with John Wayne leading the pack); and folk songs ("Streets of Laredo") all promoted this rugged kingdom. We were excited by Texas even before Ferber planted her flag. Both my parents recalled that the family was always encouraging; we were her tightly knit fan club who praised her work and gratefully accepted its results. The *Giant* project felt special; to tweak the Paul Simon song title, it had diamonds on the soles of its shoes. It was a palpably exciting time. I was still very small when she began her travel research, but I do recall the fun postcards she sent to me—particularly the "sew cards." On these cards were drawings stitched in colorful thread. There were rodeo cards with riders on broncos; there were high-stepping Texas dudes and gals; and there were the Mexican cards depicting dark-skinned children playing in the street looking extra happy, men in sombreros, and pretty black-haired ladies in bright dresses. I loved these cards so much I took naps with them.

I think we all felt a delicious sense of purpose in Ferber. It was as though she had been renewed, which she, as well as most Americans, had felt in the not-so-distant past with the occurrence of V-J Day. Not that she would ever be able to sidestep the atrocities that befell millions of innocent people. Her luck was in her gift of phrase and the discipline to repeat the lonely execution of three pages a day over and over. Aside from telling a ripping good yarn, she was able to speak for the inarticulately oppressed. She never took this power for granted and was exceptionally articulate about the way to the means:

> In all these years there was rarely a waking moment when I did not think, consciously or unconsciously, in terms of writing;

of dialogue, character and situation. On a train, as I prepare to hang up my coat, the metal hangers strike the one against the other with the motion of the car. Immediately, like a mechanism which turns itself on, the mind goes to work. What was that sound? How would you describe that sound? Uh—the coat hangers whispering sibilantly together under cover of the train noises . . . mmm . . . too elaborate . . . uh . . . the thin whining music of the metal hangers singing in tune with the train . . .

She was convinced that this struggle provided her with the right to enjoy her success. And once she had secured it, her enjoyment was fleeting before the struggle reasserted itself. She talks about the years following the war and what led up to clearing the way for *Giant*:

> These years of successful writing have given me a false idea of my own importance. A very large number of people have read my books. I have enjoyed the kudos that goes with successful writing. It has been pleasant indeed to have that little edge of advantage in a highly competitive world . . . Had I made the circle and was I right back at the starting point? Or had I arrived at my final destination; and must I set forth again on a new journey, or be content to stay here forever looking back on the road I had traveled for so many years?

Ferber had always had a penchant for drama. When she was in her teens, her family would tease her by calling her "Sarah Heartburn," mimicking Sarah Bernhardt, supposedly the greatest actress of her time.

Ferber took her only thespian bows when she got to play a role she had written: Fanny Cavendish in *The Royal Family*, in a 1948 summer production at the Maplewood Playhouse in New Jersey. Her reviews were mostly respectful. *New York Times* critic Brooks Atkinson was somewhat less so: "As an amateur actress, in the tradition of Charles Dickens, who also wrote novels, Miss Ferber ranks about half-way between Sinclair Lewis and Alexander Woollcott . . . She settled down into a workman-like performance that did not disturb the drama very much . . . After she gets this whim out of her system she can settle down to the writing of a novel which we can all enjoy without reservations."

It is a dramatic occurrence for a writer to begin a new project—yet one that the true writer cannot help repeating. Ferber describes this form of "catechism":

> I knew that the old habit was still with me of translating everything I saw and felt and heard into terms of writing. I was busy as ever tucking bits of lace and silk and feathers and ribbon and muslin into the old trunk in the mental storeroom. Perhaps that is why writers grow old and gnomelike rather early in life. The impact of life against their emotions is so constant. It is like constantly being fed with a stimulant . . . It is a gift that makes life richer and more difficult at once, for having it one must cherish it and protect it, as is true of all possessed treasures.

Ten years had gone by since her first attempt at Texas. She was sixty-three when she took her next trip. Her personal life had never changed during that world-changing decade. She and her mother, Julia, were, as always, almost constant companions. Her celebrity friends were, for the most part, the same true-blue friendships she had maintained for years. By that time fame and its trappings were encrusted in Noël Coward, Alfred Lunt and Lynn Fontanne, Helen Hayes and Charles MacArthur, Marc Connelly, Richard and Dorothy Rodgers, George and Beatrice Kaufman, Moss Hart and Kitty Carlisle Hart, Mary Martin and Richard Halliday, Oscar and Dorothy Hammerstein, Katharine Hepburn, Katharine ("dear Kit") Cornell and Guthrie McClintic, George Oppenheimer, Margalo Gillmore, Louis Bromfield, Rebecca West, Fanny Butcher, etc. Ferber's address changed occasionally from the Majestic at 115 Central Park West to the elegant Prasada at Sixty-Fifth Street and Central Park West to the accommodating Lombardy Hotel on East Fifty-Sixth Street to the luxurious 730 Park Avenue. Her eating and sleeping habits were etched in stone. She ate deliciously prepared "healthy" meals and slept a solid eight hours with her face and neck coated in Elizabeth Arden night cream.

Her paramount requisite was the ability to keep a routine. The consistency of work and output was her life's blood. A quote of hers supports her raison d'être: "Life can't defeat a writer who is in love with writing, for life itself is a writer's lover until death."

When she lived at 730 Park Avenue during the last portion of her life, Ferber and her neighbors Richard and Dorothy Rodgers would entertain each other with frequent floral offerings, leaving bowers at each other's doors—that is, when she wasn't feuding with "dear Dickie."

Naturally, she loved reading but was particular and persnickety regarding fellow writers. She was not necessarily generous toward other women novelists. She had no tolerance for Pearl Buck, Virginia Woolf, or Fannie Hurst; she rather admired Edith Wharton, Rebecca West, and Willa Cather; and blatantly adored Louisa May Alcott, setting up an altar for her at an early age. *Rose in Bloom*, a little-known Alcott novel, was one of her favorites, with Rose, the heroine, uttering what could be a Ferber mantra: "We've got minds and souls as well as hearts; ambition and talent as well as beauty and accomplishments; and we want to live and learn as well as love and be loved. I'm sick of being told that is all a woman is fit for." And years later Ferber echoed this sensibility: "If each woman from eighteen to eighty would quietly take stock, determined to live up to her mental and physical and spiritual potentialities for one hour a day—even for two hours a week—our frantic world of today could be saved from itself."

So, in 1949, nothing had changed except much of the world, which, according to Ferber, excluded Texas: "Viewed near and from afar, this

Researching in Texas

giant commonwealth seemed not so much a Southwest state of the United States as a separate kingdom with its own laws, speech and mores; and, above all, its apartness other than geographically, from the rest of the nation. It was insular, it was bombastic; naïve, brash. And fascinating. Quite without conscious plan I read everything I could lay hands on about Texas."

She absorbed the outrageous stories. Between the two World Wars, the outlandish became the norm in Texas. Mind-blowing reports described million-acre ranches and oil wells gushing millions of gallons worth zillions of dollars. These were the ranches where only barren desert had been.

She read about "vaqueros complete with Mexican-Spanish chinstraps and silver spurs and a foreign speech; strange new breeds of cattle, humped and creamy-coated like creatures out of mythology; bizarre palaces rearing their grotesque turrets on the plain; million-a-week incomes; privately owned planes in a day when even public planes were still a special mode of transportation; huge men in roll-brimmed fifty dollar Stetsons; bejeweled women whose fingertips had only recently lost their washtub puckers."

Ferber's ability to reach for the stars in her imagery, switching up grammar to suit herself, was extremely particular. It was as if she played every instrument to her own compositions. And the curious thing was that she talked the way she wrote. Even though she may have thought that her work exposed her true expression, she was funny, pithy, and visually imaginative in her verbiage. Every sentence was essential. When she called me "Miss Gomit" (Goldsmith) or "Dollface," and when she said "Let's eat some icky cream," it conjured a child's existence, where the surroundings are all fun, often silly, playful, and delightful. When she describes Texas and her early efforts to inch toward it, she reaches as high and wide as possible: "The whole thing was larger than life. Notes and notes and notes piled up and became notebooks. Magazines were read and stored away. Newspapers. Photographs. Idiom. Clothes. Characteristics. Ten or more years, really, had gone into this, for I had become Texas-conscious with a writer's instinct for the dramatic, the important and the bizarre long before that first brief and rejected glimpse of Houston Dallas San Antonio Austin Corpus Christi and all the rest of the giant state."

It feels as if all her experiences as a writer had been in preparation

for a larger task. She is eloquent in describing herself as a searcher and
as a conduit:

> Often, in these many years of my life as a writer, I have been
> drawn to this or that section of the United States and even of
> Europe by a compulsion that was stronger than mere curios-
> ity. It was, unreasonably, like an urge to return to something
> I never actually had known. Reincarnationists may have an
> explanation for this. The places to which I travel with a pleas-
> ant excitement born of anticipation I invariably enjoy with a
> double enjoyment of inexplicable recognition. Love San Fran-
> cisco, don't like Los Angeles; found Charleston enthralling,
> rejected Florida; think Canada dullish, crazy for Alaska; fasci-
> nated by big burly Chicago, can't face Detroit; sometimes go
> to Boston just to be there, have no emotion about the rest of
> Massachusetts.

The big drumroll here is Texas. As it seems to turn out, she had not
rejected it a decade earlier. She was saving it: "My rejection of Texas on
that initial visit had not been on the grounds of pre-formed opinion
or inexplicable emotion. On the contrary, I had been vastly interested,
astounded; confused and startled; repelled and attracted."

She had said that writing about this state was a man's job, that it
was more suited to a male writer. She had mentioned Faulkner and
Hemingway—neither of whom she particularly admired—as potential
candidates. It is extremely unusual to come across her having thought
and talked this way, especially in print. She was a precursor of feminism
in outlook, deed, and lifestyle. It seemed as if there was nothing she
could not tackle, nothing that she would not fight for, nothing that
would suppress her. And by the end of the decade this proved true.

Eliza McGraw, in her highly intelligent book *Edna Ferber's America*,
delves into Ferber's grasp of this longhorn project. In her chapter titled
"Big Spaces, Big Problems: *Giant*," she writes, "More directly than any
of Ferber's other works, *Giant* tackles a larger and more fundamental
question: who is an American? With *Giant*, Ferber strives less to answer
this question than to expose its many ramifications."

So, she went back to Texas toward the close of 1948, arms wide
open.

One might think that when Ferber researched, she considered luxurious conditions a priority. She enjoyed topflight everything, of course, but was a true when-in-Rome person and preferred to absorb the essences of a culture. Her sister, Fannie, would often say that "Edna's celebrity got in her way." I think that is true in the abstract—that she wanted to be the "mole" burrowing for the story—but in truth, anonymity wasn't her nature; it didn't become her. She liked to be greeted by rooms with views, with flowers, with good champagne—"champers"— icing in a bucket. She had earned her high life but never forgot to relish it. She recalled the early sensations of feeling like a tourist in her own country—sometimes pampered, sometimes not: "The weeks spent in this great Southwest region of the United States were exhilarating and absorbing. Oddly enough, there was almost the impact of traveling in a foreign country. Certainly the Spanish language was common to south Texas. In spite of heat, cold, vast distances; insufficient sleep, fried food, Mexican food, humidity; over-exertion . . ."

This last is a strange sensation for Ferber to report. The only thing I can imagine it signaled for such a high-energy person was age. At sixty-three, the girl explorer in her might have been waning a bit. The first memory I had of her was that she was an old person, mostly because she had gray hair. It was beautifully groomed, silvery gray hair that smelled like cabbage roses, but aging went with the color and very young children make broad deductions. Her trips were vigorously planned; even reading about them makes one feel the mental and physical exertion: "There were new and strange situations, constant contact with strangers . . ."

Although this is no doubt true, these "strangers" immediately attached themselves. Wherever she went, they wrapped around her, these clinging yet often helpful vines. An example of this "appropriation" was a woman in San Angelo, who writes a funny and proprietary letter:

> When the news came out that you had been here, the press and my very personal friends simply tore into me, doing away with the present altogether and threatening my future if anything of the kind ever happened again . . . Dick Waring, the friend who wanted us to come to his ranch on Sunday afternoon, was very disappointed. He has a real showplace and is very gra-

cious and generous . . . However, those you met naturally all wanted to know what you thought of them . . . "Marm" went off delighted, and Dickie said you were the only person who had ever accused her of having any beauty. The "Battle Axe" thought you were the most gracious person she had taken to the Bar S and told it all over town "for shore, cowboy."

And then there is this, which is rather touching; it shows the penetrating effect Ferber could have on people: "Outside of the pleasure it gave me, meeting you did a lot for me. Your alertness made me so hideously aware of my appalling indifference. I was quite shocked when I realized it. I have thought of many things I wish I had talked to you about."

Ferber might have seemed quintessentially successful and resolved, which was half an illusion. In preparing for this next novel she had

swarms of doubts and fears that lurk in the mind of every writer as a new book is gestating—in spite of—and even rather savoring all these—I had on each Texas journey a sensation of refreshment and stimulation. Literally up and down this gigantic region I bounced; planes, automobiles, trains, afoot; from the Mexican border on the south to the Panhandle north; Corpus Christi to Dallas; Brownsville to Austin; Fort Worth to Lubbock; Kingsville to the Davis Mountains. Houston Galveston San Antonio. Theatres. Ranches. Hotels. Mexican shacks. Oil rigs. Grapefruit groves. Roundups. Barbecues. Dinner parties. Shocked. Enchanted. Repelled. Delighted. Locutions I never before had heard gave tang to conversation.

She learned that "come down to our country for a visit" meant come to their ranch, which could be a hundred miles away and fifty or five hundred thousand acres. When you left someplace, "come back quick" meant au revoir in "Texanese." She found that "Texas talk made two syllables of a one-syllable word. "Had" became "hay-ud." Somebody's husband Ed was summoned to her side by a plaintive call of "Ay-ud!"

Ferber enjoyed knowing about and commenting on varieties of wind: the Oklahoma kind immortalized by Oscar Hammerstein II that "comes sweeping down the plain," Chicago's "blow your hair straight back" kind, Arizona's "thimble breeze" in winter. She loved New York's "fall gusts," Alaska's "icy jolts," Connecticut's "leaf swirling," and "battling the stiff wind that buffeted you as you walked along the Corpus Christi waterfront facing the Bay and the Gulf of Mexico." Her critical detractors have accused her of hyperbolic prose. Of course, I am biased and feel that she is one of the champion writers at capturing essences. When she calls the Texas wind "hot, humid, and breathtaking," it feels like a sucker punch. We simply get it in one.

Ferber was a great walker and therefore at odds immediately with Texas ways. In fact, she says, "Texans didn't walk. They hopped into their private planes for a bit of shopping in Dallas or Houston or to visit the folks upstate or down. They drove their cars at eighty-ninety-one hundred miles an hour over the thousands of miles of flat country. They rode, but horses were no longer used as a means of actual transportation. They were for ranch work, for horse shows, perhaps for a quick dashing quarter-horse scamper over the range."

Ferber courted Texas and Texas Ferber during these early research forays. Her commitment continued to deepen, and her experiences and sensations convey this:

> Huge ranches, middle-sized ranches, north south and central, offered me hospitality. At some I spent a day, two or three days, or more. The famous King Ranch in Kingsville is so world-renowned that its owners, the Kleberg family, are constantly bedeviled by strangers, tourists, acquaintances and would-be acquaintances from Egypt to Alaska who innocently wish to view and celebrate empire, view the mythological-looking Brahmans originally imported from India; and the Gertrudis breed of cattle, almost cherry-red and fabulous, scientifically originated on the Kleberg ranch itself.

Robert Justus Kleberg Jr. was a quintessentially tall, lean, leathery, good-looking Texan. He was legal counsel to Richard King and his 1.2-million-acre King Ranch. Then he married King's daughter, Helen, and when Richard King died in 1925, Kleberg took over the management of the ranch of more than eight hundred thousand acres after it had been divided among the family.

There is somewhat of an analogy between Kleberg and his ranch and James Adams and his Floating Theatre, which served as the template for *Show Boat*. Some thought the King Ranch was the model for Reata, the ranch in *Giant*, and Ferber would indeed glean some lore from Kleberg just as she had done decades before when floating on Adams's boat in North Carolina. She recalls this new professional courtship—though this one was limited and far more curt:

> Here at the King Ranch I had lunch with Robert Kleberg and his wife and his daughter and a few visiting branches of his famous far-flung family. I told Robert Kleberg about the curse of Treasure Hill that produced only male offspring, seemingly, and this interested him as a breeder of livestock. I had a half hour ride jouncing in a station wagon over an infinitesimal bit of the gigantic ranch. I recall that a few head of the choicest stock intended for family consumption were kept in a small corral of their own and one of those was so overbred and overfed that it could no longer rise to stand on its own four legs. It lay sprawled flat on the ground and had to be raised by ropes and pulley in order to regain a standing position. Privately, I thought I'd relish no steaks from that cholesteroled carcass.
>
> On my return to the main house Robert Kleberg queried me politely regarding the possibility of my writing a history of the King Ranch. With equal politeness I told him that I was a writer of fiction and that I hoped to write a novel of Texas background. The visit had been of two hours' duration, or less.

Ferber had a substantial amount of vanity. Naturally proud of her accomplishments, she was surprised when others didn't sufficiently recognize them. Not that they should fawn—she detested that—but she did expect acknowledgment. Clearly neither Robert Kleberg nor his wife nor any of his family were fans of the celebrity interloper, and so she made short shrift of them, her eye grabbing only what it needed, and not a nicety more.

It had been obvious to Ferber shortly into the interview with the Klebergs that they had frosted up. Later, the way Robert told it to his daughter, Helenita, Ferber had "informed" them about her plans to tell the story of the King Ranch, whereupon Kleberg had explained that he preferred nothing "inaccurate" be written before he had time to gather a complete history of the ranch. Ferber proceeded regardless.

Kleberg's daughter saw things somewhat differently regarding what had been, according to her, a lunch visit:

> . . . I arranged the meal. Soon after we sat down, Ms. Ferber told my father she was going to write a novel based on him, my mother, and King Ranch. After listening patiently, Daddy said that sometime in the future there would be an accurate history written which she and others could reference, but he did not have the time at present to devote to it. Furthermore, he added, he did not want an inaccurate book written. Ms. Ferber insisted that she would write the book anyway and became rude. Daddy turned to me and said, "Helenita, please call for Ms. Ferber's driver. He's in the kitchen. She wants to leave now and won't be coming back."
>
> I know we hadn't had our coffee when Daddy took Ms. Ferber's arm and escorted her to the door. She never returned.

According to Ferber, "the so-called Benedict Ranch called Reata in the novel *Giant* was not one ranch but a blend of many Texas ranches I saw—and some that I not only never saw but that never existed." It is generally surmised that the Benedict family was actually based on the prominent Texas Briscoe ranching family, who began amassing land in the early twentieth century. Eventually, by the late 1970s, they owned 650,000 acres and more than fifteen thousand cattle. Their net worth in 2015 was $1.3 billion.

In retrospect, it is curious that Kleberg was so seemingly blasé about a visit from a celebrated writer. However, he could have had no idea how lucky his disinterest would fictionally turn out to be. My conjecture is that Ferber used him as a model for Bick Benedict, her leading male character in the novel, or perhaps he was somewhat of a blend of Bick and Jett Rink. Kleberg was not to the manor born, but married into it, and simulated it, whereas Jett was a rough-and-tumble punk who remained so even when striking it rich. Neither character was meant to be admirable. If Kleberg had used some charm to dazzle Ferber, who knows creatively how he would have turned out?

Dorothy Parker, who certainly could be asp-like, somewhat respected

Ferber and understood the power of her pen, terming her the "most successful 'writeress.'" Kleberg obviously didn't care.

Ferber left King Ranch and powered on, more conflicted the deeper she burrowed. She said that if she had been a sociologist or an economist she would have gotten nowhere. Contradictions, obscurities, and obtuseness were everywhere, which didn't mean that she developed intolerance. To the contrary, she absorbed all that she got as great grist. The food, however, made her mad. She found it to be "the worst I had ever encountered in a general public way throughout my travels in the United States. Texas steaks are a test of tooth endurance. Texas fries everything but ice cream." Wherever she went, she continued to be a good sport and gracious, but blatantly stated her intentions:

> From the first I made it clear that I had come to Texas as a writer. I did not pretend to be a visitor or a tourist, merely. I intended to write about Texas as I saw it and felt it. When a Texan, in the hospitable tradition of that region, invited me to his or her home to dinner, to the ranch for a stay of a day or a week, I painstakingly made clear my position. "I am here as a writer to make sure that my background is accurate for the novel I intend to write about Texas people and Texas." This was waved aside as though I had said I was about to write a colorful brochure for fast-selling Texas real estate.

It took from the close of 1948 to the early spring of 1949 to gain verification and reaffirmation that this was the right state for the book she would "dearly wed." For almost a decade her conscious and subconscious were "quietly drawing up the blueprints and assembling the stones and bricks and mortar and metal that must go into the structure of a novel. Now I knew that the theme, the background, the characters, the motivation, the flavor of speech of dress of temperament of food were firmly established in my mind. I knew my subject and I knew what I wanted to say." She was sure.

Dorothy Parker had already predicted the outcome: "The United States is, as somewhere it has been said before, a big country, and there are still reaches of it Miss Ferber has not attended to. And in every one, there awaits a gold mine for the lady."

Ferber gratefully retreated to the crisp eastern weather of Connecticut and Treasure Hill.

"Nothing seemed unsurmountable or even difficult," is her blithe account of this period of submersion into her commitment.

> Things that went awry were fitted back into line. It wasn't that the fields outside and the rooms inside were filled with girlish laughter. It was just that the task of writing was going well and that, as always, cast a rosy glow over the dourest object.
>
> The autumn and winter, the spring and now the present summer saw the pages sliding off the typewriter and into the little tidy stack that was growing so slowly—but growing.

Ferber's editor in the nascent stages of writing *Giant* was Daniel Longwell at Doubleday. He had been working with her through the 1930s and into the 1940s, on *American Beauty, Come and Get It,* and *Saratoga Trunk.* He was the man who, tapped by Henry Luce to create *Life* magazine in 1936, convinced Luce to turn it into a pictorial account of the world's events. His idea was at the forefront of photojournalism.

Another of Longwell's novelists was Sinclair Lewis, whose depictions of America were darker and more wretched than Ferber's. His first novel, *Main Street* (1920), brought forth his central theme of the hypocrisy and parochialism in small-town midwestern society. He refused the Pulitzer Prize for *Arrowsmith* in 1926, a year after she had welcomed it for *So Big.* He then outdistanced her and in 1930 became the first American writer to receive the Nobel Prize in Literature. It is intriguing to note that in Lewis's acceptance speech he comments on the writers who were mentioned within the American Academy of Arts and Letters: "But it does not include Theodore Dreiser, Henry Mencken . . . Willa Cather, Joseph Hergesheimer, Sherwood Anderson, Ring Lardner, Ernest Hemingway, Louis Bromfield . . . Fannie Hurst . . . Edna Ferber . . . Upton Sinclair . . ."

Giant would not eventually become another of Longwell's books. Although a competent editor, his real talent was as a supervisor. Judith Haas Smith, Longwell's biographer, wrote that "Dan had a way of managing people to make a team. He was soft spoken but got people to do things together." He did, however, set up the contractual terms of

Giant, about which Ferber commented to her sister, Fannie, "When we are next in Pareee, doll, we'll still be able to splurge on Mainbocher." This was a family in-joke, because the *très chic*, supposedly French couturier, whose most famous client was Wallis Simpson, aka the Duchess of Windsor (for whom he named a color: Wallis Blue), was actually Main Bocher from Chicago, Illinois. He also dressed Mary Pickford, Constance Bennett, Kay Francis, Claudette Colbert, Irene Dunne, Loretta Young, Miriam Hopkins, and Helen Hayes, and society belles such as Brenda Frazier, Doris Duke, Gloria Vanderbilt, Bunny Mellon, and Babe Paley. He was a fashion legend, but to Ferber and Fannie he was a homeboy.

———————

At Doubleday, a lanky, bespectacled fellow named Ken McCormick would inherit Ferber, taking over editorial duties on *Giant* in 1949. In May of that year he had prepared the contract, sending it along to one of Ferber's legal representatives, Harriet Pilpel, at the prestigious firm of Greenbaum, Wolff & Ernst. The last line in his brief cover letter is quintessential McCormick-dealing-with-Ferber: "I hope everything is all right and if it isn't, we will make it so."

McCormick was just beginning his tenure as Ferber's editor. but he would grow to have a deeply felt relationship with her and instinctively understood her need for elevated white-gloved treatment as she got older. He was a kind, gentle, erudite man, who, as luck and irony would have it, was the editor for my Ferber biography three decades later.

It was now July of 1949, and Ferber had settled down to her novel's demands and to being a landowner and cultivator of flora, fauna, and livestock. She always needed a caretaker, and when her original one, whom she simply called Curtiss, left, she hired another "capable enough young farmer-caretaker to take charge of the Treasure Hill acreage and all its problems from cows to swimming pool."

The bucolic was certainly contrapuntal to the horrors that Hitler had wrought, or as Ferber put it, "that malaise that had made the business of living more violently interesting throughout the world, and more difficult and hazardous at the same time."

As always, a lot was on Ferber's mind and heart. I happened to find, catalogued in this period, but undated, an extraordinary piece that perhaps she was working on for a speech or article, or perhaps it was simply a necessary stream of consciousness.

Everybody wants to belong to something or somebody. In our infancy we want to belong to our parents. In our youth and later life we join a school, a club, a union, a profession, and we work for them! We pay dues, elect officers, enlist new members. We belong. Lawyers, doctors, merchants, engineers, teachers, laborers—how we love to belong!

But the most important organization in the world has been allowed by millions of its members to get along as best it could without their help. This club is known as the United States of America. Its dues are called taxes, its officers are elective. Its password is Liberty, Equality. But lately there's a tendency on the part of old members to push new would-be members out of the way. They say, "We've been members a hundred years—fifty—twenty-five. We don't want new blood. We don't want new energy, new loyalty. The old is good enough for us. We don't want foreigners."

Just a few years of that policy in any organization and dry-rot sets in, and the club dies.

We here in the United States of America are made up of Protestants and Jews and Catholics—we're made up of every country and every religion and every race in Europe, Asia, Africa, Australia. That's what we're made up of. These varied people didn't come here because they found their native land exquisitely perfect. For more than three-hundred years they've been coming here because they found here something they couldn't get in their own country—it may have been a material or a spiritual thing. But it isn't the weak who break the bonds that bind them. The people who come here from overseas are the men and women who have had the courage, the ambition, the energy, the persistence to escape from the thing they hated. So then, courage, persistence, ambition, energy—those are the qualities on which this country was built. Are they the qualities which now we want to cut off!

Today we are confronted with a strange new Hitler-spawned tendency to call these newcomers foreigners. Don't let them in, we hear. If that had been true years ago we wouldn't today be gifted with the incredible perfection of Toscanini's conducting; with Jascha Heifetz's violin; we wouldn't possess the clear burning genius of Thomas Mann's prose; the giant brain of Einstein; the lilting voice of Lily Pons; the inventive minds of Seversky and Sikorsky; the legal humanitarianism of Felix Frankfurter; the creative beauty of Maurice Maeterlinck, the dramatic power of Henry Bernstein. What is a foreigner in America? Aren't we all, all foreigners? Who but foreigners build the railroads that criss-cross the country? Who else built the skyscrapers, the reservoirs, the mammoth dams! Who else handles the great steel ingots that are formed, white-hot, in the steel mills! All this has been done by the toil of refugees, for these were refugees though they may not have come to America in war time. They came, as these newer ones have come, for refuge from poverty, or persecution or frustration. They came and they want to belong and they have the right to belong. Among them there may be those who are dishonest. But that is true of any group of human beings in vast numbers. You can't condemn all for the few.

The hideous war that raged abroad has sent to our doors the cream of the old-world culture. The result is that we now have here in America such riches as no one country has ever had in the history of the world. The most talented and brilliant physicians, surgeons, actors, painters, lawyers, scientists, sociologists, inventors, writers, composers, musicians, dancers, merchants of the civilized world are clamoring to be here. Brains and talent were not what Hitler wanted. He wanted slaves. And men and women of brains and ambition either escaped from slavery or died. We needed them. We needed them as much as they needed us. These new members of the club of the United States of America come to us with their precious gifts in their hands. If we, through stupidity, or bigotry or selfishness fail to take them the loss will be ours—a bitter loss—and the fault will be ours. Yours and mine.

As much as she was aware—usually hyperaware—of the world around her, she was always content when her work was going well. She explained it: "This blissful state is that frustration is not present to sap the vitality; no drear-desolation of non-accomplishment is poisoning one with doubts and fears."

Shortly before the Fourth of July in 1949, she went off to collect Julia Ferber in sticky, hot Manhattan and drive her up to Treasure Hill. As she entered her mother's apartment in the Lombardy Hotel, the doorman stopped her, saying that the doctor wanted to see her before she went up to Julia, who for several decades had turned to Christian Science, but recently had gone to a traditional doctor with some complaints.

"The physician saw me at once," recalled Ferber. "He did not mince words. 'Your mother has cancer. She may live two or three weeks.' In a kind of cold shock I said, 'She'll live forever . . . Operation?' and he said, 'Even if it's successful—in a temporary way—it could only be six months—a year at the most.'"

She took Julia to Connecticut and entered into a thicket of tests, a great deal of rest, and specially prepared foods from which Julia turned her head away. Then there was an operation in the city and then up again for autumn in the country, where Julia had a wonderful remission. They walked; they ate everything; they laughed. But then, as Ferber wrote, "October saw the end of that temporary bravado." The next sequence tells of a major watershed in both of their lives:

> During these past months the writing of the novel *Giant* had been put aside, perforce. With the approach of late autumn the ambulance carried her back to her New York apartment, high up and sunny.
>
> She did not speak once during the seventy-five mile ride. I thought she was in a semi-coma induced by the pain-reducing drugs. We drew up at the entrance. The men prepared to carry the stretcher. She spoke, clearly.
>
> "Edna, cover my face."
>
> She always had a wholesome pride and proper vanity in her own good looks. Her arrival today was expected, her apartment had been made ready, the hotel staff and perhaps some resident

friends might be waiting for her in the foyer through which she had passed so many times with a little rustle of silk and a discreet breath of perfume; her step firm, her handsome head held high. "Edna, cover my face."

So I untied the scarf that I wore and with it I covered the noble face, now reduced to a parchment-yellow mask.

Ferber said no more in print about that day or the one, soon after, when Julia breathed her last. Julia reached out for Ferber's hand, saying, "Oh, Edna I ruined your life, didn't I? I ruined your life." Whereupon Ferber turned away from her mother's confession, walked over to the window without a word while Fannie was left to hold Julia's dying hand. Ferber never turned around, and Julia Ferber died holding the wrong daughter's hand.

Ferber, never silent, was now silent. She wrote nothing about Julia's death in her diary, in a family letter, or anywhere other than the brief description in her second autobiography, *A Kind of Magic*. In the years to come—especially in her dotage—she would go on a bit about the "amazing" Julia. She was burnished, then bronzed, finally gilded. The *incredible Julia* was the only one from then on.

My guess would be that Ferber was suddenly free of being tied to her mother, of "owing" her, of having to be heroic. She could forevermore feel the way she did when she took off to research a new book in a new state. She could expand her roving reporter's nature, and perhaps expand in other ways as well. And socially she was free. She wasn't encumbered with the obligation of bringing Julia along, seeing to it that she was entertained, seeing that she was always seated next to the most illustrious or amusing guest at a dinner party. No longer would she see to it that Julia was dressed in the height of fashion, living in luxury, provided with the best of everything.

Conversely, I think that the mourning was bone deep, as deep as Ferber's early identity as Ed, Julia's rock. Ferber had a vivid childhood, in many ways because of Julia. They shared an aesthetic language, several personality traits, a shrewd appreciation of food and fashion, and a deep reverence for the United States. Losing Julia was the largest and most liberating loss of her life.

It was not until three years later, in 1952, after Julia's estate was finally settled and closed, that Ferber's grief seemed to be exhumed. She used this monetary event as a springboard to summarize her mother to the family women:

By this time, dear Fan and Mina and Janet, you probably have had a final letter about the closing of mother's estate. Though I was named executor, together with Morris Ernst, I took no active part in the settling of the estate . . .

There never was a clearer and less involved estate. Highly negotiable stocks and bonds made up the bulk of it, as you know, together with thirteen thousand or more in cash. It seems to me that the jewelry, furs, etc., need not have been listed in the assets. They could have been handled as personal belongings, but legally Wolff was correct. I note that he did not, however, list the dime found in a scuffed little leather purse which he took with him as an item in effects. A plodding and dull fellow.

. . . The entire estate ran to about $157,000, as you will see . . . During the months of mother's illness I had deposited all of her incoming dividends, etc., and I paid out of my own income all hospital, doctors' and other expenses, such as hotel, rent, nurses, etc. This I wanted to do and took some comfort in so doing. The funeral costs were left as estate charges because taxes were somewhat reduced by this. Mother left no other debts or obligations of any description whatever. She had left everything in order—her bank accounts, her investments, her correspondence, her few belongings. A miracle of order and clear-headedness and intelligence in any human being, not to speak of one who was eighty-nine, and very nearly ninety when she died.

So here, for you, ends the story of Julia Ferber. Because of circumstance I knew her better than any of you. I knew the faults and the virtues. The virtues far outbalanced the faults. I always have regretted that, by some mischance of judgement or understanding, you never appreciated the actual dimensions of this unusual woman. I never spoke to you about her to any extent because the mention of her was always met with disparagement. Psychologically, there are certain facts in her life that are clear and explanatory as a chart. She married in her very early twenties. She married a man she did not love. She didn't mean to. She didn't know how not to. She married Jacob Ferber, a decent, dull, rather handsome man because her mother said she must. She was in love with a man named Will English, and he wanted to marry her. He was not a Jew, there was the most terrible brouhaha, she was bullied and threatened and browbeaten. Will English became a nationally known figure of his day, wealthy and distinguished. Mother would have made a wonderful wife for him, high-spirited, intelligent, quick to learn and evaluate. Jacob Ferber failed in his business, became blind, lost everything, his life insurance and his shop goods were mortgaged, there were two small daughters. Julia Ferber took over somehow, there was no one to whom she could turn for help. Her life, from the time she was twenty until she was about fifty-seven, was a tragic thing. How she emerged from it, fun-loving, life-loving and high-spirited I cannot imagine. But she did.

The qualities Julia Ferber possessed were admirable ones. She had self reliance, courage, fortitude, humor, intelligence, and a sense of values that was almost too keen. She knew values all the way from Meissen china to human beings, and her judgements were often harsher than they need have been, but she hated shoddy. At any age when all her contemporary friends were being pampered by maids, companions and the like, she "did for herself" as the old saying used to go. I want to help myself she said repeatedly. I call this a spirited thing in a woman of almost ninety. An admirable character. Very often families know less about each other than outsiders know about them. It's a case, usually, of not being able to see the woods for the trees.

This, then, is just my little obituary to Julia Ferber who is very much alive to me.

Ferber's so-called spinster demeanor was a longtime topic. Why hadn't she had beaux or married or had children? Why was she such a career woman, so smart, so salty, so successful, and so rich? How could she have possibly survived and accelerated in the world all by herself? Wasn't she sad? Wasn't she lonely? Was she a lesbian?

My mother had trouble pinpointing exactly when it was that a young newspaperman named Bert Boyden began to court the brainy and witty young woman, who had not yet published her first novel. As a reporter on the *Milwaukee Journal*, Ferber covered the Republican-and-Democratic Conventions of 1912 in Chicago, and that is where the two probably met. The only evidence of their arduous relationship comes with several rather plaintive letters from him, found among her personal papers after her death. In these he expresses his hopes for a deeper, longer-lasting relationship, which, of course, they never had.

What happened to spoil it? Was it that Ferber didn't return his feelings? From the spiral of his intensity through the small stash of his correspondence, it would seem she did.

Boyden went out of her life as fame came in. In 1926 Ferber published a short story called "Mother Knows Best." It depicts a team of stage mother and star daughter. They are inseparable until the daughter meets a young man and falls hard for him. When the mother discovers her daughter's "betrayal," she literally breaks them up. After a time, at the height of her success, the daughter dies relatively young, conceivably of a broken heart.

If the short story had personal validity, then Julia Ferber's deathbed lament makes sense. She did help ruin Edna's chance at love.

———

Perhaps too soon after Julia's death, Ferber resumed working on *Giant*. Work was always her salvation, but salvation from what, one wonders. Her demons were impacted, rarely surfacing in her fiction as psychological quandaries. *Giant*, however, seemed to confront and expose some darker familial themes. For instance, in so many of her other novels the generational saga includes parents or a parent of the protagonist. In *Giant*, neither Bick nor Leslie confronts an ongoing parental situation with their own parents. It could be noted that the motherless Edna was creating two main characters who were on their own.

So, in 1950 Ferber was on her own and welcoming an incoming watershed while hard at work.

My back to the View and my face in the typewriter the decision that must unconsciously have been forming for months in
my mind came to a final resolution. The summer and autumn
lay ahead. I could see every step of the way with my eyes shut,
May to November. The glorious rotation of color and scent in
the garden; the rotation of crops, of stock, of cook's day out; of
sun moon stars in the heavens, of the furnace-needs-cleaning
the road-needs-mending; of the emotional struggle between
the writer's compulsion to work work work and the feeling of
guilt at not inviting those weekend guests to share the cool
comfort of Treasure Hill . . . But writers do not work a five-day
week. They work (by choice or compulsion) a seven-day week.
Perhaps it is the one form of employment in the world of the
arts professions sciences and business in which work is more
exciting and exhilarating and sustaining than play . . . (therefore) you are giving time and thought and energy to something
that actually is no longer important to you—at least, not that
important. You are a compulsive perfectionist which means
that you are uncontrollably compelled to do the best you can
with everything you do from books to broccoli, from trees to
Texas. And it's never quite as good as you hoped it would be
and that makes for jitters and you're Jittery Jill all right. Listen:
do you want to be a successful amateur farmer and weekend
hostess or do you want to continue to be a writer? You can't
have it both ways. Come on. What do you say?

The reply came sharp and clear: I'd rather write one excellent novel than be the owner and manager of the Garden of
Eden and all points east and west.

Ferber put Treasure Hill on the market in 1950, recording in her
diary, "No qualms of regret about the house." Julia Ferber had just
died. Her mother's death and her subsequent ridding herself of her
prize were not unrelated. Treasure Hill was the reality of Ferber's tremendous success. It was also used as scarlet evidence to her mother of
her achievements. Building that house was the first thing she had truly
done on her own, without the meddling of Julia Ferber, and doing
it was tantamount to saying, "I'm going to run away with this man,

Mama, and there's not a thing you can do to stop me!" That house was the most symbolic factor in Ferber's fairly literal life; she knew it and flaunted it. There would always be room for Julia Ferber, but it was Edna's house, had been her seed, her creation. It was husband, children, responsibility—the whole ball of wax—and Julia Ferber, like a jealous mother-in-law, resented it. With Julia's death, the proof of the house turned into dust. There was no need for it anymore; its time was over. A small postscript tucked in her diary read: "J.—It is difficult to say whether she was a help or an obstacle in my life as a writer. Probably a good deal of both. Full of small faults. Possessed of almost all the great human virtues."

A couple and their three "sturdy" sons became the new owners, who, like Ferber fourteen years earlier, saw the manifestation of her vision. The following description from the *Easton News* captures its largesse.

> The two-story stone residence is built on long low lines. The floor plan includes a large center hall extending through to a rear court. On one side is a 34-foot living room, and a windowed library. The opposite wing contains the dining room, utility rooms and an attached three-car garage. On the second floor are four master bedrooms, each with a bath, a balcony, study and servant's quarters. A 50-foot swimming pool and a two-section stone pool house are on the residence grounds. A four-room guest house is of white clapboard in farmhouse style. Estate buildings include a barn with horse stalls and cattle pens. There also are provisions for sheep, pigs and chickens, a hay barn, equipment shed and a tool house. From Maple Road, on which the property fronts, a private road winds for a quarter of a mile to the residence. The surrounding 140 acres are in fields, pastures and woodlands.

Now she was faced with dismantling one household and finding a permanent home in the city. Previously she had rented, but now she needed a larger place to lodge at least some of her household treasures from Treasure Hill. It seemed as if in solving one problem, she inherited larger ones. Her equilibrium was challenged:

The ghastly problem was the novel, *Giant*. Writers write in the midst of every sort of turmoil. But a measure of inner serenity or merely cool collectiveness they must have in order to set those right words down on that piece of paper . . . Certainly during Julia's illness and death, work on the Texas novel had been virtually abandoned. I now was a year, more or less, out of my original schedule. I should have been deeply upset but somehow I wasn't. It would be finished if I lived; and I meant to live.

This last statement is a curious one. It seemed she had been felled by sorrow after all. Neither I nor any other family member that I know of ever encountered a depressed Edna. Occasionally we would see her fret about this or that; but, first, she seemed too busy and, second, too successful to be down in the dumps. Perhaps the one who would know "another Edna" was my grandmother Fannie. Just before she died in 1975 I went to see her.

Fannie lived not far from Ferber, at 950 Fifth Avenue. She was lying down, covered by a light blanket. The older women in my family always had gossamer blankets.

"I never knew what was eating away at Edna," she said. "She seemed so angry and upset at times, especially at me. I have no idea why. She had everything, and yet . . ."

"What about love?" I asked. "Do you think she ever had *the* great love?"

My grandmother gave a sharp toss of her head, as if she was irritated.

"I don't know. I just don't know. There was something . . . but I can't say what. She could be very gay, you know? And there were men who wanted to be suitors."

"And?"

"Nothing went further that I know about. Edna was a closed person."

It was an elusive interview: Fannie held firm about being mystified. My feeling about Ferber's cryptic statement regarding finishing the book if she lived, and being determined to do so, is not all that profound. Ferber wrote about the demons she could put into words.

When Ferber moved back to the city from Connecticut in late 1949, she stored most everything and rented a couple of rooms for a month at the Stanhope Hotel at 995 Fifth Avenue. Providence came in the form of Richard and Dorothy Rodgers, who phoned to say that a six-room, fifteenth-floor apartment in their building at 730 Park Avenue had just been vacated and was up for sale. Ferber hurried over, grabbed it, and spent the rest of her life there.

Her last words about the sensation of leaving Treasure Hill indicate an uncomplicated, graceful exit:

> . . . I went out to the terrace and breathed deep and looked long and said . . . Goodbye sky, it's been lovely knowing you, and went indoors and slept eight dreamless hours . . . Next day I said goodbye to my neighbors and drove down the hill toward New York and I never once looked back. I had lived out a childish, romantic dream and I did not regret it. I knew I needed no mansion, no swimming pool, no orchard, no cows, no acres for assurance . . . I had it in my mind's eye and could take it out and look at it forever.

For another year she was devoted to working on *Giant* seven days a week. This purity was often interrupted by the daily complexity of her success. She was bound up with her editor, Ken McCormick, at this time. He acted as advisor/sounding board in matters inside and outside the book. He fielded early title ideas she was considering—*Little Giant, Big Hat, Life Size*—with his dry comment of "OH DEAR!"

And she would relay her personal stresses: "My life is still (more than ever) fantastically complicated and I must find a way out soon. It is frightful to be unable to have just the few hours of quiet and necessary peace each day to put down the words of a book. Perhaps it is largely my fault. I have spoiled every member of my family and that was a sort of vanity on my part."

She was still collecting information while drafting her story. New leads and facts would come to light. She had the reporter's need to dig as deep as possible in order to get the biggest scoop, deserving an authentic exposé. Being a true gumshoe, she knew that the scrap of paper tucked within the stones in the wall was never merely happenstance, and to confiscate it had consequences. Ferber was more than willing to take flak for what she found and what she revealed. She expected it—almost welcoming the fight to defend her freedom of speech. And even under the cover of fiction, she was still held accountable. This was especially true for *Giant*.

She found a report that had originally been drafted in 1949. It was bluntly called "Wetbacks." It was termed "preliminary" and was drafted by the Advisory Committee Study of Spanish-Speaking People. The report was gathered by George I. Sánchez and Lyle Saunders and issued by the University of Texas. Reading it today, some seventy-five years later, it is uncannily current. It was just what Ferber needed to make her case for the authenticity of shame.

Here, then, is what she found in its opening pages:

In 1948 the "wetbacks," so-called because most of them wade the shallow Rio Grande under cover of darkness in search of the good Yanqui dollars, swarmed into El Paso and its adjacent irrigated valleys as never before. Estimates have placed the total crossing, within a single thirty-day period, at between 20,000 and 40,000.

One of the most serious problems facing the people of Texas is the presence in the state of a very large, but as yet undetermined, number of wetbacks—illegal aliens who cross the border from Mexico mainly in search of agricultural employment, but who are to be found in many cities of the state, and in many non-agricultural jobs. The Spanish-speaking Texans are not the only ones affected. Every citizen of the state, Spanish and English-speaking alike, shares, to a greater or lesser extent, in the evil effects and devastating repercussions that derive from the presence in the state of from a hundred thousand to a half a million homeless wanderers—men, women, and children, without legal status, without skills, without knowledge of our ways and customs, without protection, and without opportunity for improving their condition. No citizen of the state, or of the other states into which many of the wetbacks eventually drift, can escape the consequences which appear in the form of poverty, disease, slums, ignorance, dependency, low wages, and social and personal disorganization, not only for the wetbacks themselves, but for the Spanish-speaking citizens whom they displace, and the English-speaking Texans in whose communities they, and the thousands of displaced persons, come to live.

No one knows how many wetbacks there are in Texas, but everyone who has given thought to the problem is aware that the number is almost unbelievably large. Low as are the wages which they can command for their services, these low wages are still several times greater than could be earned in Mexico. This economic differential becomes a powerful attractive force, drawing the laborers across the border in numbers which the Immigration Service and Border Patrol, with their present staffs (approximately one patrol officer for each forty miles of border), could not control, even if they always wanted to . . .

With about 200,000 Mexican aliens being caught and returned to Mexico each year, it is evident that several times this number must cross the border during the course of any given year. Some are caught, most of these are allowed to leave voluntarily. Some few are deported. Many immediately return. There are many stories—possibly apocryphal, but certainly revealing—of Immigration Service officers who escorted Mexicans to the bridge, turned them loose on the Mexican side, and then, later, on their way back to headquarters, found the recent deportees thumbing a ride on the highway. Some probably return the way they came and never get into official records at all. Others, no one knows how many, remain for years or even permanently, living on farms along the border or drifting up to San Antonio, Dallas, Houston, Austin, or even on out of the state to Chicago, Detroit, New York, and other Midwestern and Eastern cities. Forty, who had ridden for five days, packed under a false bottom in a truck, were arrested in Chicago last June; fifty-six, who had walked more than seventy five miles through the brush, were picked up near Falfurrias in September . . .

The life of a wetback who escapes the attention of the Immigration Service is not pleasant. He has no rights and no privileges. He must stay off the highways and out of the towns.

He must work for whatever is offered under whatever conditions the employer chooses to provide. His home is a shack or a brush shelter, or a blanket thrown beside a ditch. He owns nothing except that which he carries. His wife and his children, when he has them, share his life.

When Ferber came across this next part of the report, it was so terrible that only fiction could somehow soften it. The text, describing a wetback camp housing some thirty families bordering Hidalgo County, is from a social worker for the American Friends Service Committee.

Each had one narrow bed built of two sawhorses and planks, covered with no more than a flannel sheet or blanket. The small babies slept in a suspended wooden box. The large families had nothing else but the hard earthen floor on which to sleep and eat . . . Most shelters had a makeshift bench, stool or chair. Each had an indoor fireplace with no chimney outlet. Thus the interior of the hut soon blackened, darkening the already cave-like atmosphere. The two unprotected openings, serving as window and door, are the only source of light other than burning candles . . . There are no cupboards . . . I saw no ice box or even any food, with the exception of frijoles and tortillas . . . A main irrigation canal borders the camp on the East. This is the only source for washing, drinking, and cooking water . . . All men, women, and children in the camp, who work in the fields, put in equal hours and receive equal pay—$2.50 per day. A day consists of twelve hours of labor.

The report continues for many more gruesome pages. It allowed Ferber to fully absorb the plight of the Mexican coming to America and to be able to accurately create her scenes of their existence, which were to cause one of the uproars upon the book's publication. She conveyed the depravation and squalor through the eyes of Leslie, her heroine. It mirrors the "Wetbacks" report:

She must have taken a wrong turning, what with the heat, the glare and her weariness, for she found herself off on a smaller, rougher road lined with rows of shanties, small and tumble-down. Flimsier, even, than the Negro cabins she had seen so familiarly in Virginia . . . A thin wailing sound. From within one of the hovels an infant crying . . . She brushed aside the paper strips, she entered the dark, close-smelling room . . . The infant's shrill cry came from a tiny second room at the rear; the lean-to kitchen of the shack . . . The child's wailing pulsed through the hot low room. Leslie went to him. He lay in a basket, very wet . . . There was no water tap, no pump, no sink. He smelled badly . . . The floor of the little wood and adobe hut was broken so that you actually could see the earth over which it stood. Rats must come through those gaps, Leslie thought, looking at the squirming infant. Rats and mice and every sort of creeping thing.

Ferber knew by the reports of living conditions of most Mexican Americans living in Texas and working for landowners that whatever she wrote couldn't be bad enough to capture the reality. This was an area where her research was extensive. Injustice appalled her, and she knew that there could be no gag order in her chosen form of fiction.

Many of the Mexican Americans lived in huts in so-called labor camps. They were situated there by a committee of well-meaning citizens. Among Ferber's research notes was found a 1948 record of one such camp in Mathis, Texas. The families who lived in this camp were not migratory. Where they were placed served as their home. The report cites the conditions found in this camp. Here is a sample:

1. Ten families. Total of sixty members.
2. Two water hydrants for the whole camp.
3. Camp approximately one third filled up.
4. No lights. No bathing or washing facilities, no heating or cooking facilities unless brought in by families themselves.
5. No screens in the houses, no windows to speak of.
6. All open pit privies with no screening, no rat-proofing, no fly-proofing. Majority of pits already full and overflowing.
7. There are no wooden floors. People lived and slept on bare ground.
8. No garbage cans. No facilities for sewage disposal.
9. Garbage littered all over camp.
10. No cleaning equipment like brooms, brushes, water carriers.

Of the eight camps visited and reported upon, seven had members sick with dysentery and diarrhea.

Whenever new information came to Ferber during her writing process, she was always thankful to incorporate it. People were generous about giving her leads, no matter how grim. My intuitive mother thought there was a vicarious thrill about seeing their contributions in the published book, and that everybody always wanted to help "our own" best-selling author. Mother (the actress) would give an imitation of the druggist, the podiatrist, the butcher, the hairdresser. They all seemed to know a Texan or a Mexican.

Although there was an anticipatory flurry around *Giant*, Ferber didn't—and never did—neglect her other literary works. Most of her books, except for the very early ones, remained under copyright for her lifetime. A great many of them resided with the supposedly tried-and-true Doubleday & Co. The dustup that she had had with Nelson Doubleday between *Saratoga Trunk* and *Great Son* had left her gracious while firmly holding the reins.

She never attempted to move from Doubleday again, but in the early preparation days of *Giant* she continued to send queries and comments to Ken McCormick at least once a week. Some contained humor:

> Thanks, dear Ken, for the Penguin Books Company check.
> [An experimental deal had made for a line of inexpensive
> paperback editions.] I find it rather upsetting to know that
> the books didn't catch on as well as expected in the cheap
> edition. [Attorney] Morris Ernst says that this is true of all
> books (or almost all) other than the bosom-and-crime type.
> I'm thinking of doing one in which Mae West murders Dean
> Acheson. That ought to have about everything.
>
> (April 30, 1949)

Some were outraged:

> It was the SRL (Annual Bibliography of English Language and
> Literature Column) you know, dear Ken, that raised the howl
> against the weekly Best Seller lists, claiming that they were
> unverified and unedited and unreliable.

If Henry Seidel Canby "does very little editing of the SRL in any case" why is his name on the masthead as editor?

The omission of *Show Boat, Cimarron,* and *So Big* from that list is a serious omission or the list itself is a dishonest piece of work and should be corrected. I have had letters about it [from her fans, who noticed this slight], by the way. One came from Chicago, so the SRL lists can have a harmful effect.

By the way, I resent being relegated to the past. Henry Canby says (I seem to be full of quotes) "It needs no list to tell the public how popular she was."

He, or the editor who neglected to verify that list or to read it, should publicly state that an omission has been noted. The three books I have named sold far into six figures the first year of their publication, and this was before the day of the book club . . . Oh, well, maybe it doesn't really matter enough to get upset about.

(September 5, 1949)

Obviously, her literary relevance was much on her mind. Heretofore, she had given her life to her mother and to her career. Now, with her mother dying and then gone, her books were her "children," as she once said to me. Her clucking was often loud, as in this November 5, 1949, letter to McCormick:

I'm returning to you the copy to be used on the jackets of the republished *Cimarron, So Big, Show Boat* . . . These books are still alive after a quarter of a century. There must be a reason for that. The reason is that they have vitality; they have color and movement; they have a feeling for life and for living and for the emotions of human beings which somehow communicates itself to the reader. If this were not true they would have died the year after they were born. But they didn't.

By the way, a new motion picture is being made of *Show Boat* and of *Cimarron* and of *So Big.*

Some of the letters to McCormick were intimately chatty: "How are you, my dear? I missed you very much. Now the old Doubleday ship seems again on an even keel"—she finally felt that her business at the firm was secure again. "By the way, everyone has you engaged to marry practically everyone from Eleanor Roosevelt to Hedy Lamarr" (October 5, 1950). Others were scolding, somewhat modified by her desire to maintain her standards:

> My thanks for the revised copy to be used for the book flaps. It's no use my saying that I think this copy is good, because it isn't. I get letters from grade-school children, which are more compelling than this; but up in the office you must think his work adequate or the young man wouldn't keep his job. If you haven't anyone in your office who can't write better copy than this, something has happened to the world of young men and women with writing ambitions. *So Big*, *Show Boat*, and *Cimarron* deserve better than this dreary and incompetent school-boy writing.
>
> I wish I could keep our November 30th lunch date, but I now know that I cannot. I'm really in a very bad spot . . . [Julia's death and the subsequent sale of the house and relocation to the city had greatly interrupted her work schedule.] I must make no day-time social dates—at least, not before mid-afternoon or later. Perhaps you people [meaning Ken and his new lady friend, Joan, or Ken and his two children] can come in some afternoon, or we can meet at the Carlyle or some such place for a cocktail, if you can't come up here; but I must hold myself to a day-time schedule, or I shall fly to pieces. I know you understand, dear Ken.
>
> (November 21, 1950)

Few people instinctively knew how to handle some of Ferber's stances and not get in the way by trying to dodge or placate. Ken McCormick stood and took it until it was over, surviving one of the biggest literary coups of the decade with the upcoming *Giant*.

———————————

When I was researching my biography of Ferber, Harriet Pilpel gave me access to many boxes of Ferber files prior to their being shipped to the Ferber archive at the University of Wisconsin's Historical Society.

I was burrowing and reading until I felt blurry when a wondrous sheet of foolscap appeared. On it, Ferber had scribbled many names that were possible candidates for the odd, somewhat sullen character of the young ranch hand who works for Bick and his sister, Luz, at Reata. "The eyes that were too small, very blue; the curiously damp-looking curls with one lock falling across the forehead," the novel describes his look. "Those pagan goatlike young gods in the Greek pictures—that was it." I now saw in front of me Ferber's search for the right name for this pivotal character: Chet Jepson, Zeke Lint, Teak Riley, Clint Fiske, Bo Polk, Reg Rinker . . . Jett Rink. She had circled the last.

If she wasn't writing it, she was researching, thinking, dreaming it. This was a character she had designed and yet, once she'd named him, he became more real to her than many people she met—and I'll wager she was as intrigued by and attracted to Jett Rink as her character Leslie was.

———

In 1950, after Ferber had moved into the penthouse at 730 Park Avenue, her work on *Giant* seemed more gratifying. She was digging deeper into her thematic ground, becoming freer in her indignant depiction of the Mexican American situation. Late into her on-site Texas research, she had been introduced to Dr. Héctor Pérez García. Affectionately referred to as "Dr. Héctor," he was a champion of Hispanic causes, founder of the Corpus Christi–based American GI Forum, which fostered his insistence that Hispanic Americans have the right to participate in all facets of society.

This forum came into the spotlight with its involvement in the case of Felix Longoria, an Army private killed by a Japanese sniper in the Philippines in 1945. His remains were not returned for burial until four years after World War II had ended. The story gained national traction when his hometown funeral parlor in Three Rivers, Texas, did not permit the family to use its chapel because he was Mexican American. In a communication to then Senator Lyndon B. Johnson, Dr. García appealed to correct the atrocity. Johnson then offered the Longoria family a burial at Arlington National Cemetery with full military honors. The publicity made for a successful inroad, bringing an expansion of the GI Forum into New Mexico and Colorado. The forum went on to expand its reach into the areas of education, farm labor, desegregation of schools, jury selection, public swimming pools, hospitals, poll tax reform, and other equal opportunities.

Dr. García made his mark as a leader because he was both a physician and a civil rights champion. He barely escaped being a victim of what he fought against all his life. Born in northern Mexico in 1914, he moved to Mercedes, Texas, in 1918 when his schoolteacher parents escaped an attack on their village of Llera during the Mexican Revolution. He went on to graduate with honors from the University of Texas at Austin and then proceeded to medical school. He served in the Army during World War II and was awarded the Bronze Star.

When he returned home, he set up his medical practice in Corpus Christi and became the go-to doctor in the area. In 1948 he founded his American GI Forum, combating discrimination in jobs, housing, and education for all veterans. Soon enough his special focus was on Hispanic rights.

Dr. García was Ferber's kind of guy. She became friends with him and his wife, Wanda. When she was in Texas researching, she traveled to Corpus Christi, setting up talks with him into the early evening and then dining with both. He soon became the model for the character of Dr. Guerra in her novel. In director Hector Galán's documentary *Children of GIANT* (2015), Dr. García's daughter Daisy Wanda is interviewed and reflects on how Ferber, "fiercely curious about the segregation and isolation of Mexican Americans in Texas," visited for long periods with her father.

Ferber's earliest impression of Mexico in an undated letter to her family is candid, as personal correspondence tends to be, but it also forecasts what she would later use in *Giant*. Her impressions feel youthful here, in retrospect, compared with the complex layers she would gather later.

> I'm sitting on a train of the National Railways of Mexico, and I must say I've had the most beautiful time in the last twenty-four hours. At least it has been a grand time for me, though I have done literally nothing but stare out of the window. I am

writing just one letter for the Ferbers and the Foxes because I neglected to put a sheet of carbon paper in my brief case, and two letters are just too much. So pass this on, will you, Mom.

It is nice to be alone. I think I love travelling alone better than anything—for a time, at least, though I'd probably get lonesome after a while.

Just now it is divine . . . Mexico is amazing . . . but it takes a rugged girlie to stand it. Madeline [Connelly] is just out of the hospital, Marc is sick with dysentery, and [Howard] Weaver, the newspaper man, is hardly able to crawl. I was lucky, or perhaps sensible. I ate very little and as plainly as possible. The food in Mexico—all over Mexico—is almost inedible. There's one restaurant called Sanborn's, in Mexico City where the food is clean and good and decently served, and one simply comes down to going there day after day. It is the only restaurant in Mexico that serves absolutely no drinks of any kind and it's the most popular, strangely enough. Or not so strangely, considering the vileness of the food in other places. It proves, at any rate, that both Americans and Mexicans (as well as the British) would rather eat well than drink well. It's owned by an American—a little dried up grey haired spectacled fellow who is very rich indeed.

We have rolled over desert and desert and desert all day. So beautiful. Every now and then we come to a Pueblo, a tiny settlement that isn't more than a cluster of adobe huts squatting on the mesa. Men in rope sandals and enormous straw sombreros and serapes, women in rebosas, babies, dogs, chickens, mules . . . every time the train stops at one of these little water tank stations . . . swarms of beggars spring up out of the earth. We had a 20-minute stop at Canitas and I got out to walk up and down. The inspecting conductor opened a little sort of iron chute door in a box under the train—part of the car, I mean—a metal contraption about three feet square—and there crouched a young Mexican boy who had been riding there for twenty-four hours. He was the most desolate and stricken looking creature, blackened with smoke and grease and desert dust, stiff and feverish. He crawled out, on command, hardly able to stand, and reached in to bring out his shoe-blacking kit.

He was trying to bum his way down to Juarez. They dumped him out, and I gave him two pesos and he made a bee line for the terrible little station eating house. On the way he stopped to thank me with the most melting Mexican look and courtly bow you ever saw outside a Spanish court.

Although Ferber didn't revise her original manuscripts much, she would research throughout the writing process. She followed a certain narrative trail, making room for any tips that might come her way. It was akin to a reporter drafting a story while tracking a new lead. Dr. García was a major, if late, addition to her work. He also advised her about all the medical issues that arise in the narrative. In an early scene—an enhanced version of what had happened to Ferber—Leslie as a new bride attends her first Texas barbecue and faints when some cow's brains, directly out of the cow's head, are plopped on her plate. Dr. García gave Ferber the sensory cue for just when a faint would occur and how the body collapses. Later, when Leslie visits a sick Mexican baby living in one of the hovels on her husband's acreage, the description of the baby's condition was coached by Dr. García.

The medical information from Dr. García was useful, but the biographical case of Felix Longoria went directly into *Giant* as the character of Angel Obregon, who was played in the movie by Sal Mineo.

When Ferber was accelerating the writing of *Giant,* she was in fact still researching as well as corresponding regularly with her sources and her "support team," which included her editor, lawyers, family members, and trusted friends. She writes to the illustrious acting duo the Lunts in 1951: "Do you suppose I'll ever finish this endless-seeming novel of mine. I'm truly tired of it, yet I can't stop and wouldn't for the world. Sometimes I think it's good and sometimes it seems terrible."

When the accusations and brickbats greeted the emergent novel, one of the most insulting was that her research was faulty and skimpy, that she failed to depict the "real" Texas and its inhabitants. What was gravely misunderstood in this criticism is that novelists are not genuine historians; they function as interpreters. Accuracy at all times cannot and should not be an expectation from a novelist. That is not to say that facts can be misinterpreted or misrepresented. But with research in the bag, substitutions can be made. The novelist doesn't have to have experienced every ounce of what he or she writes for the work to "assume" validity. Illusion is the key.

It is not commonly known that Ferber never was afloat on the Mississippi River, or even visited its banks, while she wrote *Show Boat.* The vessel that had been her model for the *Cotton Blossom,* the James Adams Floating Theatre, had been anchored in North Carolina. But her feel for the Mississippi was as accurate as any author's for any body of water featured in fiction.

She kept a kind of daybook, a diary-type journal, while drafting *Giant.* It vividly sketches her options. One can see how she whittled out what she wanted—at least for that day—and what was canceled. This is as close as one can come to understanding a novelist's process. The following samples give ample glimpses of the meticulous Southwest choreography forming. In terms of a writer searching for new exposure, this represents a panful of gold.

THE FAMILY—Characters—Characteristics—Background

Where was the LINK (?) Library, the LINK Hospital, the LINK School? The money was put into land and land and land.

LUZ managed the ranch for forty years. She rode in divided skirts, in long skirts, she rode side saddle when this was considered a social crime.

He was an emperor, but he was destroying his empire by his own greed.

Sometimes a rancher's daughter would fall in love with a cowhand through boredom or propinquity or love of horses. It was a possibility against which all ranch parents fought.

By this time Sukey was 16. "You going on being an old maid," Maw threatened her, "I'll dress up Louetta and put her in the parlor."

Uncle Moke (Marcus) had taken the young Jordan along. "Don't forget now. Don't never put your hand in your pocket, or near it. Keep 'em kinda loose hung, front of you. But if you do by mistake put a hand in your pocket, or toward it quick, then don't wait. Shoot. Or else you won't be the one to stay standing." [This last was crossed out. There would be no Uncle Moke but an Uncle Bawley, who was eventually brought to finely weathered life in the movie by the character actor Chill Wills. Ferber did keep the "young Jordan," who became Jordan Benedict, played by Rock Hudson.]

Drinking this Coke and sweet sugary stuff. Best thing when your thirsty open a can of tomatoes and eat 'em with a spoon. [This sentence was crossed out and replaced with "drink it down. Squenches, right off."]

By reading these notes and meanderings, one can feel the early sensory stirrings of the novel as well as trace what will be retained and what will be discarded. It is definitely a code for an emerging language. She writes: "(Luzita talking) . . . Jett Rink—she has danced with him. He has a kind of male draw, very violent. Leslie shocked, then remembered her early days; it was undeniable. 'He talked about you. He said he's been in love with you—stuck on you was the elegant way he put it—he went on like mad—he'd been drinking. He said that was why—he babbled a lot of stuff about his failure & Dad & I got fed up and walked away. Oh, yes, and how about—he wanted to know—how about me marrying him.' "

Translated—at least to me—this is on the brink of a large plot point as well as an entire scene. Luzita will become Leslie and Bick's daughter, Luz, named after her late aunt, Bick's sister. Luzita is recapping an evening spent in the presence of the now all-powerful Jett Rink, where, she tells her mother, all he talked about was being in love with her back in the day. Leslie recalls this with a kind of a flush. This one handwritten, scrawling page presents two generations seeing and feeling the same tug toward one man. Jett Rink is probably the most vividly carnal creation in Ferber's fiction. His urges gave a jolt to all the women of *Giant*, seemingly including its author.

Ferber visualized her characters in such detail that the clarity of what she saw became a certainty, undeniable. When that character was thought about and discussed in terms of movie casting, she, like many writers, was often far ahead of all the ideas tossed about. Ferber knew that if a movie should evolve, Robert Mitchum or Burt Lancaster was her Jett.

Even her notes convey that everything she would write would have a specific look; she would see it distinctly first and then be able to say it. She was never an abstract writer, and the negatives of her photos are in her notes, which when developed would have color and motion. For example: "The girls. The club. Mexican Day. Costumes. Mexico— Land of Flowers and Song." And "These men were unlike Washington men or Ohio men in that they were very big nervous men instead of smallish or just medium sized nervous men. Hard-bitten and terribly competitive."

She had developed a "note" style for herself that, even early on, was quite mature, full of character insights, snatches of dialogue, colors, textures, designs. Her details were such active snapshots, they sometimes appeared as blurry candids. There was lots of motion involved that would later be more crafted. Sometimes, however, the details stayed the way they were, as if they were precious signatures, and got transported into the novel: "A Leslie-Bick snippet: Leslie's subtext is: It was the beginning of that period in which one heard the phrase 'socially conscious.' Texas was completely unconscious, socially. It was like a limitless cupboard into which you reached and brought out a fistful. Bick, as if reading her mind says, 'Listen, Les. Just you go and enjoy yourself and leave the ranch to me, will you? You talk like that Dobie fella over at Texas U.'"

And then she sketches a small scene between a middle-aged Leslie and Bick discussing their daughter, Luzita.

> She wore exquisite hand-made underwear beneath her levis and brush jacket. Leslie said, "I think she does it to prove to herself she isn't masculine."
>
> BICK: "She's got character from you. Bossiness from Luz. Sweetness from me. You're always saying I'm sweet—it used to burn me up . . . She's a mixture of Texas and Ol Virginny."
>
> LESLIE: "Luzita is a little masculine, you know. The way she walks and stands and holds a cigarette."

There is a note taking a huge leap in plot coming toward the end of the story: "Leslie goes to restaurant (or her son's Mexican wife and their blonde little girl) and are refused service by a tobacco-chewing old Texan. 'We don't serve Mexicans here . . . I wouldn't serve the president of Mexico himself!'"

Eventually in the novel this scene evolves as important and dramatic but not as cathartic as it is in the movie. Ferber chose a foursome of Leslie; her daughter, Luz; Juana, her daughter-in-law; and Polo, her Mexican American grandson. Bick was not present. Three of them enter the diner as Luz parks the car:

They stood a moment, Leslie, Juana, the child, in the bright steamy room with its odors of coffee and fried food. "That table in the corner," Juana suggested. "Perhaps there is a high chair for you, mi vida."

"I don't want a high chair, I am a big boy."

They sat down. "What's keeping Luz?" Leslie said, and tucked in a paper napkin at Polo's neck which he at once removed.

"We don't serve Mexicans here."

They did not at first hear. Or, if they heard, the words did not penetrate their consciousness. So now the man came from behind the cash register and moved toward them. His voice was louder now. "We don't serve Mexicans here."

Leslie Benedict stared around the room, but the man was looking at her and at Juana and at Polo. Leslie was frowning a little, as though puzzled. "What?"

"You heard me." He jerked a thumb towards the doorway. "Out." The men drinking coffee and the people at the nearby tables looked at the two women and the child. They kept on eating and drinking, though they looked at them and glanced with sliding sideway glances at each other.

Leslie rose. Juana stood, too, and the child wriggled off the chair and ran to his mother's side. "You can't be talking to me!" Leslie said.

"I sure can. I'm talking to all of you. Our rule here is no Mexicans served and I don't want no ruckus. So—out!"

The worried-looking woman behind the lunch counter said, "Now, Floyd, don't you go getting tetchy again. They ain't doing nothing."

Leslie felt her lips strangely stiff. She said, "You must—be out of your mind."

"Who are you talking to!" the man yelled.

Luz came blithely in, she stared a moment at the little group on whose faces was written burning anger; at the open-mouthed men and women at the counter and tables.

"Heh, what's going on here," she said.

The man glanced at the golden-haired, blue-eyed girl, he pointed a finger at the two women and the child, but Leslie spoke before he could repeat the words.

"This man won't serve us. He says he won't serve Mexicans."

Even the jaws at the counter had ceased champing now.

The scarlet surged up into Luz's face, her eyes were a blazing blue, Leslie thought, with some little portion of her brain that was not numb, why she looks exactly—but exactly—like Jordan when he is furious.

"You son of a bitch," said Miss Luz Benedict.

The man advanced toward her.

"Floyd!" barked the woman behind the counter.

"Git!" shouted the man then. "You and your greaser." And he gave Polo a little shove so that he lurched forward and stumbled and Luz caught him.

Luz reverted then to childhood. "I'll tell my father! He'll kill you! Do you know who my father is!"

In the original notes, the child was blond, which would have been more improbable and less powerful.

———————

By the time she drafted her book, she knew her Texan men, and their horses, and the derivation of their horses! Here, she clipped an excerpt of an article that later she used in order to be exact:

The Spanish horses that were sent over to the New World in every ship that left the Spanish ports were the kind that Velasquez painted—strong and stocky (as they had to be to bear all that weight), and far different than their descendants of today with their long, stilty legs. They were stable fed and domesticated, but once on these shores they soon went wild. As the conquistadors and their descendants settled on the land, so the horses made America their own. Nature seemed to be ready for them. In fact, no other country in the world has proved more suitable for horses than the Americas. Into Northern Mexico and to the great prairies of Texas . . . the horses brought from Spain wandered and multiplied in countless herds.

Ferber seemed to have a thing about cattle, which, as a subject, doesn't seem thrilling, but her notes are quite entertaining. She titles this batch "LONG HORNS, CHARACTER STUFF. TEXAS":

There is a glass case in front of the court house. It is near the road of the wide street, wide as are the main streets of all small Texas towns, meant for the driving of cattle herds to market. There is a huge, plate glass case, roofed, where there was a stuffed and mounted Longhorn staring moodily out at you. His horns measured easily nine feet from tip to tip, Copper welded glass, copper roof. Wrinkled horns. Meeting a friend not seen in years: "You've got wrinkles on your horns."

In 1854 Congress appropriated money for the importation of camels from Syria, Alexandria and Constantinople to Indianola, Tex. A camel train of 125 camels, Armenian c. drivers and their families. CAMELS IMPORTED. YOU SAW THEM DISDAINFUL CREATURES LOOMING UP LIKE SOMETHING OUT OF AN ALCOHOLIC DREAM IN THE AMERICAN PRAIRIE.

DALLAS, HOUSTON, SAN ANTONIO, FORT WORTH. YOU SAW MEN WITH BOTTLES UNDER THE ARMS ENTERING RESTAURANTS. THEY ALWAYS LOOKED SHEEPISH, AS THOUGH CAUGHT IN MISCHIEF.

HEAT, DUST, HUMIDITY. SCORCHING SUN, BITTER NORTHERS. THEY HAD SURVIVED THE CLIMATE, THE FITTEST OF THEM ONLY HAD BEEN ABLE TO SURVIVE, AND LIKE THE BRITISH, THOSE WHO HAD TRIUMPHED OVER NATURE WERE NOW PRACTICALLY INDESTRUCTIBLE. IMPORTANT.

The oil lamps in the kitchens of the little Texas town of

Indianola blinked amazed at the sight of these humped ships
of the desert, chewing their cud in the backyard in the quiet
star-spangled Texas night.

Ferber was a stickler for accuracy and didn't believe in "divine inspiration." She would double back in her writing process if she felt her
facts were shaky, and if a new morsel was presented, she would redraft
a portion to fit it in. Such was the case of the cattle. She researched
ranch cattle in various portions of the state, and because Texas was so
vast, there were myriad breeds grazing according to where the grass was
growing. She finally zeroed in on the right breed for the early portions
of the novel when Leslie first arrives at Reata.

Though Ferber denied that Reata was a direct imitation of the King
Ranch, she did plunk down its herd into her novel. It was the Santa
Gertrudis breed of cattle, which would develop a "good beef carcass
when finished on grass, and which at the same time would do well
under range conditions." This was a critical mandate for a saga of a
ranching family dating back to 1852.

She also delved more deeply into the character of Jett Rink, the
ranch hand turned oil-rich mogul. The hard-core rumor was that her
model was the fabled Texan Glenn McCarthy, owner of Houston's
Shamrock Hotel. Ferber, who had rather enjoyed McCarthy's company
as well as his luxury hotel, denied this. Hers was a cleverly disguised and
embellished fictional account, but one can detect the association. It was
hard to deny the Glenn proclivities that appeared in Jett. The following
is taken directly from a *Time* profile of McCarthy:

> He . . . drives his royal blue Cadillac at 100 m.p.h., often with
> a whiskey bottle at his side. He likes to shoot craps at $1,000
> a throw, and has a longshoreman's uninhibited propensity for
> barroom fights.

In the next paragraph of the profile, I feel, Ferber found the essence
of her Jett:

> McCarthy's incessant, explosive extracurricular activities, plus
> the luck, deadly nerve and ferocious vitality with which he has
> sought and found oil, have made him one of the most highly

Texas mogul Glenn McCarthy,
model for Jett Rink in *Giant*,
circa 1949

publicized Texans since Sam Houston. This does not mean that he is popular; many of his fellow citizens grudgingly envy him his wealth and audacity. As many more deprecate him, and point out, correctly, that he is hardly typical of the Texas millionaire. Nevertheless, Glenn McCarthy is as peculiarly a product of Texas as the famed San Jacinto monument: the Lone Star State is one of the few places left in the world where millionaires hatch seasonally, like May flies.

This incisive source material continues to trigger more of a rationale than an inspiration to write this story. Here, essentially, is the arc:

Texas throbs with prosperity. In a fevered decade of war and boom it has not only produced new fortunes in crops and cattle, but become one of the nation's great industrial areas . . . Oil (plus natural gas) has been the catalyst. The presence of potential bonanzas under the soil inspired the beginnings of Texas industry . . . And the steady stream of oil wealth, along with the income-tax generosity of the U.S. government, sprayed money off in dozens of different directions.

. . . Both Texas industry and Wildcatter Glenn McCarthy were born at Spindletop—a gently sloping salt dome near Beaumont, from which gushed the first big flood of dark, heavy Texas oil. Like many another boom field which was to follow, the Spindletop discovery was the result of one man's faith, energy and stubbornness.

These were the bones of the story of Ferber's *Giant*. Glenn McCarthy, in a July 21, 1957, conversation with Mike Wallace on *The Mike*

Wallace Interview, readily agreed to the character of Jett Rink having been based on him, but denounced Ferber's novel. He didn't care for it. He thought it was opportunistic: however it bent the truth, it would sell. It disturbed him because he had a fine family who might be caused to suffer. One of the themes of the book was great wealth. McCarthy— who didn't seem happy in the interview—doesn't think that any man who corrals a tremendous amount of wealth also doesn't do a tremendous amount of good. One could say this is where he departs from Jett Rink. Ferber portrayed Jett as a scoundrel through and through. So, apparently art stopped short of imitating life.

In her notes about the corrosively evolved McCarthy-like Jett Rink, she sketches a Texan Dorian Gray:

HE HAD A BOMB SHELTER IN THE GARDEN BEHIND HIS HOUSE IN TOWN AND ANOTHER AT THE RANCH STOCKED FOR A FOUR MONTH SUPPLY OF FOOD AND NECESSITIES. [One can see how ahead of her time Ferber was in creating this dystopian scenario.] PARKED HIS CADILLAC AT THE BUS STOP REGULARLY EVERY DAY. EVERY DAY THE COP ON THE CORNER GAVE HIM A TICKET. EVERY DAY HIS SECRETARY PAID THE FIVE DOLLAR FINE AS THOUGH IT WERE PART OF BUSINESS EXPENSES.

IT WAS THEN EXPLAINED TO HIM THAT BUS PASSENGERS HAD TO WALK TO THE MIDDLE OF THE STREET TO REACH THE BUS OR TO REACH THE SIDEWALK THROUGH RAIN, WIND AND TRAFFIC. WHEN HE HEARD THIS HE SAID QUITE WITHOUT HEAT, "TO HELL WITH 'EM."

THE VAST WAREHOUSE GATES WERE LOCKED AND BARRED AND A GUARD, ARMED, STOOD BEHIND THE METAL MESHES. AS HE APPROACHED WITHIN THREE BLOCKS OF THE PLANT AND WAREHOUSE WITH THEIR VALUABLE METAL PARTS AND EQUIPMENT OF OIL WELLS, HE OR HIS BODYGUARD PICKED UP THE TELEPHONE AND CALLED THE GATEMAN. FROM THE CORNER OF VINA AND CABALLERO. THEIR SPEED NEVER SLOWED,

THERE WAS NO THOUGHT THAT THEIR PROGRESS
WOULD BE STOPPED. AS THE CAR APPROACHED AT
HIGH SPEED AT THAT SPLIT SECOND THE GATES
SWUNG OPEN, THE CAR TORE IN AT TOP SPEED,
THE GATES SWUNG SHUT AND THE BIG CAR
STOPPED WITH A SHRIEK OF BRAKES AND WHEELS.
THE FEUDAL LORD AND HIS DRAWBRIDGE.

WHEN THEY SPOKE OF HIM THEY DROPPED
THEIR VOICES AS IF THEY SPOKE OF THE
DEITY—OR THE DEVIL. THEY WHISPERED AND
LOOKED ABOUT THEM, FEARFULLY.

Ferber maintained that her Jett was made from whole cloth. However, when she was looking to create a dominating sister for her ranching heir, Bick Benedict, she freely took right from the column of a small
AP item that read:

> William S. Hart's sister ruled his household back in the 1920's
> and even the bride couldn't compete with her, says a witness in
> the will contest of Bill Hart, Jr.
> The witness taught Mrs. Hart to play the harp. She related
> a dinner conversation in 1922 where the sister said to the bride,
> "We're having cookies tonight. Who said you could bring
> home a lemon pie? I'm doing the ordering here and we're hav-
> ing cookies. This is my house."

Ferber's creation of Luz Benedict, later to be indelibly depicted by
Mercedes McCambridge in the movie, was a fearsome woman; she was
lovelorn and jealous of anything that might take her brother's attention. She ruled Reata and its household with an iron hand. When Leslie
first marries Bick, she is gently appalled in an early scene where she is
trying to adjust:

> "Darling, you Texans have a kind of folklore, haven't you?"
> "Why I don't know exactly. What—"
> "Nothing. Uh—look, dear, I must order a lot of books
> from Brentano's in Washington."
> "Oh, you won't do much reading out here."

"But I always read. I read a lot. It's like saying you won't do much breathing out here." Her tone was a trifle sharp for a bride.

"Here in Texas there's so much more to do. You won't have time to read."

"The house, you mean? Yes, I suppose there must be a lot to do, just running a big house like this."

"Oh, I didn't mean that. Luz runs the house."

"But Jordan! I mean—I'm quite good, you know. Really. I know about food and servants and furniture and I'm even a pretty good cook. I'd like to—"

"We'll let Luz tend to all that. She wouldn't like anyone else to run the house . . ."

"But I'm your wife!" Her sense of the ridiculous told her that she was talking like a woman in a melodrama. She began to laugh rather helplessly. "Let's not be silly. This is my—this is our house, isn't it!"

Leslie's question was not rhetorical.

A long-held rumor that Ferber didn't get along with or was contemptuous of most other women was simply untrue. That she found certain women insufferable was accurate. Like anyone else, her proclivities and tastes were formed early. She was drawn toward resourceful women because her family was full of them. Her mother, her sister, and her favorite aunt Jo were all handy, high-spirited, humorous, and intelligent. As a result, Ferber sought out these traits in other women. I can't think of a woman character in Ferber fiction that was thick, insensitive, corrupt, or, in an extreme case, villainous. In *Giant*, Luz was territorial and indomitable but certainly not evil. One can understand her aggressions, and when she gets thrown from the horse that happens to be Leslie's champion, her precious souvenir from Virginia, it is a tragic event and not remotely justified.

In fiction Ferber was more lenient with a female character than when she took exception to one in real life. A big pet peeve of hers was the playwright Lillian Hellman. Ferber thought she was overdramatic and phony. She liked neither the woman nor her work nor her abstract, theatrical politics. In fact, she would cross the street if she spotted her, which she frequently did, since they both lived near each other in

Harriet Pilpel, circa 1950

the East Seventies. Once when I was walking with Aunt Edna, it was quite hilarious to see these two aging, mink-coated women spotting and practically running from each other.

Added to her list of dislikes were silly or vain women who either were or pretended to be useless. She backed up her preferences by never writing about this sort of woman in her fiction, except as an ancillary character. When she began to diagram her women characters for *Giant,* they all were given substance and appeal, some of which was transmitted via Leslie Lynnton Benedict, her protagonist. In an early draft showing the kind of life Leslie had inherited by marrying Bick Benedict, Ferber lays out their root differences and how Leslie navigates her female family members through them:

> Bick Benedict insisted that all that grease in the back lot—as he contemptuously termed it—had made no difference in the Benedict way of life at Riata [the early spelling of the ranch's name]. He was deep in talk with Uncle Bawley and Judge Whiteside and Gabe Klick and Pinky Snythe. All these visitors except Uncle Bawley were guests at the Big House. Uncle Bawley would have none of it. The Big House had now become a sort of private free hostelry at which might be found a bewildering assortment of guests. Bick's modern machinery and daring methods had turned Riata into a vast laboratory. The world came to see and learn. East Indian potentates were put up at the Big House; Calgary ranchers, Kansas farmers, English cattle men, South Americans. They ate, slept at the Big House, were brought there, departed from there. Leslie insisted that the Main House was a place for privacy, for peace, for the Benedict family life; she long ago had resolved that visiting strangers at the Big House must never invade it. It was a place for her husband and herself, for their daughter Luzita and their son Jordy

and his wife Juana and their child Nancy. Nancy named for Leslie's mother Nancy Lynnton. "She's no Benedict," Bick had said bitterly of the little girl with the dark Mexican eyes and the abundant strong black hair and the café au lait skin like the skin of her handsome grandfather, old Polo, the Caporal. "Call her Nancy. Call her anything you want to. She's no Benedict."

Leslie Benedict had lost none of her spirit. "You've always had delusions of grandeur, Jordon. A lot of Texans have. But now you really sound like a father in a melodrama."

The judgment about theme often comes from the literary professor or critic and not the writer. However, perhaps because Ferber had been turning out novels so long, she decided upon her theme while still in the note-drafting stage. I found this simple, clear "THEME" page among the collection:

I am trying to present the growth and decline of the great landowners. From the day of the early Spanish explorer (this sketched in only) through the rich land grabs, to the great cattle fortunes, then the discovery of oil, the breaking up of the vast ranches into smaller ones, the lonely day of the great ranch king who must decide between money and the land and takes the money.

It may be that people act much the same who have too much room as do those who are too crowded. Too big is as bad as too little. Too much is as bad as not enough.

———————

Some of the ancillary rights to the new novel were presold. *Ladies' Home Journal* was to carry installments; *Reader's Digest* was to print a condensed version of the novel after its initial Doubleday & Co. hardcover publication; the British and French rights were sold quite far in advance, as Ferber had a large readership in both countries. It was not infrequent that as Ferber entered into her business transactions, whether domestic or international, her tone was dead serious, occasionally vituperative, or sometimes merely wry. Since Ferber was never a mellow person, one could expect a definite response from her, as in a letter she sent to a Miss Byles, who was fielding European offers from her office at the Curtis Brown agency in London. She would often take the bit between her teeth, settling her own business instead of letting others do it when she felt something was particularly idiotic.

Dear Miss Byles,

On July 9th you wrote me regarding an offer which you had received from a magazine in Copenhagen. Your letter refers to what you term the "serializing of my short story, *Giant*."

Your office has repeatedly been notified by my lawyers, Messrs. Greenbaum, Wolff & Ernst, 285 Madison Avenue, New York, that the firm of Curtis Brown, Ltd. have no longer the right to act as my agents in any matters except such as still exist from arrangements made in time long past. In fact, I believe that even those have been transferred, but I shall have to verify this with my lawyers. You will hear from them within the next few weeks.

No transactions in the matter of *Giant* are to be made by Curtis Brown, Ltd. You will please notify the senders of any communications showing an interest in that work, that the contact is to be made through Mrs. Harriet Pilpel, of Greenbaum, Wolff & Ernst.

Incidentally, *Giant* is not a short story. It is a novel of about 150,000 words. Certainly your offer of $12 must appear even to you as something that you should not have incorporated in your letter to me.

Very truly yours,
Edna Ferber

Harriet Fleischl Pilpel was a major force and comfort to Ferber around this time and for the rest of her life. An attorney and women's rights activist, she upheld freedom of speech, freedom of the press, and reproductive freedom. Counsel to both Planned Parenthood and the American Civil Liberties Union, she helped shape the arguments protecting these freedoms. Pilpel was a full partner in the international law firm of Greenbaum, Wolff & Ernst, and she also maintained an active practice in copyright law with clients including, at one time or another,

Paul Robeson, Alger Hiss, Erich Maria Remarque, Alfred Kinsey, Benjamin Spock, and Svetlana Alliluyeva—Stalin's daughter.

Simply "Harriet" to our family, she was Ferber's guiding light, and ours, for several decades. Whatever might go wrong, it was always "Call Harriet." Prior to her inheritance of Ferber as a client, her senior partner Morris Ernst was the sole responsible one. He and Ferber were respectful but scratchy with each other, so when Harriet ascended and smoothed the waters, everything appeared brighter. Not only did she attend to Ferber's large and small business matters and snags, she was an expert advisor on everything. She literally became her family practitioner of good sense.

Harriet lived with her kind and nearly silent husband, Bob, in a sprawling apartment on Manhattan's Upper East Side. More than occasionally we were invited for dinner, where we would always find a luminous guest. After Ferber's death, as I gradually ascended into a responsible role in her estate, Harriet and I became quite close.

At one of her intimate dinners, I was seated next to Alger Hiss, a government official accused of being a Soviet spy. He had been convicted of perjury in 1950. Ultimately, he served three and a half years in federal prison. Arguments about the case and the validity of the verdict were manifold. Many critical files were deemed unavailable, and his case would be debated for years to come.

I was intimidated by Hiss's presence at my elbow until Harriet said, "You know, Alger, Julie also went to Dalton," at which point his gentle focus turned to me as we discussed the merits of the Dalton School, which his son, Tony, had attended.

Harriet Pilpel was part of Ferber's support system during the *Giant* years. She and Ken McCormick were the troubleshooters whenever trouble appeared. And there would be plenty of it wherever *Giant* was concerned.

The initial reactions to the new novel came concurrently with the supplements published in *Ladies' Home Journal*. But Ken McCormick had sent out advance copies to the designated few whose opinion Ferber valued. As anyone might be when judged, she was fallible—deeply injured by what she perceived as imbecile criticism and feeling sleek when praised. She was less likely to be critical of the variety of praise she received.

One of the first "outsiders" to respond was Ferber's former editor,

Daniel Longwell, who in a letter dated April 29, 1952, gave the book what could be perceived as a thumbs-up.

> I read the sweep of *Giant* at a lolling. It is enormously good. Someone should really write an adequate piece about you sometime as the great story teller that you are.

Ferber could not accept his applause, feeling it was half-hearted, and that he used an expression—"story teller"—that diminished her. Longwell was abject:

> I am sorry my letter about *Giant* upset you. I think it is the best book you have done. . . .
>
> I am sorry, too, about the "story teller." I happen to admire people who can write stories. So few can.
>
> Did you ever know that I collect first editions of your books and that I do not have an autograph in any of your books on my shelves? I have always been too shy to ask for one, but am going to be just like any other reader now and am sending you a copy of the first edition of *Show Boat*, which I hope you will sign for me.

He first signs the letter, "Sincerely, Daniel Longwell," then crosses out the "Sincerely" and replaces it with "Affectionately."

———————

Reactions to the supplemented novel from the public and from friends and colleagues were swift and varied. They were thoughtful, loving, waspish, vituperative, threatening, and fawning. She had clearly hit a major artery with Texans, sometimes extracting lava, sometimes oil. One from a Texas woman was pungent: "Your descriptions of Texas, that incredible, fantastic 'country,' is complete and magnificent. From the torrid winds and the Cadillacs to the startling idioms and the voices of the women—it is all there, a living and powerful picture. I love your choice of the name Jett Rink. The very sound of it is mean and vulgar—it stings and jives me into exquisite feelings of repugnance."

Another one was eloquent:

The first few paragraphs of *Giant* delighted me, for I thought, here is something slyly but good-naturedly poking fun at our massive ego and as a native Texan, I relished that!

But *Giant* is more than Texas with its sprawling, nearly formless way of life. Your power is utterly boundless, magnificently strong and ruthless, yet gentle and tender. It is so good to feel each moment of the story as though one were living it.

Miss Ferber, I salute you and love you for every word of *Giant*. (Beaumont, Texas, July 27, 1952)

And from the manager of the Anson Chamber of Commerce:

My what a thrill we Ansonites got when we read *Giant* in this issue of the *Ladies' Home Journal*. Of course we knew that all Texas loved our Cowboys' Christmas Ball and that many people from all over the United States visit us each Christmas to enjoy our Western Festivities, but it gave me a special "bang" when you referred to Cowboys' Christmas Ball at Anson, Texas, in the marvelous novel *Giant*.

I am sure that Texans from everywhere are writing you letting you know what a grand novel they think *Giant* is but I especially want to thank you in behalf of Anson. I have a seventeen year old son that looks forward to each issue of the *Ladies' Home Journal* now that *Giant* is running; not often will this boy read a continued story but he really loves this one.

Again let me thank you for giving our town a boost in *Giant* and I hope that all of your novels meet with the success that we Texans feel for this your latest novel.

(August 5, 1952)

Ferber saved these choice letters because she celebrated her articulate, enthusiastic women readers. She saved a great many of her favorites from the correspondence forwarded by Doubleday, positive and negative. She seemed open-minded to bile as well as to praise. These early reactions from the public were to the portions of the narrative that had been published, and so when someone cried fraud, it had to be only a partial judgment.

According to the late Texas-born writer Don Graham, "Texas overwhelmingly despised the Texas epic novel penned by an outsider who played to all the stereotypes of their land and people."

It would seem by her positive and often effusive fan mail that not all Texans took umbrage at her depiction of them. Her book was endorsed by a Mexican American contingent of readers as well, which is rarely mentioned when discussing critiques of a novel that blatantly points to racial inequity. In one early letter, she is commended for her insight: "I notice that you have studied Texans and their relationship with Mexico. Especially in their adoption of Mexican customs." The letter goes on to propose a possible collaboration in writing a film with a deeper geographical slant on Texas and Mexican land rights and their violations. "This subject should be filmed," it is suggested, "but RKO said they could not at this time."

Ferber, and eventually Doubleday, her editor, and her lawyer, took her negative mail seriously. Some of it was vicious, as well as the more insidiously damaging charge of violent ignorance. This from a woman in Tyler, Texas, responding to the initial installment in *Ladies' Home Journal*. She copied the magazine's editor as well and addressed Ferber as "Dear Madam."

> I have just waded through the first installment of your most boring novel *Giant*. I feel impelled to criticize this far-fetched, so-called Texas tale. You misinterpret so grossly Texans and their way of life that it is not even ludicrous. It is an insult not only to the oil and cattle people of Texas but to the United States in general.
>
> You have no doubt been entertained at one time by some pseudo "cattle king," who was in fact just a play boy, probably having come to the opening of the Shamrock Hotel; and seem to think you absorbed enough local color to write about something so vital to Texas and the whole nation, as cattle and oil production, in which attempt you have sadly failed.
>
> Having myself been born in Tennessee, a Lee of the famous Virginia family, I would probably be placed in the category with your Leslie; however since I have lived in Texas all my married life, some thirty years, I believe I know Texas and its people. To give me further insight into the lives and characters, also manners of the class you write of, my husband

is engaged in the production of cattle on a large scale. These are shipped by Armour to Kansas City to produce the meat you spoke of being served at your party. He fattens the cattle so our steaks are ready for consumption here. My husband also produces oil. Over and above these activities, he is a lawyer of some attainment. I tell you this to show you that I have been about all over the state among the cattle people and know them first hand. I would like to say they are among the finest men God ever created; they are the salt of the earth people who are at the grass roots of this nation. They are men of integrity who pay their income tax without complaint. I do not believe any cattle man has ever carried on as you paint their activities in this *Giant*.

The hottest novel of 1952!...

Book-of-the-Month Club
Selection for October

The novel *Giant* (1952)

Aside from your misrepresentation of a fine group of people, I also note that you are trying to weave in the race prejudice you northerners, especially Jews, are always raving about. You mention such an inappropriate item, if even true, as that at the hotel there were signs "Ladies" and "Colored Women." I know such things as toilets so designated do not exist in hotels in Texas for the simple reason that colored people do not go to the best hotels, as they are not permitted at the best hotels in New York or anywhere else. You northerners are always preaching about segregation when there is more flagrant segregation in the north than in the south. We have separate schools, yes; the Negroes want this as much as we do. By giving them equal opportunity in schools of their own, we give them a challenge to take pride in their race, to try to achieve higher standards as a race. Since we have so many Negroes in the South, it would not be practical for all to attend the same school, therefore, we provide equal but separate schools.

Your incident of the Mexican girl being excluded from the beauty parlor is a flat misrepresentation. I know this is not true anywhere. As a rule these matters take care of themselves for the ignorant, dirty, poor type of Mexican would not think of going into the beauty parlor in a fine hotel. On the other hand, a refined, well-dressed girl such as you describe your Juana to be, would most certainly have been admitted. I have seen just such characters being served at your oft-quoted Neiman-Marcus.

It was really amusing your describing the Texas women as lacking confidence, and allowing this to reflect in their manners, even in their manner of speech. Of all things lacking in confidence! I have observed they seem rather over-confident. If money and all things it buys, such as education, travel, etcetera, is at the rest of this class you write of, it would seem rather incongruous that the women who are in reality placed upon pedestals, lacked confidence. Also along this line, you speak of the women being down the line in order of importance—you missed it there too. My dear, they are first! That idea comes from the culture of the old South, which is the hereditary background of most Texans.

This first installment in the June issue of the *Ladies' Home Journal* is all I shall read of your book for I do not care to waste my time on such bunk.

Very truly yours . . .

This letter shows such swaggering hubris that it reads like it comes from a concocted Ferber character—and she could skewer behavior on paper with cold and deft precision—which is perhaps why she preserved it. It is a kind of reverse flattery. That voice, its intonations, and its anti-Semitic jab would become part of her collection.

The wicked letters kept coming—even those that threatened to do Ferber bodily harm: "Lynch her!"; "Let splintered glass cut her to ribbons!"; "Shoot her if she ever sets foot again in the great state of Texas!" She seemed to take these ugly sentiments somewhat in stride. My guess would be that she felt a million miles away from it all up in her pent-house on Park Avenue. What irate Texan could shoot his way up fifteen floors to git her there?

What did bother her were things said in print—reviews, damaging articles, dishonorable mentions, such as the one by a columnist named Westbrook Pegler. He championed everything Ferber excoriated in *Giant*, as one can see from this item in "As Pegler Sees It":

> Poor Texas has stood up proudly through an actual campaign of abusive sneers and belittlement. Consciously or not, Edna Ferber threw the biggest rock in that barrage in her hateful and, I thought, envious novel, *Giant*, which got publicity far out of proportion to its worth as writing just because it smeared Texas.
>
> Miss Ferber has neighbors within a mashie shot of her own home in Connecticut [he hadn't known she'd sold it] who are evil by comparison with the clumsiest parvenu of the Texas aristocracy. But they are, as a group, New York Reds of various shades.

Book critics in general offered few bouquets along the swath of her career, which was rosy despite them. She was slotted as a popular yarn spinner whose work, not unlike soap operas, was followed religiously by primarily stay-at-home women. This was the illusion. There were male readers who adored her work—older and retired, men of the church, and gay men. There was also a surprising contingent of GI fans during World War II. With her midwestern slant and her epic familial sprawls, she reminded them of the heartland, of home, of family, of faith. For many men in the service, she was performing a service.

She was certainly performing a service as far as Doubleday was concerned. They capitalized on *Giant* being her first novel in eight years by issuing its emergence as a major event in their PR campaign: "The name of Ferber means storytelling magic. Her books are American classics—*So Big, Show Boat, Cimarron, Saratoga Trunk . . . Giant*, her newest, is the explosive story of a Virginia girl who married a fabulous Texan, and discovered she'd married not only a man but a mania—the mania for bigness that some Texans believe is greatness." Even this description was sideswiped by a phrase in the *San Angelo Standard-*

Times that read: "THESE are the giants of Texas—not the straw men set up by a female."

No one could refute *The New York Times* and its best seller list every Sunday. For more than twenty weeks it landed in that newpaper's top ten. *Giant's* popularity was certainly nudged along by John Barkham in the *New York Times Book Review* of September 28, 1952:

> If you haven't read Edna Ferber's name on any new novel lately, it isn't (as you might have suspected) because she was relaxing on the royalties from *Show Boat, Cimarron, Saratoga Trunk* and other movie masterpieces made from her books. On the contrary, it was because Miss Ferber was brewing the biggest witch's broth of a book to hit the great Commonwealth of Texas since the revered Spindle blew its top. Miss Ferber makes it very clear that she doesn't like the Texas she writes about, and it's a cinch that when Texans read what she has written about them they won't like Miss Ferber either. Almost everyone else is going to revel in these pages.

"Mr. Barkham," his byline notes, ". . . has made a study of best-seller writing techniques."

In several of the lists of best-selling fiction of 1952, *Giant* came in at number six, sandwiched in between Frances Parkinson Keyes's *Steamboat Gothic* and Ernest Hemingway's *The Old Man and the Sea*. On her overseas agent Victor Gollancz's foreign sales list, *Giant* went from third to fourth editions on succeeding days. Doubleday ran an early campaign that paid off in spades: one free copy for every ten ordered before publication. In 1952, the book was selling briskly in Swedish, Dutch, Norwegian, Portuguese, Spanish, Japanese, Danish, English, German, Italian, French, and Czech.

But Ferber was always vulnerable to dismissive reviews and rather frightened of a bad press, as she expresses to Ken McCormick in August of 1952, as she was about to leave for Elizabeth Arden's retreat, Maine Chance, and he was about to vacation as well. In an early short story called "Nobody's in Town," she had written about the dog days of August, when most people "of consequence" fled. But before she left:

> Did you read the Laura Hobson piece in the last *Sat. Review Lit?* Texas. We can run into real trouble if the *Times* or the

Tribune assign a Texas writer or so-called literary figure (local) to review *Giant* . . . If a resentful Texan reviews my book it will be a bad business. Much of the published comment I have seen (Texan) is real Nazi stuff. For that matter, it has just occurred to me that the set-up down there reminds me more the Nazi ideology and behavior than any community I've ever encountered. I like, by the way, Governor Shivers placing his state above his country in the matter of the oil tidelands. Nice boy.

I shall need quite a few copies of *Giant*. Aside from the copies that Doubleday is kind enough to send me. I should think I ought to have twenty copies in all. And of course I'd love to have them before publication if possible. Some must go to Texas people who were so helpful and generous—Doctor Hector Garcia, Colonel Sterling, and others. I hope this can be managed. Of course, mailing out books is a hideous business, what with wrapping and all that. But who am I to complain! I'm glad to have been able to finish it, hot or cold, reviewers or no.

Have a fine holiday.

In the winter of 1952, *The New York Times Book Review* requested twelve authors with new books to identify another book published that year that they wish they had written. John Steinbeck praised Al Capp's dialogue in the cartoon *Li'l Abner*, Tallulah Bankhead said she envied Adlai Stevenson's written campaign speeches—and Ferber singled out her own novel, *Giant*. I would imagine that this was because her sensitivity was elevated during this stressful time when some critical cudgels were raised.

Her northeastern, midwestern, and southeastern reviews were mostly positive. She brought in the majors, hence her best-selling status. She was pleased when a well-known rural-area critic brought home the bacon, as W. W. Baker did in *The Kansas City Times*:

Since her first novel was published in 1911, Edna Ferber has turned her attention to such typically American matters as the show boat, small-town and farm life, and the travelling saleswoman. Now, tongue-in-cheek and pen in hand, she goes beyond matters American and delves into the modern-day folklore of that strange land to the south known as Texas.

It is a well-drawn plot, with the usual Ferber niceties; the characters, though mostly of the race known as Texan, emerge as essentially human beings, as loveable or unlikable as Miss Ferber's people usually are.

During this time, her favorite Texan, Joe Linz, had intelligently tried to ameliorate the blows from his own state, which had already started bashing her. His words were balm to her wounded creative temperament.

How very wonderful and heartwarming for you to send me *Giant* . . .

Can you agree that it is your best novel? That is my opinion. Perhaps because of my relative closeness to the subject; perhaps because it is an angry book, and I am often angry about the same things . . .

I understand . . . that vilification has already been heaped upon you by the *Houston Press,* obviously by somebody with a sense of guilt. And although we deserve a good cussing, no one likes to be cussed, and this will be only the beginning. I seem to remember the storm that broke over you with *Cimarron,* and you are probably beginning to think this is where you came in.

Let them say what they want. *Giant* is a great book. It would have to be to bear the weight of its very apt name. The bigness and littleness of Texas is all in it. No one has ever caught it before, and I wager it will never again be put down so magnificently nor so poignantly, the latter because I think you love it and hate it all at once.

I am glad that you ended it on a note of hope. A hundred or so years is not, unfortunately, much time in which to teach people about decency and tolerance and spiritual honesty. Maybe we'll learn in time how to live with Mexicans. It won't happen until about the time we learn to live with Negroes and Jews and Japanese, here and everywhere. Our most popular employee is a Mexican lady. She isn't in the shipping department hidden away like they are in many stores. She is a saleslady right out where we can be proud of her. Maybe this doesn't prove anything, because we are in a firm owned by Jews, maybe it does.

I'm sorry for all this. You didn't ask for a critique. You only made a beau geste. You also made me very happy. I can't answer for Texas, but I can certainly say I hope you'll always love me as much as I love you.

Ferber's darling "Mossie"—Moss Hart, 1932.

Moss Hart, circa 1938

Ferber had many devoted friends, but no one else quite like Joe Linz. He seemed to bridge all of her needs in another person. He was familial—almost filial; he was kind, thoughtful, loving, romantic, helpful, therapeutic, amusing, clever, honest, honorable, generous, loyal, and consistent. They never lost touch, and they never feuded.

When she finally wrote back to him in October, she seemed almost jaunty from being a veteran of her own book.

> The early reactions and reviews have ranged from very good to savage. I have developed the hide of a rhinoceros. The book is selling fantastically. For me it is a piece of work finished and that is that. If you had resented my writing it I'd have regretted it all of my life.
>
> Orville Prescott in *The New York Times* and [Lewis] Gannett in the *New York Herald Tribune* wrote the most understanding reviews. The *Chicago Tribune*, too. I wish Texas could have seen them. For these reviewers saw and spoke of my admiration for Texas and its fascination for me, as well as the other side of the picture.

Ferber approved of her work on *Giant*. She was not prone to self-flattery. On the contrary: she would often berate herself for actions or behaviors, taking a certain comfort in fessing up: "*Giant* is a much better novel than *Ice Palace*"—its successor, in 1958— "in theme, characterization, execution. I think that in order to write really well and convincingly one must be somewhat poisoned by emotion. Dislike, displeasure, resentment, fault-finding, indignation, passionate remonstrance, a sense of injustice, these are perhaps corrosive to the container but they make fine fuel."

The Blaze

In the early summer of 1952, just prior to publication of the novel in the fall, preceded by the installments in the *Ladies' Home Journal* and the Book-of-the-Month Club, Ferber went to Europe for two months.

First, she was exhilarated by the act of finishing, which was followed by exhaustion and anxiety about its critical reception. All this psychological activity made escape mandatory. She went to England, France, and Switzerland in June and July, and then in August she returned to the States and hid out at Maine Chance. She also patronized its sister spa in Phoenix, Arizona, where she was pampered, massaged, oiled, and buffed. She would eat nourishing foods, beautifully prepared, with an occasional cheese or chocolate soufflé thrown in for kicks.

She recovered from all that ailed her: back problems, arthritis, ulcers acting up, occasional but fierce headaches, and general rheums. Although Ferber had a sturdy, orthodox health regimen, she was susceptible to physical invasions. No matter if they were categorized as relatively minor, they were frequent. She was a woman of many maladies. Now, she would renew her resistance to the critical—mostly Texan—brickbats that were starting to bludgeon her. As indicated in the following letter to Ken McCormick, written in August 1952 from Maine Chance, there were always new vexations.

About the *Reader's Digest* contract. That must not be signed
with any finality until I return. I'll be back in New York about
the 23rd or 24th of August. There are many things that I must
do during the last week in August. I suppose Morris [Ernst]
won't be back until after Labor Day. But I must in any case
write his office. If all *Giant* payments are piled up next year
I'll be busted after years of working on this book. Income
tax. [Ferber's dramatic streak escalated around financial
matters and, coupled with her early working-to-middle-
class upbringing, resulted in an unrealistic but abject fear of
poverty.]

What with the B.O.M. [Book-of-the-Month Club] and
the *Reader's Digest*, Doubleday will be in the clear and out
again before the book is published. I do hope this won't in
any way cause your organization to relax on promotion and
sales plans.

I am a bit bewildered by your figures on advance sales.
When I saw you a week ago you said that the advance was
about $29,000 and as this seemed to me to be less than
colossal I was somewhat depressed. Now suddenly you write
that advance sales will be 65,000 or 70,000.

The Steinbeck [*East of Eden*], Hemingway [*The Old Man
and the Sea*], and Texas guy's [probably Madison Cooper,
whose epic novel, *Sironia, Texas,* was published that year]
books should make a very competitive setup.

Even if you have a finished book perhaps you'd better not
try to send it up here. I'm dying to see it, but as I'll be leaving
in a very short time now, and probably will stay one night in
Boston, the book might miss me.

How good of you to send me the Texas letter. I have had
a number of pleasant ones—or perhaps I should say a few.
Strangely enough, they were written by native Texans.

This place is good for me, but the inmates and the
conversation are for the most part almost unbearable. But
anything's better than New York just now.

You'll be very rushed next week, before your holiday.
If I don't get a glimpse of you here are my good wishes for

a happy cool restful sunny time. I'm going to the George
Kaufmans in Bucks County over Labor Day.

My love to you, dear Ken.

Edna

She loved abundantly and protectively . . . until she didn't. She
was a great one for feuds. Her tempers were massive, sudden, and felt
permanent. She didn't speak to Alexander Woollcott for nine years.
Although their friendship had never really been a generous one, it held
some nostalgia, dating back to their halcyon days as Algonquin wits. In
1933, George S. Kaufman had written a play with Woollcott called *The
Dark Tower*, which turned out to be a meager offering at best. Ferber,
who was invited to the opening, went totally against her grain, arriving
in the middle of the second act, as she had been delayed by an illustrious dinner on a yacht owned by businessman Stanton Griffis, who
later served as a special envoy to FDR and Harry Truman as well as
the United States ambassador to Poland, Egypt, Argentina, and Spain.
After the play, visiting Woollcott backstage, he dressed her down so violently that she finally retorted: "You New Jersey Nero! You mistake your
pinafore for a toga!" And that was the curtain line on their friendship.

Her feud with Moss Hart lasted four years. It began during the filming of *Giant*. Ferber and Hart were beginning to work on the libretto
of a musical version of *Saratoga Trunk*. Rodgers and Hammerstein had
already turned them down, whereupon Hart suggested a composer
named Harold Arlen. Ferber had never heard of him and would have
none of him. Hart sensed that the project was doomed and wanted to
beg off it. The day came that he broke it to her. Kitty Hart recalled that
he was gray with fright. But when he came home, he reported that he
felt all had gone smoothly enough. The phone rang sometime later that
day. It was Ferber, who ranted to Kitty about how Mossie had called
her "an old granite face," and how she couldn't see her way clear to ever
forgiving him.

Her two-year feud with Margaret Leech Pulitzer came after the
publication of *Ice Palace* in 1958. Peg, as she was known to Ferber, had
written to say how much she was enjoying reading *Giant*, obviously
confusing the two novels. A few days later, Pulitzer received an enve-
lope addressed to her in Ferber's hand. Inside was the letter that she had

written to Ferber, who had circled the word "*Giant*" and in the margin written, "If you haven't yet, why not read *Show Boat*, or *So Big* if you get a chance."

With Louis Bromfield, the feud was on the other foot. Being old friends and living in different states, they would arrange to meet up for an occasional adventure. In 1940, it was New Orleans. As they were driving to the Oak Alley Plantation, Bromfield told her his concept for a new short story. Some months later, he picked up an issue of *Cosmopolitan* to see his idea as realized by Edna Ferber. Bromfield did not forgive her until 1951, when they met in New York for dinner at 21, where they had a pleasant, forgettable time. The rapture was gone.

To quote Katharine Hepburn, with whom she never feuded, "She was definitely a violent person. I watched my p's and q's with Edna." Hepburn, who also had a temperament, admired Ferber, according to all evidence. Perhaps her use of the word "violent" was, in a sense, a compliment—that Ferber was a maverick, who exploded at what she saw as injustice—or perhaps she had observed that Ferber could become volatile by random provocations.

Ferber could be gallant, especially when it came to American causes. Although steeped in all the odds and ends connected to the emergent *Giant*, she found the time and energy to go all out for Adlai Stevenson's 1952 bid for president of the United States. She wrote speeches and they were either delivered or printed and published. I came across this one among her personal papers. I have no idea where it was "speechified," as she would say, but its message feels uncannily prophetic:

> Right now I may as well break down and confess to you that I'm not on this program today because I wanted to talk about my novel *Giant*. People seem to be reading this book and find-ing it interesting and that's wonderful for me. I wrote it because I wanted to write it, and I wrote it as honestly as I knew how. It took me [thirteen] years because it was a difficult and com-plicated book to write.
>
> What I really want to say is so much more important to you and to me than any book written by me for your reading. There's a subject about which we're all talking and thinking and debating in our minds and souls. I've lived through a lot of presidential campaigns but I've never witnessed anything like

this one. The men and women of the United States are searching the very spirit within them to decide who shall be the next President of the United States. We know that these next four years will not only be important in the history of our country. They may decide the fate of the world. What you decide is vital to billions of people. Not millions. Billions. It will be vital to the people of India. Of China. England. The captive countries of Poland, Hungary, Czechoslovakia. It may well be the test of the survival of civilization itself . . .

There is a saying that when a great man is needed in time of crisis in the United States he always somehow, miraculously, appears. And he has appeared. The man, Adlai Stevenson, fits the period in which we live. Here is a man of compassion, courage, wisdom and deep integrity. . . .

. . . Ours is a free not a captive country. Adlai Stevenson is a free, not a captive man . . . If you don't know that a revolution has been going on these past twenty years you'd better learn it now, because it has been and it still is. The old boys are not only trying to turn back the clock. They can't even tell the time.

Being combative didn't mean she was tough. How thick could her skin be against scathing reviews of a book she had lived and breathed for years? Across the Lone Star State galloped hang-her-high reviews of *Giant*. *The Houston Press* suggested a match to burn her and the book. *The Dallas Morning News* called *Giant* "a slander on Texas." *The Texas Observer* pronounced it "a richly-conceived and rottenly written book." *Houston Press* columnist Carl Victor Little proclaimed that Ferber had written "a gargantuan hunk of monstrous, ill-informed, hokum-laden, hocus-pocus." And even light-years away from the initial *Giant* slumming, Don Graham wrote in his book *Cowboys and Cadillacs: How Hollywood Looks at Texas*, "For a while a joke circulated that Ferber had done her research on Texas by having a commercial plane fly low over the state."

Perhaps the howl of indignation was a form of the highest recognition. The characters in *Giant* weren't stereotypes as much as they were hyper-recognizable to the Texan. The ruthless, wildcatting Jett Rink was uncomfortably similar to the rags-to-riches mogul Glenn McCarthy. The entire Benedict clan seemed to echo the Briscoe clan. The Conquistador Hotel was definitely Houston's—and McCarthy's—old Shamrock Hotel. Reata was a stand-in for the King Ranch. Ferber's heroine, Leslie Benedict, could represent every out-of-state bride surveying her new home with a critical eye. Bick Benedict, the generationally rich star rancher-patriarch, was a prototypical gallant Texan hero, lauded by every family lucky enough to have one. Vashti was every girl ever left behind who accelerated back with status and wealth. Uncle Bawley was the rich-boy would-be artist, forced to capitulate to the family business. Luz, daughter of Leslie and Bick, was the headstrong younger generation. Her brother, Jordy, was the shame of a Texan boy who didn't like to be on a horse and became a doctor; he was the "turncoat." Bob Dace was the young throwback to an older generation who appreciated ranching. These main characters might have been too close for comfort.

In retrospect, Robert Leleux of *The Texas Observer* mused in August 2011:

> At the time of *Giant*'s publication, many reviewers suggested that Ferber's exaggerated choice of fictional subjects had resulted in a boorish, overblown book. But looking back on it now . . . she did a fairly commendable job of conveying the truth and spirit of our state. One of Ferber's most admirable insights is that Texan-ness is essentially performative. That Texans "talk Texan" when abroad, just "as a certain type of Englishman becomes excessively Oxford." It's a secret that all great Texans know . . . After all, as *Giant*—in its broad, unsubtle strokes— yelps and yee-haws from the rooftops, Texas possesses magic. Texans are magicians, and no magician wants published the secrets of his tricks.

Most of the mainstream presses were protective without being slavish:

> "Her vocabulary is rich and vital; she sees material objects with a penetrating and delightful vision." —*New York Herald Tribune*

> "A brisk, slick, clever, constantly moving story . . . *Giant* makes marvelous reading—wealth piled on wealth, wonder on won-

der in a stunning, splendiferous pyramid of ostentation . . . No one can deny the explosive impact of this story."

—*The New York Times*

"Miss Ferber at her best, and that's very good indeed."

—*St. Louis Globe-Democrat*

"A powerful story . . . truly as big as its subject."

—*Los Angeles Times*

Fresh from her vacation abroad and then time at the Arden spa, Ferber ceased immediately to be ironed out and became choleric: "Hardened though I thought I was to literal-mindedness on the part of the readers, I was not prepared for the violence of the Texas assault following the publication of the novel *Giant*. The virulence of this attack was so libelous in character that merely to start proceedings on the grounds of libel would have snared one forever in a mass of degrading filth. It was scarcely believable that such obscene matter would be permitted in a publicly distributed newspaper in the United States."

In the novel, Ferber did not intend Jett Rink to have any vulnerability or sex appeal: "His face was grotesque with smears of dark grease and his damp bacchanalian locks hung in tendrils over his forehead . . . He came on, he opened the door of the screened veranda, he stood before the company in his dirt and grease, his eyes shining wildly . . . The man stood, his legs wide apart as though braced against the world. The black calloused hands with the fingers curiously widespread as they hung, his teeth white in the grotesquely smeared face."

This quote, citing Jett's Black-Mexican-Anglo appearance just after he has struck his mother lode of oil, could be equated to the racial invective of Black testosterone. And with Jett, Ferber makes a point of deconstructing Texas hierarchy. Although the Texas critics didn't seem to home in on this, their abuse bordered on a verbal lynching. Here was this small, older Jewish woman crossing their masculine territory and mixing it up. In the *San Angelo Standard-Times*, a book critic named Jack Allard wrote: "Many Texans . . . are calling for a burning at the stake of Miss Ferber. Instead of faggots, they would pitch copies of *Giant* on the fire." Carl Victor Little in his *Houston Press* review suggested that she be lynched. He dismissed her and her " 'brand of fiction' as steeped in backstairs gossip and what girl-novelists call local color."

Aside from swatting at daily horseflies from the Texas press, she was confronted in her own backyard by one she least expected. Norman Cousins, editor in chief of the *Saturday Review of Literature*, was a well-liked colleague, if not quite a friend. They found each other at the same dinner parties. A man named William Kittrell was assigned to write a review of *Giant* for the September 27, 1952, issue. It is, or was, standard procedure for writers to silently take the medicine of a bad review. Not Edna Ferber.

Kittrell's infamous review was titled "Land of the Boiling Gold." "Boiling" was the operative word for her reaction to this excoriation of her handiwork.

Miss Ferber's new novel is certain to be on the required reading list of the Texas Folklore Society, for it deals with the habits of those mythological creatures, the free spenders from Texas, the Land of the Big Rich.

According to Miss Ferber's account, the really well-to-do Texans have four-motored planes, while their earthbound poor relations are restricted to Cadillacs in a limited range of colors. One of Miss Ferber's typical female Texans wouldn't think of going out for an armload of stove-wood without throwing a sable stole around her shoulders, and she usually leaves her old worn-out diamonds around on the washstands of her primitive home.

Miss Ferber's fable shows that she shares the feelings of most Texans toward their noted if not noteworthy neighbors who like publicly to display their purchasing power. There are some seven million Texans who aren't millionaires.

Despite the disclaimer in the front of the book, the characters in *Giant* will strike many Texans as bearing a remarkable resemblance to actual persons . . . It is about as difficult to identify the characters and places in *Giant* as it would be to recognize the Washington Monument if it were painted purple.

Miss Ferber has done a lot of homework on this book, and there is some meat in it. Her discourses on grass, while not the last word on the subject, reveal diligent study. Her dislike of the treatment of the wetback and the discrimination against Latin-Americans is shared by many of us.

While there was a touch of genuine Texana in the mountain oyster feast Leslie ran into on her first day at the Reata Ranch, Miss Ferber surely dug up something out of this world when she wrote about the barbeque where the pièce-de-résistance was a cow-head cooked whole for eighteen hours, no less, and greedily devoured by the primitive plainsmen. [George Stevens had no problem with the authenticity of this food rite when he filmed this scene.]

Giant will be joyfully received in forty-seven states and avidly though angrily read in Texas, for if Miss Ferber and her publishers think they are going to make Texans so dang mad that they will stage a book-burning and hang Miss Ferber in effigy, she and they just don't know the residents of the state whose flag floats a single star.

A proper postscript is the writer's biography attached to the piece: "William Kittrell, a Texan of pre-Revolutionary stock, operates the Texas Press Clipping Bureau, a peanut farm, and a peach orchard."

An anonymous editor's supercilious note prior to the review reads: "Few of the novels we review this week will be remembered after this season has run its course, but a number of them will provide pleasant enough reading until something important comes along. The most keenly awaited of the lot because of its author's reputation is Edna Ferber's *Giant* . . . As our review suggests, it is going to arouse the wrath of all good Texans and entertain most readers in the other forty-seven commonwealths."

What ensued was a firestorm initiated by Ferber, who bit right back at the snake in the grass. Her reaction was certainly worrisome to those who wanted to protect her—and themselves. Slander suits can be wildfire or catnip depending on the perspective. Ferber first approached Henry Seidel Canby, a founder and former editor of the *Saturday Review*, in a letter dated September 28—a good example of her unique method of charm laced with fury:

Knowing you as I do, dear Henry Canby, and knowing Norman Cousins, I think and hope that the man who reviewed my novel *Giant* in the *Saturday Review* of September 27th was not of your choosing.

Beneath the article on page 15 of that issue your magazine has stated the qualification for book reviewing possessed by a William Kittrell. He is, one is told, a Texan of pre-Revolutionary stock. I assume that this refers to the Texas Revolution. To a few people outside Texas the term pre-Revolutionary may sometimes refer to the American Revolution. Mr. Kittrell is further equipped for literary criticism through being the operator of a Texas Press Clipping Bureau, a peanut farm, and a peach orchard. This I quote literally from your note.

This list of occupations is an honest and interesting one and spiced with the flavor of variety. It is not one which ordinarily would be considered sufficiently literary in its background to fit one for book reviewing.

Book reviewers are privileged to say that they like or dislike a book; approve or disapprove; and why. This is sound and good. But your reasons given for the choice of this particular reviewer are an affront to you and to your editorial staff and to your subscribers and to your readers and to me. The *Saturday Review* is generally considered the foremost magazine of literary criticism in the United States. Literary criticism does not stem legitimately from press clippings, peanut growing, peach raising, or even from pre-Revolutionary Texasism.

Your choice seems to me inconsistent as well. Else why did you not choose a communist clerk and farmer living in Hungary or Russia today as a reviewer of Arthur Koestler's book on how he arrived at Communism? Or a Cuban sugar planter for Hemingway's short story? Or a Salinas California lettuce grower for Steinbeck's novel?

Can the choice of Mr. William Kittrell have any connection with the fact that Mr. E. DeGolyer, whose financial relation to your magazine is so well known, and who

is chairman of your Board of directors, also happens to be a
wealthy Texas oil man?

Sincerely,

Edna Ferber

Perhaps, in fairness, you will use this letter in your Letters to
the Editor page.

Canby's response remains unknown. Norman Cousins offered to
print her letter, but she refused at the advice of her lawyer.

The connections that Ferber made to this "good ole boy" network were
solid. Everette Lee DeGolyer was a prominent oilman, geophysicist,
and philanthropist in Dallas. He was known as "the founder of applied
geophysics in the petroleum industry," as "the father of American geophysics," and was a legendary collector of rare books, according to
Wikipedia. He was of particular fascination to oilman Glenn McCarthy, of Shamrock Hotel fame, whose admiration and emulation were
no secret. It has been suggested that a combination of these two men
was rolled into the character of J. R. Ewing, head of the fictional Ewing
Oil Company in the epic television series *Dallas*.

Ferber was fearless in taking on an irksome issue. She was used to
getting a speedy, forelock-tugging response. This was not quite what
she received from Norman Cousins two days later:

Dear Edna,

I am deeply sorry that it turned out the way it did. In the
last several years I've lost six friends because of things that
appeared in the magazine. Please don't make it seven.

The note on Kittrell was in extremely bad taste, I agree,
and I don't blame readers for thinking that the editors have
either gone off their nut or have deliberately embraced a
policy of frivolousness. Someone on the job thought that
it might be amusing to write a note in the same vein as the

review itself. That was a mistake in judgement. I'm sorry it
happened.

We'll be glad, of course, to publish your letter. With
your permission, however, we would like to delete the last
paragraph. The reference to Mr. DeGolyer is gratuitous and,
I hope you will agree, may weaken an otherwise strong and
effective protest.

With all good wishes, my dear Edna, I am

Sincerely,

Norman

In the interim, Morris Ernst, Ferber's troubleshooting lawyer when
called upon, had been consulted and advised her to essentially cool her
jets. This was her attempt three days later:

Dear Mr. Cousins:—

You state in your letter to me, dated September 30, 1952, that
in your magazine you have done something in extremely bad
taste; that this thing justifies your readers in thinking that
the editors have either gone off their nuts or have deliberately
embraced a policy of frivolousness; that mistake in judgement
(as well as taste) was made; and that you are sorry it
happened.

I say to you that in this case, and this being true, you owe
an apology to your readers as well as to me, and couched in
exactly these words.

Certainly I would not consent to the publication of my
letter with the deletion you suggest. And I now do not wish
the letter to be published at all.

If your note on Kittrell was in extremely bad taste,
as you admit, and if its statement was the truth, then you
must realize that my objection is not to the footnote alone
but to the selection of reviewer as well. If the footnote
was meant to be what you call "amusing" then the review
which was (you say) meant to match, also was meant to be
"amusing."

Only brave people admit their mistakes when they are

wrong. You have admitted yours to me. If you are a brave editor you will admit this error to your readers as well. The review and its footnote were meant for them, not for me. The character and standing of the *Saturday Review* call upon this.

    Edna Ferber

One must remember that these missives were not emailed and therefore could be considered an unusually rapid-fire process. Cousins's response came on October 8:

Dear Edna (I hope I can still call you Edna despite the formality of your own reply):

In my letter to you, I tried to be as candid as I knew how, and to express my very sincere regrets that the incident worked out as it did. In the light of your reply, I am afraid I failed to make myself clear, about one point at least. I was addressing myself to the biographical note and not to the review itself. I thought the biographical note was in poor taste, and I have raised hell about it in this office. It would be a distortion of my intentions to say that my letter equally condemns the review on the basis of my reference to the ostensible effort to write an author's note "in the same vein as the review itself." This was intended to refer to the intended whimsicality of the review.

    My own feeling about the review itself, or, for that matter, about a number of reviews that appear in the magazine are irrelevant. It happens that I do not assign the books for review. The fact that I happened to be away on vacation at the time the book was assigned is not pertinent for even if I had been here I would not have reversed my "hands-off" policy with respect to the operation of our book review department.

    As for the editor's note in the magazine in which I acknowledge the bad taste of the biographical note, I agree with you completely. I will see to it that such a note is published.

    Once again, I ask that however great your denunciation of me as editor of SR, you try to think of me as someone who continues to have the highest regard for you as a person and friend.

Sincerely,
Norman

Ferber was now advised by her trusted advisors and her editor, Ken McCormick, to drop the matter. She couldn't, as she wrote McCormick on October 12: "You may be surprised to learn, dear Ken, that I didn't drop the *Saturday Review* thing after all. I found that my indignation was deeper than my caution qualms. Caution, perhaps unfortunately, never has been one of my characteristics. Norman's letters have been interesting." She must have written another upbraiding letter, which unfortunately is missing; but Cousins's seething and yet abject response of October 13 is not:

Dear Edna,

I'm going to make one more stab at this, with as much good grace as I can muster under the circumstances.

First, I am not trying to get out from under. Your "I only work here" reference was uncharacteristically unfair and inappropriate in the present instance. I accept responsibility for the *Saturday Review* and for everything in it. If on the basis of that flat statement you wish to denounce me for the review or for anything else, please do so. But I wrote you on the assumption that you would make a distinction between the editor's ultimate responsibility and the necessary spheres of authority within the organization. I also thought—and I should hate to think I made a mistake in this—that you were entitled to know that someone who considered himself a friend of yours did not deliberately set out to attack your work. It was in that connection that I told you about the mechanics of book review assignment and publication. Next, without commenting on the review itself I said that I didn't like the autobiographical note. I did not thereby condemn the review; what is inappropriate in an autobiographical note may not necessarily be inappropriate in a review. I

The New Yorker, November 30, 1952

said we would publish an editor's note apologizing for the inappropriateness of the autobiographical reference; we have done so.

Second, your reference to Mr. DeGolyer. He didn't write the review and I can think of nothing more unfair than to attack him because he happens presently to live in Texas. Edna, I don't know who your informants are in this case, but you ought to know that he is considered one of America's leading scientists. His field is geology, and he is ranked among the top three or four experts in the world. He is also a bookman. I can think of few men in this country who have done more for books without public fanfare than he. Years ago, when the *Saturday Review* was run down and practically bankrupt, we tried vainly to get help from the people who were identified in the public mind with cultural activities. One or two of them offered modest help but on terms involving impossible conditions and loss of editorial independence. Mr. DeGolyer listened carefully to our story, brought in no lawyers for exhausting sessions, drew up no

conditions, said that he felt the *Saturday Review* was worth
continuing, and insisted on the editors being given ownership
control. Since that time, ten years ago, we have been on our
feet. And in all those years, Mr. DeGolyer has made not a
single demand on us. Now comes a letter which kicks him
in the pants for something of which he is entirely innocent.
Certainly I would ask that it be deleted. And I felt equally
certain you would, too, if you knew the facts.

There goes the bell ending round three.

Sincerely,

Norman

The whole issue seems to have been dropped—at least in what Ferber saved in her papers. Win, lose, or draw, it was an imbroglio of some proportions and conveys how deeply she would go for what she considered justice, but which could be perceived as bullying. And when she felt that, at least here, it amounted to an even steven, hell broke loose again—for in came the Lon Tinkle review in *The Dallas Morning News*, headlined "Ferber Goes Both Native and Berserk: Parody, Not Portrait, of Texas Life."

As Ferber knew, Tinkle was a fifth-generation Texan whose ancestor fought in the Alamo, and a longtime book editor for the paper. By choice she had sidestepped interviewing him early on. His supposed stature was that "he understood the tradition of Texas and its writing with all its elements of frontier myth and its hard reality."

With Tinkle's byline came the review that hurt more than all the others combined. It seemed to edge too close to whatever writer's frailties she might have as he jovially blackened and charred her craft. He seemed to be thoroughly enjoying himself in hoping to make her squirm, and he succeeded:

Writing about Texas (or a fragment of it) in her latest novel *Giant*, Miss Edna Ferber has gone native. Trouble is she has spoiled it by also going berserk. . . .

What Miss Ferber finds wrong with Texas is precisely what is wrong with the rest of the world. But having gone native, she reduces our Texan braggadocio to absurdity: she gives us a monopoly on everything. Texas, first in oil, in cotton, in cattle, in size—and first in villainy. Now, now, Miss Ferber, you aren't writing *Uncle Tom's Cabin*.

But part of Miss Ferber's confusion is that she doesn't seem really to know what she's trying to write. Her novel sounds off about Texans in general, but obviously this is a "key" novel written out of hatred . . .

Many readers will buy *Giant* because of the quick identity of many conspicuous and prominent Texas names, some mentioned directly—such as Glenn McCarthy, the Klebergs, King Ranch, Neiman-Marcus and others disguised but as recognizable as your pastor playing Moses in the church pageant this National Bible Week.

All we can tell you about that is that the chief villain, one Jett Rink who built the famous Hotel Conquistador on the outskirts of the big city of Hermosa from his oil profits, is clearly Simon Legree. Not since the days of Little Eva has American literature harbored such a ruthless heel. . . .

On a deeper level, Miss Ferber scores two direct hits. What she says about voting practices and political combines in South Texas is almost daily verified in the news; and her resentment of the exploitation of Latin-Americans will find an echo in most Texas minds. But it is deplorable that Miss Ferber has made of race discrimination a sensational and implausible factor in her plot, dragged in by the neck and not organic to her story. This is sentimental cheating.

As a novel, indeed, *Giant* is a triumphant parade of platitudes, with almost no real sensitivity to people as such.

Miss Ferber's whole problem as a novelist has been that she is powerfully responsive to situations (wife versus jealous sister-in-law, say) and insensitive to the people in the situation.

This weakness is appalling in *Giant*.

For every swipe there seemed to be a counterswipe. Ferber saved this little Band-Aid of a clipping sent to the *Dallas Morning News*:

I have read the review by your book Review Editor, Lon Tinkle of Edna Ferber's *Giant*, in which his defense of Texas pretty largely rests on his attack on the heroine of the book.

Sir, it is just like a Texas reviewer to defend the men of Texas by attacking a woman—and not just a woman—a lady. And not just a lady—a Virginia lady. It is typical of the degeneracy of a state which has the effrontery to call itself Southern.

This review is complete proof of the contention that in Texas cattle come first, then men, then horses, then women, with oil above all. I understand that Texas reviewers have a rope ready if Miss Ferber should ever turn up. Well, if any Texas reviewers should ever turn up in the Old Dominion, they can expect pistols at ten paces.

And then there was this forward-thinking review from *The Texas Observer* that helped to settle her down: "A powerful novel and a gripping read, and very much ahead of its time regarding South Texas race relations. It has charm and intelligence and swagger, and even some fairly profound sociological insight."

Autumn in New York

One of Ferber's great loves was walking—and if she was in New York, window shopping along the way. A good, stout pair of shoes and she was off, rain or shine, striding and stopping to gaze. However, this practice became somewhat fraught after the initial release of *Giant* in the *Ladies' Home Journal* and then in *Reader's Digest*, and then, with huge fanfare, the commercial release of the novel in hardcover.

During the late fall of 1952, she was stopped everywhere she went. This was a day of different New Yorkers. They were polite, sometimes hesitant or shy, but determined to be heard. No one was rude, pushy, possessive, or a show-off. They approached as supplicants, thrilled to be in her presence. But it was tiring. Like many established writers, she craved anonymity and yet not too much of it. I once witnessed her being simultaneously flattered and exasperated when, while she and I were walking ahead of my parents after a dinner out, a woman about to pass us stopped and blocked us instead. "Oh, Miss Ferber," she gasped, "I absolutely loved *Giant*!" Ferber gave a wintry smile and said, "Did you? Tell me why?"

After a new book came out her sociability level was high. The letters of approbation poured in from her illustrious friends. She had requested that Ken McCormick send advance copies, but not so much to pals as to the people who had helped her assemble her information along the way. She hoped that her friends would buy the book, which they dutifully did. Humorist Frank Sullivan wrote:

> I finished *Giant* at four this morning and merely wish to say that if you will step into the conservatory behind the palms I will give you the very warmest embrace of congratulations and affection within the power of a Sullivan to bestow. I heard enraptured reports about *Giant* last spring, from a lady on the *Home Journal* editorial staff, but I didn't want to read the serialization, so I waited for the whole book, and it was worth waiting for, and more . . . You've done it again, like the champ that you are, and all I can say is that I have an awed respect for you for being able to sit down and write a novel of such sustained power and good humor and good indignation. Everything in it is real and every character walks and not a one but isn't alive. And that thing you have said about Texans so needed to be said . . .

Screenwriter George Oppenheimer sent this:

> I have just this moment finished reading *Giant* and am embarking on one of the few fan letters I have ever written. I should be cursing you. Your damned book has so completely held me that I've neglected my work for the past four days to live in Texas . . . If we beleaguered Liberals are looking for a definition of the word "liberalism," it can be found in *Giant*. And there hasn't, as far as I know, been such trenchant social criticism since *Main Street* . . . and if you have any trouble whatsoever with any Texan, I will gladly wrestle him or her (preferably her) two out of three falls . . .

From playwright Paul Osborn:

> I just finished reading *Giant*. I enjoyed it so thoroughly that I can't help writing to tell you so. I think it's a wonderful, comprehensive, exciting book.
>
>   It also put the fear of God into me. What if Judy [his daughter] should fall in love with a Texan?

Richard Halliday, theater producer and husband of Mary Martin, wrote to say:

> You didn't I'm sure, deliberately write *Giant* in order to cause serious friction between husband and wife.
>
> But—! I happen to be married to a certain girl . . . I've just lived through five days of the worst hell I've ever known. Not a moment alone, of privacy. This girl, my wife, has followed me around with *that* book in her hands, exclaiming, "Oh, isn't this wonderful, listen," and then she reads paragraphs, even pages aloud. She roars with laughter and expects me to join her, becomes furious if I don't. Another moment, "my how vivid and accurate this description is," later, "Oh! I know, I know this character."
>
> The climax came only last night. She had just finished the book at 1:30 a.m., handed it to me and said that I had to read it immediately . . . On top of that she started talking about what a wonderful film it would make—and before long she had cast Katharine Hepburn, Clark Gable and Gregory Peck, and she practically declared *she* bought the rights and the picture was almost completed!
>
> You'll have to agree she has proven to be a very trying, disappointing wife—to us both. As soon as possible I plan to come live with you and look forward to our evenings together while I read *Giant* aloud.
>
> I do think this is a wonderful solution—Mary has inadvertently done a really beautiful thing—thrown me right at the woman we both admire and love.

And from Katharine Hepburn:

> I have been meaning and meaning to write you about the book which I read immediately, when I got back from Lausanne, Switzerland. It's wonderful—fascinating characters and atmosphere—a really fine plot—how proud you must be. You can present such a vivid and moving picture. If it wasn't it wouldn't be a most agonizing but satisfying means of expression. It may have taken you a long time to do, but it is

certainly worth it. I was completely absorbed and so proud to know you.

Ferber also received praise from Blanche Knopf, the wife of Alfred Knopf, renowned head of the publishing firm. When I read it, I had my first new perspective of Katharine Hepburn's saying "unicorn women." The correspondent reflects a certain wistfulness and the ambivalence of that phrase. It is also documented that the wife was open to triangular relationships, so perhaps, just perhaps, she was referring to a bygone invitation in her note.

> Dear E.F.,
>   Reading the Book-of-the-Month-Club News about you, and remembering our very early acquaintance, and friendship I hope, I am starting *Giant*. I am so impressed that I want to write to you and tell you congratulations on all of your accomplishments. I wish . . . I wish . . . but it never happened. But I think your path has been one strewn with glory and hard work and all I want to do is offer my small congratulations along with the world's.
>   When we have a chance again one day, we must meet and talk over all the nice old days and perhaps those coming along.
>   All good wishes for this Texas book, and for you.

It is clear how deeply Ferber affected those around her—some of the more timid were often on tiptoe. During the early months of *Giant*'s release she seemed more easily injured than usual. Her defenses were down, and as a result, praise was headier and stings became wounds. She took umbrage when Harriet Pilpel wrote to her about discussing *Giant* with Abel Green, the editor of *Variety*, the movie and show-business bible:

> I told him that there is big interest in the book in Hollywood but you didn't want to sell it until after publication . . . He did mention to me, however, without giving names, that his files show that at least of the big companies none at this time see a movie in the book, all of which means little or nothing because

if there is a good movie in the book or if they think there is one they're not going to be scared off by anything on earth.

Frankly, I am surprised that even though the policy was to indicate no dealings at the moment that some company didn't try to put on some heat and make a definite offer. Incidentally, Abel thought it was very wise not to sell before publication, particularly in a case like yours, since Book-of-the-Month and *Reader's Digest* will enhance the value as compared to a sale before publication.

On one hand good news, on the other bad news—but then maybe potential good news after all . . . This letter made Ferber peevish, but there was a respect between the two women that she never disrupted. Harriet never received a "spiral."

When Ferber saved a letter, it was because it represented something. She especially had a penchant for saving letters from the public that got under her skin, as this one did:

You might say that I border on being an irate Texan. I am at present engaged in reading your latest book, *Giant*.

There is one question I would like to ask you. On what and how many trips to Texas do you base the material in your book?

My home is in the Panhandle, but at present I am living in Dallas. My father is employed by one of the larger ranches of Texas and I feel that I know ranch people well enough to say that your picture is grossly overdrawn and brutally unfair to this wonderful group of persons.

Not everyone in Texas owns a Cadillac or has his own personal plane. Neither are the women as tactless and shallow as those in your book.

Perhaps you wonder why I continue to read *Giant*, well, I really don't know any reason except that it is a wonderful exercise for one's emotions. Especially if you are a native born Texan.

Hoping you'll make a visit to Texas soon.

Not all native-born Texans were against the novel and Ferber for writing it. She not only saved the following letter but acknowledged it by having her longtime secretary, Miss Garden, send a polite thank you.

> This is a fan letter from an ex-patriate Texan for twelve years now a Californian thank heavens. I have just finished reading your wonderful novel, *Giant,* and although I must admit that months ago when it was first given to me to read I almost threw it in the waste basket over that line, "I'll just be a minute, I want to pick up a little ole mink throw." I'm glad now that I didn't. I did, however, sit it to one side and picked it up again a day ago and didn't put it down until I'd read every last word of it.
>
> It is a thrilling book and brilliant piece of writing . . .

The harsh criticism coming out of Texas seemed to be infecting the movie-sale chances. The kind of infamy that the book was generating was not what Hollywood moguls liked to take on. Although her representatives—editorial, legal, foreign and domestic—reassured her that her novel was outdoing itself in sales, Samuel Goldwyn and fellow movie moguls were conspicuously silent—almost. The director King Vidor was blatantly hat-in-hand chasing a deal to form an independent film company, as his lawyers put forth in a letter to Ferber's representatives. He would like to enter into a deal whereby he can obtain the film rights on an option basis for a period of six months to enable him to prepare a screenplay and to arrange for its production, release, etc. Afterwards, if the option is exercised, a deal wherein Miss Ferber would receive a percentage of the film profits would be arranged."

I can imagine Ferber sniffing and saying, "Two et ceteras too many."

Then, without advance warning, at least where she was concerned, Houghton Mifflin published a novel called *Sironia, Texas* by Madison Cooper. The novel took place in the early twentieth century, its author was a Texan, and the setting was a fictionally disguised Waco, his hometown. What distinguished the novel—other than the potential competition with *Giant*—was its size: it would be remembered as the longest novel in publishing history at that time. It was originally brought out in two volumes, with an estimated word count of 840,000 and a page count of 2,119. Although it won the Houghton Mifflin Literary Fellowship Award, most reviewers and readers found the novel heavy going—and heavy lifting.

Any rivalry that Ferber might have felt was quickly quelled by the size of this tome. After Ken McCormick reassured her that her novel was still the "giant" one, she wrote back pleasantly, "I am delighted to hear that *Giant* will be number one on the *Herald Tribune* week from Sunday and I'm sorry that the *Times*, which is, as you say, far behind in its listing process, still gives me only third place. I know that *Sironia, Texas* at $10 a throw must need quite a bit of strategy." On November 16, she was in second place on the *Times* list, between *East of Eden* by John Steinbeck and *The Silver Chalice* by Thomas B. Costain. The price of *Giant* was $3.95.

Ferber occasionally reaped what she sowed when one of her "sources" became overly proprietary. She had stayed with a family in Dallas in the early days of her research. They went all out in giving her a gala time. The missus of the tribe wrote Ferber several cozy family chronicles over the years. A couple of them were politely answered by Ferber's secretary. All hell broke loose when the novel was read, digested, and regurgitated. The woman was vitriolic: from her point of view she was an injured party.

At that time there was a stark division between the haters and the lovers of *Giant*—there was no in-between. However, the haters were not every single Texan: "You have done a wonderful job which needed to be done," wrote a "good Texan." "You have held the mirror up to us and if we do not like the picture it's up to us to change it. It should help the cattle, the cattlemen and the Mexicans." This was the reader for Ferber, who was quoted as saying, "A closed mind is a dying mind."

Although *Giant* was Ferber's third novel addressing racism—*Show Boat* dealt with the subservience expected of African Americans as well as the issue of miscegenation, while *Cimarron* portrayed the transformation of the Oklahoma Indians from impoverished loiterers to wildcatting millionaires—its portrait of Mexican Americans would stir up the boldest reaction of the three for years to come. Leslie, Ferber's fictional heroine, led the way for this.

Around 1954, Ferber began to show early signs of a condition called trigeminal neuralgia. A jabbing pain on one side of the face, ruthless, and then gone for weeks or months. It is a relatively rare affliction, more particular to women, and to those with tightly wired psyches. It was no wonder this happened to Ferber when one reads the following passage from *A Kind of Magic*:

> Headlines in black letters two inches high streamed across the pages of Texas newspapers. This Ferber is a liar and a criminal. We think she ought to be caught and hanged here in Texas and we'll arrange the hanging and choose the people to hold the rope. The drop should send her through a sheet of glass below the scaffold so that she'll be cut into hamburgers when she falls. She's an idiot. She doesn't know Texas. . . . Letters. Telephone calls. Animal rage.

Author Pamela Smith Hill sums up the legacy of *Giant*:

> This kind of attack sounds unsettlingly familiar more than sixty years later. The themes and ideas Ferber tackled are still with us—but they've spilled over beyond *Giant* into a larger, more polarized national debate. . . .
> . . . As Leslie advises in *Giant*, we must just keep on working to create a more enlightened, compassionate, and diverse society with opportunities for all. There's nothing dated or old-fashioned about this idea.

If it was annoying to others that Ferber involved herself in every aspect of the novel's aftermath, her professional associates never countered her frontal approach. When she called, they sprung—even their verbiage sprung. Louise Thomas, director of promotion at Doubleday, answered a Ferber inquiry with: "Sales are leaping ahead beyond expectations, and it's necessary to get another edition on press immediately. *Giant* is 'getting away very fast,' as they say in the sales department." Doubleday's advance order of 100,000 copies had all but sold out.

Kate Steichen, daughter of the photographer Edward Steichen, was the copy editor on *Giant* and assistant to Ken McCormick. She was the ideal acolyte, knowing precisely how to please an exacting writer. Ferber liked and trusted her and therefore was easy on her, deferential in her tone. Steichen added considerably to Ferber's well-being and through the years built a funny and true relationship with her. Ferber fans were incredibly loyal once they understood and appreciated her character. She was then able to relax, allowing a relationship to grow. Although Steichen left Doubleday for Macmillan in 1959, the two remained in contact. From Steichen:

I loved her from the very first minute and in all those years at Doubleday. She was a devil to work with. She was a heller, but I kept saying that she's worth it. That was to me the key-stone of Edna Ferber. She was worth it. She was so damn real. Always. With even the little things. I know when I used to set up the luncheons—the long luncheons that she and Ken had to have when they were working—when they were "in book," and I'd call up and say, "Good morning, Miss Ferber." "Dear Kate, how are you?" Then, I'd say, "Now, about lunch . . ." and I would propose whatever was the best place then—Baroque, Pavillon—whatever it happened to be. "No," she'd say, "I'll meet Ken at Schrafft's." I would say, "Schrafft's??" And she would say, "You know, they make the most delicious chicken hash available."

One time over lunch with Ken, he told Miss Ferber that Carol [Kate's partner] and I were finally going to build our own house, and she said, "You know Ken, I would like to do some-thing really nice for Kate. What do you think I could do?" So Ken thought about it and he said, "Well Kate's father is giving them a whole hi-fi music system thing for the new house. They have no long-playing records, so why don't you pick some out and send them to her." And Miss Ferber, Ken then told me, draws herself up to her full height, which I think was probably to my shoulder, standing there on the corner of Madison Ave-nue after lunch, and says to Mr. McCormick, "I wouldn't ever think of choosing books or records for my friends." Where-upon I assume Ken threw himself under the nearest taxi and evaporated. Well, a few days later, with a beautiful little note, came a check. It was a check for one hundred dollars to use to start our record collection. I was really shocked and I went into Ken with this check—and of course at Doubleday we just didn't take any lagniappe or gravy from authors—let alone agents. There was really none of the stuff at Doubleday, which was one of the things I loved about it. So, I went into Ken and I showed him the check and I read him the note and I said, "Ken, I simply cannot accept it, and how can I gracefully refuse?" And Ken looked at me and he said, "Look, dear, take it because it will give Edna so much pleasure." And so the basic collection was started at that time, and I mentioned it to her several times, for instance in a little Christmas card I'd say, "The music is still resounding, thanks to you."

During the book's gestation time, its reception and outcome, Ferber heard proprietary echoes from distant relations whom she had helped financially over the years. There had been an extremely dire situation during the war years when a family called Hollander, remote relatives, needed to get out of Germany. Ferber arranged their passage—cloak-and-dagger stuff—and saw that they were situated in Chicago. The most faithful correspondent among the Hollanders was a woman named Gudren, who obviously felt proudly proprietary: "Lillian is not yet through *Giant*, but I have just finished it. Edna, truly it is your Opus Magnum it is Epic it is Homeric. Do you see how I have fallen into your style of no commas? The sociologists will use it like a bible."

My grandmother did in fact agree with Gudren on the enormous merits of *Giant* but was afraid of its implications. Not that Fannie was timorous; she was brave, as were all the Ferber women, but she felt violence could come to her sister. "It was an ugly situation," she said to me so many years later during one of our last interview visits. "It was a beheading."

Ferber managed to take it mostly in her stride, as she confided in her friends the Lunts in a letter of November 1952:

I've thought of you both there in London [starring in Noël Coward's *Quadrille*], dearest Lynn and Alfred. Such weeks of turmoil here. The political campaigns have been a kind of torment. I am, of course, working and voting for Stevenson. Eisenhower has been a jolting shock to millions of people. Poor bewildered decent fellow, stumbling along at the heels of Taft, McCarthy, Nixon. He smiles and raises his arms high in the air. It's like a gesture of surrender . . . You know I had sent a check to further the Eisenhower campaign, and I thought he definitely would be a superb choice for President. It still seems incredible that a man could have changed and weakened so pitiably. Of course no one knows how the contest will be resolved . . . You'll be interested, Alfred, to know that the *Milwaukee Journal* switched to Stevenson last week. They could no longer stomach the McCarthy foulness. I sent a telegram of congratulations and thanks to the paper, as one who used to work there as a reporter . . .

I'm happy to know you found *Giant* interesting. It is going along fabulously. I thought the reviews were only fair. Of course the Texas press was savage. By the way, you had said you had loaned the book to Noel. I should have loved to send him a copy. I thought about it quite a bit. But Noel, I've always thought, doesn't particularly care about my books or short stories. I didn't want to put him into the position of being obliged to say something polite.

In a considerably more whimsical light, in October there had come word from the Texas Institute of Letters, addressed to Doubleday:

Dear Sirs:

On November 14 the Texas Institute of Letters will make a $1,000.00 award for the best Texas book of the year and a $250.00 for the best first book of fiction by a Texas author. According to our information the following books published by you are eligible for consideration:

Fuermann, George. *Houston: Land of the Big Rich*.
Ferber, Edna. *Giant*.

In order for these books to be considered for the award, one copy of each of them must be sent to each of

the following judges and should reach them not later than
October 21 . . .

In an essay for *The New York Times Book Review* in June 1971, the
literary critic and editor Walter Clemons outlined four rules that gov-
erned the awarding of the Pulitzer Prize for fiction: "Rule One, mid-
dlebrows . . . get it early in their careers"—he cites Louis Bromfield,
Ferber, Herman Wouk, James Michener, and Allen Drury. "Rule Two,
better writers get it late, if at all, and preferably after their best work
is behind them"—and he cites William Faulkner and Willa Cather.
Clemons's Rule Three dictated that moral uplift helps, and Rule Four,
that imitating your betters helps even more.

Wouk won the 1952 Pulitzer for *The Caine Mutiny*. *Giant* was not
even in contention.

It was as if she was trying to divert the maelstrom going on in Texas
by delving into her business affairs, as in a November 7 letter to Ken
McCormick:

> As you said in your postscript, dear Ken, your letter came this
> morning after we had talked on the telephone yesterday, I
> grumpily and you patiently and with the goodness and warm
> friendliness that always has been so sustaining to me.
>
> I am relieved to hear that the revised clauses in our con-
> tract have been agreeable to you as well as to the Ernst office
> representing me. As you know, a lump sum in 1953, includ-
> ing Doubleday royalties, Book-of-the-Month Club, *Reader's
> Digest*, English and other foreign publications, and a quite-
> possible motion-picture sale, would have left me with $17.62 [I
> would wager this was Ferber being facetious] out of the many
> many thousands. You know that the work itself was spread over
> a period of years. If legally, as we have arranged, the returns
> from this work can be spread over an equal number of years it
> will make life much easier for me than it otherwise would have
> been.

The next week she received a fan letter that she added to her collection of loopy ones, vicious ones, ecstatic ones, and the occasional highly
intelligent ones. This was one of the latter:

Dear Miss Ferber,

It occurred to me that you might be interested in a few
words from one who is not a litterateur or reformer but just a
desultory reader of books.

I have just finished the reading of *Giant*. Previously, of
your books, I have read *Show Boat, Cimarron*, and *A Peculiar
Treasure*. Believe me I have found all of the latter interesting
and entertaining but *Giant* is clearly something more. It is,
in truth, a devastating assault upon certain obnoxious human
characteristics falling within the generic term skullduggery—
braggadocio, smugness, provincialism, race bigotry, crass
materialism.

Recently I came across a news item in which it was said
that *Giant* had aroused a storm of indignation in Texas. Well,
this may be all to the good, for the louder the outcry the more
your book will be read, not only in Texas but elsewhere also.
The things of which you wrote are by no means confined to
Texas.

Giant bears a stamp of authenticity that is unmistakable.
You can rest assured that it will not be soon forgotten.

But then, a day later, a very dissatisfied Ferber wrote this clenched
letter to Ken McCormick:

Dear Ken:—

Since the first week of the publication of *Giant* I have seen
no advertising or publicity on this book [four months had
gone by since the first run in September 1952], other than
an advertisement galley sheet which you sent me and which
carried a penciled notation naming the *Dallas News* and the
Dallas Times Herald for October 26.

I find this situation unprecedented in my experience and
deeply distressing.

There must be, in the Doubleday offices, a good reason
for this state of affairs, and I should like to know what it
is. I should like to set a date on which I could talk briefly

and listen, too (I hope) to Mr. Douglas Black [president of Doubleday from 1946 to 1963], and to your advertising manager, and to you.

I have Tuesday, Wednesday and Thursday clear, morning and afternoon.

Yours,
Edna

Bygones must have been left in the meeting. All was forgiven in this letter written shortly afterward:

Though this is typed (for legibility) Ken dear, it's hand-written in spirit. Nothing that came to me at this Christmas time gave me the surge of pure pleasure I felt as I looked at the copy of *Giant* you sent me. So beautifully bound, so handsome and sleek with its monogram and its gold-edged leaves and its delicate tooling. I love to hold it, the feel of it is so delightful and just right.

My thanks to you, my dear. And did Gaston Pilon make it? An artist, if ever there was one in bookbinding in our day. If he fashioned it I'd like to write him.

My love and best wishes go to you for the New Year. You who did so much to make my year of 1952 happier in many ways.

Her year would have been happier had she received her usual movie interest prior to the novel's official publication. She regretted a strategy that had been put in place early on when excitement about the "impending birth" was escalating. Ferber's team of advisers, Morris Ernst, Harriet Pilpel, and Ken McCormick, had decided to plant an aura of exclusivity around the property. An announcement had been placed in Hollywood's *Daily Variety* on May 20, 1952, saying that Ferber would not permit an advance peek before the official publication. This plan backfired. Because word of mouth spread about the outrage from Texas critics, and Texans in general, Ferber was not being heavily pursued for a book-to-film marriage. The few offers that did come were turned away as unacceptable. The producer/director King Vidor wanted an option and then would shop for a studio production deal. There was also interest from RKO, which had been successful with Ferber and Kaufman's *Stage Door*, but without a signed director to steer the project.

Ferber was always occupied with those who wanted or admired her books. Everything came across her desk; nothing was unattended to. There were the Spanish and Portuguese rights to be negotiated, which would provide an enormous readership. There were the Norwegian rights, which in mid-December she told Harriet she felt strongly about:

> I feel as you do about the Norwegian rights in *Giant*. This country has been through hell and back. I am not inclined to press them for high prices. The same would be, in my opinion, true of that courageous little Finland. And I would very much like to accept an Italian offer, and there too I don't think we can expect anything very terrific in the way of advance money. However, it would be nice to get as much as possible. There are, as you know, fewer and fewer countries available for translated rights.

Ferber was always a champion of the underdog, but many Texans had attempted to make *her* the underdog—and had succeeded for a while. Each side was calling the other racist. The general tenor was that Ferber had painted Texans in a harsh light—as racists, as nouveau-riche braggarts and arrivistes who were treated poorly—especially the millionaires and even a few billionaires! This imbroglio seemed to put the kibosh on her movie chances. The major studios were wary of supporting a property that came with advance backlash. And, of course, this bothered Ferber no matter how well the book was doing, which was gangbusters.

It wasn't enough. She was steeping in what she had created, as if an obsession was beginning. Offers that came in were found unacceptable. Columbia Pictures was interested in an option, but only an outright sale would do. That was that. An agency approached, offering to show the book to a studio, and was turned away abruptly.

At various portions of Ferber's career, she had been handled for film by two outstanding agents: Leland Hayward and Irving "Swifty" Lazar.

Both did very well for her. In fact, Hayward had orchestrated a system by which she would "lease" her work instead of optioning or selling it. A rental would be put in place for a finite amount of time, with options to renew. For *Giant*, however, Ferber was flying free—except for her advisory team. This was distressing her, causing her neuralgia to flare up and the left side of her face to begin hurting, a condition my family called "the Face." No one was to telephone Ferber when she had the Face.

———

In early December a lawsuit jutted its Hydra head toward Doubleday & Co. A Texan wrote a series of threatening letters to Ferber and her publisher. These she did not answer, but her legal team did.

> . . . We are sorry to note that you resent Miss Ferber's *Giant* to the extent of becoming more personal in your comments on her motives than perhaps you intended.
> First of all: *Giant* is fiction. The book bears Miss Ferber's statement that all characters in it are purely fictitious. Notwithstanding this statement, some Texan reviewers claim that the characters are unmistakably true to life. . . .
> An official disclaimer is hard to refute.

———

The Year of the Blaze ended with a man whose opinion she valued probably above all:

> It's a hell of a good book, Edna, as witness my reading it in this short (for me) time. I predict that the Messrs. Wouk and Costain will be gnashing their teeth in envy . . . I found it utterly absorbing and a great job all around. I didn't even think it rapped Texas as much as all that—like Ethel [Barrymore] and *Royal Family*, they'll gradually come around to putting a statue

of you right next to Sam Houston . . . From now on all you have to do is take care of the store.

Love, George (as in Kaufman)

A few days before 1953 had rung in, another George, as in Stevens, came calling.

PART TWO

More Was More

There was breathing room, but not too much. Ferber did not have a project lined up following her work on *Giant*. She conveys that suddenly limp state that every professional writer is inclined to have experienced:

> Following months or years of concentrated work in a single writing project the writer, task completed, is left dangling in a vacuum. The paradoxical mad orderly routine of the compulsive worker is broken. It is no longer necessary to awaken and immediately to say to oneself: "Up, up, up!" And a little later, again to oneself, "No, don't read anything but the headlines at breakfast . . . You know what happens when you get started on the *Times* . . . the front page and Bergdorf's ads and the theatre and the obits and the next thing you're plowing through the weather and the shipping news just to keep from working . . . All right, take a little walk, but ten minutes flat . . ." Then, to the understanding and infinitely patient housekeeper, Miss Molly Hennessy, "Um—dinner?—well—lamb chops, I think, and carrots and string beans and a fruit Jell-O . . . Yes, I know, it's baby food, but it's a mass of proteins and that's what I need to get work done."

This mental and emotional Simon Legree flogs the writer on mercilessly. Yet then the book or the play is finished and the shackles fall from the slave and he stands free he hugs his chains through force of habit or through fear of striding down the open road without the terrible voice of conscience and the snakewhip of ambition to urge him on.

Hollywood director George Stevens was at loose ends following his last picture—still unreleased. It was called *Shane*. Not that he was looking for another one-word title. He wasn't remotely sure of the last one. The advance scuttlebutt was "trouble," as in uncommercial.

A perfect storm occurred when the morally and socially conscious Stevens understood the big picture figuratively and literally. He had enlisted with the necessary American optimism to fight the Germans during World War II and had returned with a new layer of gravity. "I don't think I was ever too hilarious again," he said. Although most of his films had shadows, his sensibilities had darkened, but certainly not soured. According to his fellow filmmaking friends William Wyler and Fred Zinnemann, he was quieter, more reflective, and not one for war stories. "He wouldn't talk anymore," director Frank Capra said of his colleague.

Stevens was interested in a bigger American image than valor, glory, loss, and resurrection. He was interested in what was happening to America after the war because of that war, and beyond. He was looking for something like *Giant*, and there it was, film rights free and clear.

Stevens was interested in the kind of rebellion that was Ferber's trademark. He saw in her story an extension of some of the themes of *Shane*. His altered perspective believed in social change through big-screen dramatic storytelling. Stevens was intrigued by the fact that she had pissed off the entitled Texan gentry, making her a gen-u-ine pariah.

My mother told me that Ferber liked Stevens's looks: rangy, verging on beefy, with a clear, keen, fair-deal look in his eyes. As shrewd a businesswoman as Ferber was, she was open, verging on fallible when it came to things she didn't know. She certainly knew that her book had outraged an entire huge state. What she didn't understand was why Hollywood studios, full of courageous pioneers, had turned away. And then, providentially, all it took was one—the right one.

What is fascinating is how Ferber breezed through the next four years as if she had swallowed a time capsule. Prior to investigating the movie of *Giant*, I had read her account, layered between the accounts of many others. She recalls an amusing story:

> I had been conferring with the writer, Ivan Moffat, and the director George Stevens. We had paused for lunch and were seated at a table in the patio restaurant of the hotel at which I was staying [the Bel-Air in Los Angeles]. I was paged for a message. My name was called at the pool, in the restaurant, the patio; now the message was delivered to me. We resumed our conversation whose subject was, of course, the picture script.
>
> At this moment Henry Ginsberg, co-producer of the picture, rushed up to the table, his bathrobe billowing as he sped. He had been sunning himself at the swimming pool. The paging of my name came through the loud-speaker. At that a man just next to him who had been lying face down, at the side of the pool, uncoiled like a python.
>
> "What's that!" he shouted. "Who's that he said?"
>
> Affably Henry Ginsberg repeated the name to the stranger. This one now rose. It was an impressive footage. "I'll kill her!" he said. "Where is she? I'll kill her!"
>
> He was a Texan.
>
> Henry sped to announce my impending demise. We three at the table rose. Nothing was said. Ivan Moffat, tall slim wiry Englishman; George Stevens, big brown brawny Westerner; Henry Ginsberg, medium, fiftyish; and I, five feet in height and enchanted at the prospect of meeting my prospective murderer.
>
> At the poolside he was shrugging into a bathrobe and glaring about him. His stance, his expression, the slow movement of the head from side to side, reminded me of an angry and bewildered bull I had once seen in the arena at San Sebastian. We four advanced to him, the three men a solid wall just behind me. I held out my hand. I spoke my name.
>
> "I hear you intend to kill me."
>
> Before our eyes the bull melted and was reduced to the size of a bashful and rather engaging calf. "Well, say, you hadn't ought to have gone and written a book like that about Texas. We're real nice folks down there."

And so they are—with reservations. And so are we all—with reservations. Something, some little screw or bolt that holds the huge contraption together, seems to have been jarred loose. It could be the soul, or perhaps what is called the spirit, of a country. The contraption is lacking a vital part somewhere in its makeup.

We had dinner together, the big Texan and three or four of my friends, and I. In his late forties, a family man, the pictures of his wife and the kids in his wallet; friendly, colloquial; the IQ of an average high school boy.

Stevens's pictures were meticulous and therefore expensive. According to a memo from Eric Stacey—an assistant director and production manager—to Jack L. Warner regarding the *Shane* budget, Stevens "auditioned" fifteen hundred horses before selecting the right one for leading man Alan Ladd. So, when Stevens wanted to go rogue for *Giant*, it would be an invigorating challenge.

In February of 1952, leaving Paramount, he formed George Stevens Productions, which planned to produce, sell, and distribute. He called upon former colleague Henry Ginsberg, who had known Ferber previously and who was also a career diplomat—an expert at putting a potentially ornery deal together. Stevens and Ginsberg had been estranged after working together on *A Place in the Sun*, where Ginsberg was his producer. However, their bygones faded with the promise of something entirely new.

The notion was that their company would be an independent, forming a triumvirate of Ferber, Ginsberg, and Stevens as equal partners—without compensation, and with a partnership that would last for ten years. They would put the capital raised into the production, and then would each share a third of the profits. In December of 1952 they made Ferber an offer to purchase *Giant*.

George Stevens rescued Ferber from temporary ignominy. She had never been a poor little nobody looking for a life raft, but she found it was tough to have no acceptable movie offers, especially after delivering a sensational book that was being widely sold, read, and discussed nationally and internationally. However, when the Stevens offer came through, the art of the deal initially escaped her.

Although she questioned and knew about every dollar that came in and went out, she was basically simplistic about money. She understood it in numbers that she could lay on a table. Her idea of having a good deal was when somebody would approach her and say, "I want to buy this property and I'll give you $300,000 for it." She would say, "I want $500,000," and would settle for $400,000 and be pleased as punch. The tax ramifications were beyond her. That she would take $40,000 over a period of ten years was anathema to her. What if the company failed and went bankrupt? What if they lost the contract and there were somehow no copies of it? Then where would she be?

Her trusty nephew-in-law, my father, Henry Goldsmith, remembered, not too fondly, trying to help advise her on the proposed *Giant* movie deal:

> A final part of the *Giant* deal was the selling of her third to Warner Brothers, [who had agreed to distribute if the deal were to go through]. She eventually agreed to it, but only under constant pressure from Morris Ernst, myself and Harriet Pilpel. We three would always be in touch with each other and play "you be the good guy, I'll be the bad guy" kind of game and say, "you try and press this so that when she turns I can take the other side." She took a lot of manipulating. When we said to her—whatever the thing was with Warner's—let's take that now over ten years or so—she thought that Warner's might not last ten years. And what would happen if Warner's went bankrupt in the meantime? Then she would be standing there with egg on her face and nothing in her hand. She would say, "Let's take the money now," and we would say, "Well, if you take it now you give it all to Uncle Sam." *Giant* was the single most lucrative deal that she ever made, and to her dying day she felt it was disastrous and that she'd lost money. In simple terms, she was a hoarder of cash.

Every allegation has another side. Perhaps Ferber's nickel-and-dime approach had validity. Prior to my father's membership in the family, Ferber's role had always been as a breadwinning Mother Courage. Her diaries constantly chronicle how she felt about shouldering her burden—simultaneously valiant and oppressed. For example; "Worked. To Ernst office at 3—to 5. Arranged additional sum of $1,413 each to

Fan-Jan-Mina. Fan's doctor bills, house (country) etc. I hope that in one more year of work I may be out from under this avalanche."

She rarely asked for financial advice, and even more rarely admitted to being muddled. She practiced life in general, as well as her financial life, guided by a stout, innate sense of what was best for her, which benefited others quite nicely as well. In application to her theory, my father used to quote a lyric from the musical *Li'l Abner*—"What's good for General Bullmoose is good for the USA." That there could have been more money, that she could have been shrewder, was hypothetical. Her estate still provides to this day, although the returns have dwindled because much is out of copyright. However, two movie versions of *Show Boat* still float; people still can have *Dinner at Eight*—and if they hurry, *The Royal Family*. Many student actors still sail through the *Stage Door*: the large cast is nearly all female, accommodating many a college production's needs. And *Giant* still looms large.

Although she was frequently quoted, Ferber hardly ever quoted anyone other than Dickens. However, she did have two selections— one from Kipling and one from Maeterlinck—whose themes she used in her daily life. This one comes from Kipling's "The Female of the Species":

The formation of Giant Productions: Jack Warner (left),
Edna, George Stevens, and Henry Ginsberg, 1953

But the Woman that God gave him, every fiber of her frame
Proves her launched for one sole issue, armed and engineered for the
*   same;*
And to serve that single issue, lest the generations fail,
The female of the species must be deadlier than the male.

And this one from Maeterlinck's *The Life of the Bee*:

. . . Aware, it would seem, that nature's laws are somewhat wild and extravagant in all that pertains to love, it tolerates, during summer days of abundance, the embarrassing presence in the hive of three or four hundred males, from whose ranks the queen about to be born shall select her lover; three or four hundred foolish, clumsy, useless, noisy creatures, who are pretentious, gluttonous, dirty, coarse, totally and scandalously idle, insatiable, and enormous.

George Stevens had been cautious about entering into the fray in the first place, as he suggests in this in-house Warner Bros. memo from late 1952:

. . . It is hard to say whether or not it will turn out worthwhile—it is well-written and certainly dynamic—but what the theme develops into?? It is based on Texas, Texans and their great wealth and superiority(?) and sophistication—First installment [in *Ladies' Home Journal*] brings into story names and some background of the people who will probably turn into central characters—from what I could gather it will be based on character sketches of these "giants"—their intrigues— great wealth—race hatred for the Mexicans—and one central figure called Jett Rink—who is more fabulously wealthy than all others—story starts with these people flying in their big 4-motored private planes to the opening of an airport which Jett Rink has given to Hermosa, Texas and the lavish reception and banquet to open the airport and introduce Rink to the reader.

At the end of 1952, the go-ahead was coming into focus for, as this studio memo calls it, *The Giant*:

Per telephone conversation today with Henry Ginsberg . . . the story dept. is talking to Morris Ernst, who is Edna Ferber's attorney, and Ginsberg and George Stevens are waiting to hear from Ernst now on an offer made to them for the novel *The Giant*. Ginsberg, at George Stevens['s] suggestion, talked with David Brown, formerly of *Cosmopolitan*, now 20th Century's Story Editor, to discover if the major studios had any reason for stepping away from this property. Brown, himself, thinks it is a good property, and believes that the studios have no reason not to deal with it other than the fact that it looks to be a bit of a commercial problem.

The movie sale progressed apace once Ferber realized that her best chance looked to be her last chance. In May of 1953, Giant Productions was formed, and in November the new company acquired film and allied rights for a decade. Each partner in the new triumvirate—Stevens, Ginsberg, and now Ferber—would receive a third of the profits. The three vagabonds still needed a studio to back them, and after the titan Darryl F. Zanuck of 20th Century–Fox sidestepped the project, Jack Warner stepped up, making a deal in which the director, producer, and author worked as "substantial profit participants." The deal was finalized in December of 1953, allowing that Warner Bros. would finance the production as well as handle the distribution and advertising. The three partners would go without a salary but would share 50 percent of the profits. This sounds like a hats-in-the-air deal, but there was a catch built in. This 50 percent would be collected only after the studio recouped its costs and then took 30 percent of the international box-office gross as a distribution fee. The terms got rougher: Stevens was to complete a finished script thirty days prior to when the initial filming began, and to wrap four months after the conclusion of principal photography. And there was a little, vital addition to the agreement stating that "Ferber will write additional material if requested by other two partners and will turn over rights to partnership."

Was Ferber thrilled with a deal that included one of the finest directors in film? There is no proof of whether she was or wasn't. Seeing that my family was theater-and-book-oriented, and that television was a relatively new member of the household, movies were even more magical to me than the beautiful Madame Alexander dolls in the famed wonderland of the FAO Schwarz toy store on Fifth Avenue. Movies were as spellbinding as life got.

Prematurely, the names that were being floated above the title for the role of Leslie included Audrey Hepburn, Grace Kelly, Ava Gardner, Gloria Grahame, Marlene Dietrich (imagine!), Katharine Hepburn, Joan Fontaine, Irene Dunne, Olivia de Havilland, Deborah Kerr, Maureen O'Hara, June Allyson, Anne Baxter, Ann Blyth, Jane Greer, Susan Hayward, Rita Hayworth, Jennifer Jones, Vivien Leigh, Dorothy McGuire, Patricia Neal, Eleanor Parker, Gene Tierney, Janet Leigh, Donna Reed, Jean Simmons, Joanne Woodward, Jane Wyman, Betsy Drake, Virginia Mayo, and Elizabeth Taylor. For the role of Bick there were Clark Gable, Gary Cooper, William Holden, John Wayne, Forrest Tucker, Sterling Hayden, Errol Flynn, Henry Fonda, Charlton Heston, Tyrone Power, Robert Taylor, Jeff Chandler, Victor Mature, Gordon MacRae, Charles Bronson, James Stewart, and Kirk Douglas. For the role of Jett there were Robert Mitchum, Burt Lancaster, and Alan Ladd; for the elder Luz, Judith Anderson, Bette Davis, Ann Harding, Angela Lansbury, Agnes Moorehead, Claire Trevor, and Jo Van Fleet. For the role of Jordy Benedict, there were Robert Francis, John Kerr, Jack Lemmon, Kevin McCarthy, and Leonard Nimoy; and for the role of his wife, Juana, Pier Angeli and Rita Moreno.

Early on, with the contractual ink barely dry, Ferber had long talks with her highly intelligent partner and director. She knew Stevens understood her novel but would probably make a somewhat different movie of it. The protective language of "based upon" allowed for a hopefully smooth evolution. Stevens had assured her that he did not concur with the rantings of those who felt that ultimately Ferber's men were supporting players in a world that starred women—a world where men were contractors and women were builders. Stevens knew that her work bucked against the traditional principles of the American setup, and that although she wrote about racial issues, her critics always attacked her gender and her strong heroines. Stevens knew that these would be the issues when adapting her novel.

He hired two practiced screenwriters—that they were male was not the point. He had worked with both Ivan Moffat and Fred Guiol previously, and was fond of both. Moffat had the more theatrical history, being the grandson of British actor-manager Sir Herbert Beerbohm Tree. A bit of a gadfly, Moffat took stock during World War II and began to make films to promote the war effort. While filming activities of the US Army, he met Stevens and followed him to Hollywood at war's end, assisting him in making movies for Paramount, such as *I Remember Mama, Shane,* and *A Place in the Sun,* where he had a brief affair with the movie's star Elizabeth Taylor, whom he would meet again during *Giant.*

Fred Guiol was an American film director and screenwriter who cut his teeth working at the Hal Roach Studios, directing and writing many of Laurel and Hardy's silent shorts, with antic titles like *Duck Soup, With Love and Hisses, Slipping Wives,* and *Love 'Em and Weep.* A native Californian, he had met cameraman-cum-director George Stevens early on in their careers.

Ferber had nothing against either man. Not being a film buff, she had never heard of them but deferred to Stevens. In recollection, Moffat is vaguely dismissive of Ferber, her novel, and her contributions to the movie effort:

> Most of the writing was done at George's house on Riverside Drive. We attended every story conference. He paid more attention [to the script] than any other director I worked with. We [Ivan, Stevens, and Guiol, also a longtime associate] spent a lot of time making tea in the morning to avoid getting down to work. We took our time, started in March 1954 and did not finish until December . . . Edna Ferber was with us some of the time. The basic story is there in her novel, but there was a good deal of trial and error, structural changes, scenes which worked and didn't work.

Moffat skips over some large moments in between. For instance, once the deal was signed, Ferber began preparing her own defense of issues in her novel that could be softened or whittled down. She was a production partner and had not simply sold or leased the rights to her novel and banked the check as she had done with many of her novels. She knew that grumbling at the outcome would be relatively useless as well as sour grapes.

She felt insulated with proof of the novel's tremendous popularity; the sales were consistently booming, keeping the book toward the top of some best-seller lists. For many weeks it placed on the *New York Times's* best-seller list as numbers two, three, and four. According to *Publisher's Weekly, Giant* was one of the top six novels of 1952.

While doing her research, she had read a book by Carey McWilliams that was a study of Mexican Americans called *North from Mexico: The Spanish-Speaking People of the United States.* It portrayed a bilingual world in a state mainly dominated by American white men speaking English.

Texas existed in a robber-baron past, where materialism crushed liberalism, leaving little margin for civil liberty. Ferber explored this theme of how the American past prevailed in certain states in her novels *Cimarron, Come and Get It, Great Son,* and *Ice Palace.* And she would explore it with George Stevens on the film of *Giant.*

It could be said that part of her—along with her novel's—appeal to Stevens was that the former queen of popular novelists had become, in her own words, "An Angry Old Woman." He certainly knew what he had bought into and understood that in her novel three generations of a cattle-raising and oil-rich family were seen through the perspective of a highly educated and cultured easterner: Leslie Lynnton Benedict. She was Ferber's Greek chorus.

Ferber's suspicions about infidelity to her source material were not entirely founded, as Stevens would "split the bill." He would not totally re-form Ferber's Bick Benedict and present him as "a claw-footed Victorian bathtub in a Levittown home," which is historian Jane Hendler's delightful description. Nor would he completely tilt his lens to reveal all of Leslie's perspective as she condones the megalomaniacal traditions of man, beef, land, and oil.

Stevens was shown a small treatise that Ferber had sent to Ken McCormick before publication and in case the novel was gravely misinterpreted: "Leslie does not become a listening and respectful wife. But her fine mind and her love don't make a dent on Bick or anyone else in that Texas crowd, really. I never intended they should. That's the point of the book. If that isn't clear, the book is a failure. Do you really think that I imagine a Leslie could make a dent on the hard hide of Texas! She wins—or will in the end win—through her son and daughter."

Ferber wanted not only to imprint her story's arc on Stevens, but to have him understand her premonition that her yin would never go with Texas's yang. Both Ferber and Leslie had married Texas first and then came the second thought "What have I done?" The following, straight from the novel, is this sensation dawning upon Leslie, the new bride being introduced to her new home after she and Bick have been met at the train station by a Mexican boy:

"How flat it is! And big. And the horizon is—well, there just isn't any it's so far away. I thought there would be lots of cows. I don't see any."

"Cows!" he said in a tone of utter rage.

She was, after all, still one of the tart-tongued Lynnton girls.

"I don't see why you're so put out because that boy came instead of someone else. Or the family. After all, it's so far from the railroad."

"Far!" In that same furious tone. "It's only ninety miles."

She glanced at the speedometer. It pointed to eighty-five. Well, no wonder! At this rate they'd be home in an hour or so. Home. For an engulfing moment she had a monstrous feeling of being alone with a strange man in an unknown world—a world of dust and desert and heat and glare and some indefinable thing she never before had experienced. Maybe all brides felt like this, she thought. Suddenly wanting to go home to their mother and father and their own bed.

He was speaking in a lower tone now, but a controlled anger vibrated beneath it. "We don't behave like that down here."

"Behave?"

"Making a fuss over that Mexican boy. We don't do that here in Texas."

"But this is the United States, isn't it? You were being mean to him. What did he do?"

The speedometer leaped to ninety. "We have our own way of doing things. You're a Texan now. Please remember that."

"But I'm not anyone I wasn't. I'm myself. What's geography got to do with it!"

"Texas isn't geography. It's history. It's a world in itself."

She said something far in advance of her day. "There is no world in itself."

"You've read too many damn books."

She began to laugh suddenly—a laugh of surprise and discovery. "We're quarreling, Jordan. We're having our first quarrel. Well, it's nice to get it over with before we reach—home."

To her horror then he brought his head down to his hands on the wheel, a gesture of utter contrition and one that might have killed them both. At her cry of alarm he straightened. His right hand reached over to cover her hands clasped so tightly in her fright. "My darling," he said. "My darling girl." Then, strangely, "We mustn't quarrel. We've got to stand together."

Against the brassy sky there rose like a mirage a vast edifice all towers and domes and balconies and porticoes and iron fretwork. In size and general architecture it somewhat resembled the palace known as the Alhambra, with a dash of the Missouri Pacific Railroad station which they had just left behind them.

"What's that! Is it—are we near the ranch, Jordan?"

"We've been on it the last eighty miles, practically ever since we got outside Viento. That's Reata. That's home."

"But you said it was a ranch! You said Reata was a ranch!"

Ferber's and Leslie's ideologies and behavior toward Texas and Texans serve as the novel's structure. The scene where Leslie is brought to a barbeque and faints after being served a huge portion of brains direct from the cow's head is an enlarged version of what happened to Ferber when she was a guest in a Texan's empire.

Stevens was a specialist on the perspective of the outsider in his films as ostensibly diverse as *I Remember Mama*, *A Place in the Sun*, and *Shane*. He supported Ferber's stance on racism, but she questioned to what degree. In 1953, after the contracts had been signed and discussions had begun against a Warner Bros. time clock, Stevens closely followed Ferber's extracurricular "Angry Woman" activities, applauding from the sidelines.

In the July 11, 1953, issue of *The New Yorker*, a "Talk of the Town" piece by Brendan Gill, titled "What Housewives Know," covered an incident that gained notoriety:

> . . . Edna Ferber . . . deplored New York's dirtiness when she was interviewed aboard a ship on her return from Europe, last April. She described N.Y. as the most "disgustingly filthy" city in the world. She said she was merely citing a fact. European cities are very clean she claimed, while in N.Y. you must pick your way thru refuse and garbage. Soon after Miss Ferber's statement an organization called the Greater N.Y. Citizen Clean-Up, Paint-Up, Fix-Up Committee sponsored a Clean-Up Week in May. This is silly Miss Ferber says as cleaning should be done all the time, not just in fits and starts. She rejected an award which the Mayor offered her from the Committee for her help in promoting interest in the clean up campaign. She loves N.Y. and wants to go on living here but she is fearful of the impure air.

Stevens also shared Ferber's politics. As a lifelong Democrat, she had worked for a number of presidential candidates by "speechifying," as she called it. She would write rather long, impassioned essays that occasionally she was asked to present in person, but mostly were published in what were considered somewhat left-leaning periodicals.

Prior to her association with Stevens, she had stumped for Adlai Stevenson for president in his run of 1952 against Dwight D. Eisenhower and she would come out for him again in 1956. In 1952, Eisenhower's running mate was the relatively young Richard Nixon, a lawyer for J. Edgar Hoover, head of the FBI and right-wing zealot. Ferber was on the warpath to prevent what she saw as a voter's terrible mistake to have him anywhere near the White House.

Richard Nixon's lengthy service as vice president impacted her feelings about George Stevens's winning *Giant*. Ferber was more adamant than ever that the democracies of her novel, as upheld by Leslie Benedict, remain intact. There was something about Stevens—a basic decency—that had urged her to join with him, allowing him to essentially take over her property. That's what directors did, and she'd had plenty of them. Not one to play favorites once she had relinquished a novel to be adapted, she did, somewhat grudgingly, appreciate certain directors' work. She gave the nod to Wesley Ruggles for his 1931 production of *Cimarron*, William A. Wellman for his 1932 production of *So Big*, and James Whale for the 1936 *Show Boat*. This time, however, she had made a nervy and personal deal and was determined to stand her five-foot-one ground.

Stevens, in keeping with his initial intentions, worked in close conjunction with his writers, making notes on his copy of *Giant*, highlighting the scenes of racial prejudice against Mexican Americans, just as Ferber had in her novel. He even made a pledge:

> Actually, our picture is not just a story of Texas. It is a saga of America. We are presenting a tale in which the leading characters are depicted honestly with their weaknesses as well as their virtues. Though the film chronicles the rise of a great Texas cattle and oil dynasty and its relationship to the rest of the community, it could be the story of any section of the United States, confronted with parallel problems. It is Americana.

Ferber did not agree with these parallels. She had intended her book to be idiosyncratic in the extreme. Texas was the last dinosaur, happily encased in its own vastness in an increasingly modernized country. The whole point of "her" *Giant* was that Texas was determined to remain where it always had been in the evolutionary chain, except for her heroine, Leslie, who determines her future there in spite of it. At the end of chapter 1 in the novel, Ferber writes that Reata is a kingdom. Her Leslie would be a protagonist and a heroine, but never a queen reigning over this kingdom, like Luz. She would work within it but also outside of it.

Prior to actually sitting down to draft anything, Stevens asked Ivan Moffat for profiles of the three main characters, Bick, Leslie, and Jett Rink. Moffat had been somewhat stuck from the get-go in transferring the book's logic onto the film. In fact, he challenged the source material: "Reading the novel, it's clear that Edna Ferber found it hard to write convincing dialogue to explain why the Benedicts decide to go to Jett Rink's party." So, by accommodating Stevens's request, Moffat felt that his profiles shed more light on the characters than Ferber did in her own novel. The profiles that he put forth were in-depth ones and proved immensely helpful to the eventual three leading actors: Rock Hudson, Elizabeth Taylor, and James Dean. They tell Ferber's story and show Stevens's vision:

BICK BENEDICT: A PROFILE

Bick before his marriage was a lonely man with only his sister to keep him company on the ranch. It was like the stale end of a marriage that is nothing more than a set of patterns for avoiding inactivity in the presence of the other: early morning coffee together, then Bick riding off to some distant part of his domain.

"Luz runs the house," Bick was to explain later, and ruefully add: "Some say she runs the ranch." And he felt it was true. It was a prison in which he was its captive, she its jailer.

His escape, when it came, was accomplished by marriage. He cannot have been under any illusions as to how Luz was going to feel about Leslie, or how Leslie would react to Luz's wifelike shrewishness. When Luz got killed (more than he had bargained for), Bick's sense of guilt came welling forth. Although he had spoken of the freedom which Leslie would enjoy in Texas, he was not really prepared for the fact that she would avail herself of it. She took him at his word, and he discovered immediately that it was not Luz alone whose ideas were in conflict with his wife's.

True to human nature, Bick desired Leslie's originality, but wished it to conform to his own conception of how a wife should behave. Perhaps deep down Bick had long known that some of his views were wrong, and that Leslie was right in her point of view, but he never admitted it. He indulged to his own considerable satisfaction in unfavorable comments about the appearance of his half-Mexican grandson, and relished doing so all the more because he had a sneaking feeling that in actual truth the mixture of his blood would be a pretty good one.

But Leslie's views, attitudes and behavior never affected the tremendous admiration and feeling which Bick had for her. He relished her wisdom while pretending to disdain it. He relished also the posture of ignorance which he could adopt for her. Right at the end, when Leslie was at last praising him as her hero, and concluding that the family they had made was a pretty good one, he pretended not to understand. "Leslie," he said, "I'll never understand a word you're saying." But he understood well enough. And she knew it. And he knew that she knew it, and he knew that it pleased her.

LESLIE BENEDICT: A PROFILE

When Bick Benedict first met her, there was in Leslie the elements of romantic rebellion against the mannered, circumscribed and often petty qualities of the Virginia social world. She liked to dance at Washington parties, to ride and to hunt, to argue about affairs with the men and women around Government, but this was not what she sought from life or her own married future.

She had been led into a romanticization of the West, promising a kind of freedom and richness; and Bick, sensing it, had played upon this note in her. She was soon to discover that Texas was as different from what she had imagined as her own brand of nonconformity was different from what Bick had imagined. Each of them had been guilty of self-deception, and each was to be surprised and shocked at the consequences. At one time it almost cost them their marriage, and what saved it was not realistic appraisal, but love. Knowing this full well, Leslie even told Bick at the end of their separation: "I haven't changed. I'm just the same now as when I went away."

One of Leslie's problems was not that conditions in Texas were worse than in other places, but that Texans were exceptional in their unwillingness to admit that their state stood short of perfection. They were self-conscious and touchy about anyone, especially an outsider, saying derogatory things about them. This made Leslie's rather hopeless task all the more so, although she achieved much of her goal in a superficial but pleasing way . . . But it was the same Bick Benedict, it was the same Texas, the poor remained poor and the rich remained rich.

It was in the aesthetic rather than in any other sense that Leslie's world and the world of Texas drew closer together. Her taste and flair was [*sic*] eagerly grasped and imitated by her friends, and the Reata house became a standard by which others were judged. Texan self-consciousness acted as a spur to this process, and unlike her social opinion, the seeds she cast in this regard fell upon fertile land.

And slowly, Leslie, Bick and Texas matured and aged. The young girl fill [*sic*] of vitality and zeal became a woman responsive to her surroundings, and in a way responsible for them as well. Feeling at home, rather than in a strange country, Leslie was able to enjoy and cherish the loyalty and strength of Bick; and today, when the hot wind blows from the West, or the fresh, cool wind blows from the Gulf, or the north wind sings cold and dry in the telegraph wires, they remind her that she is where she wants to be, where she has chosen to be, and where she will remain.

JETT RINK: A PROFILE

Jett had many reasons, as a young man, to be angry. First, he was a drifter in a world where he found himself one of the few underprivileged and yet non-Mexican employees of a young man of vast wealth. He had drifted to the ranch, and now he was hung up there for some reason he did not fully know. Perhaps it was instinct, perhaps he knew his future was there.

He was angry because he was smart enough to appraise the world in terms of its opportunities, and his limited access to them, smart enough to perceive that the world did indeed owe him a living, and that he could take from it, if he was lucky, ten thousand times as much. Later, he was to be angry because Leslie, who owed him nothing, was kinder, gentler and more understanding toward him than the others, but still remained a Benedict—a figure to dominate and confuse the clear horizon of his bitterness.

Jett did not dislike the Mexicans. He knew, more than most, they were getting a raw deal. But his only interest in life was to get into the same position as those who were giving the

Mexicans that same raw deal. The world was a jungle, and if he sometimes felt that its laws were outrageous, he proposed to avail himself of them, not change them.

When Jett started telling Leslie about the conditions of the Mexicans who worked for her husband, it was an attempt to prick what he supposed was a complacent conscience. Her reaction impressed him, and for the first time he sensed, in a member of the dominant class, a genuine note of compassion. He even felt that, in the well-educated, unprejudiced person of Bick's wife, he had found a kind of recognition of his sense of personal destiny.

On top of it all, Leslie was the absolute symbol, morally and physically, of the unattainable feminine goal. Unattainable, that is, in his present state. For the future, he was ready to bide his time. And bide it he did.

As a product of Texas, Jett is an example of the phenomenon of someone who believes in a legend and is in the rare position of making it seem to come true. But in his heart of hearts, he knew that his struggle had little or nothing to do with the self-congratulatory effusions of those Texans who spoke of their state as being the very cradle of opportunity and benevolence. It must have been hard for Jett to look with any great pride upon the fact that only accident had made him a native of Texas. And a secret grudge grew up inside of him. All that his early life had brought him in the way of loneliness, all that his relationship to Bick had occasioned in the way of envy and humiliation, he now blamed on Texas. All that he had earned in the way of money and power, he felt he had earned despite Texas, and he felt a vindictiveness toward his Mother State which smoldered inside of him and finally erupted with violence.

Of all the people in our story, the only one who did not grow up, or mature, or become reconciled to this earth, was (in purely Texas terms) the most successful one of all: Jett Rink himself.

There were several treatments of the characters and story line. Ferber, sympathetic to the creative process, steered clear of reading or commenting unless requested to do so. She also knew that there was a great deal of checking for libel before anything was scripted. The eagle-eyed research and legal departments of Warner Bros. were on the alert. Carl Milliken, a research reader, sent a memo to Henry Ginsberg at the end of 1954 listing potential troubles: many of Ferber's characters were based on Texans still alive—especially her Benedict family, who supposedly closely resembled the Kleberg clan and their King Ranch, aka Reata. Then there was the cozy resemblance of Jett Rink to the ruthless millionaire rake Glenn McCarthy. (My father thought that no one was really keen on a major lawsuit: the Texans because they were secretly flattered at so much attention, the producers because a lawsuit would hold everything in abeyance in the courts and stop the film cold for an indefinite time, perhaps forever.) Milliken wrote: "Edna Ferber's *Giant* is a specially worrisome property because it has been accepted, to a large extent, in the public's mind as a true document about not only life in Texas but also specifically the lives of the Kleberg family, which owns and operates the King Ranch, and of Glenn McCarthy, the much publicized oil millionaire . . . The individuals with whom we are . . . involved are very wealthy and well able to sustain any lawsuits they embark upon."

Stevens commissioned a full report on all the potential liabilities. He personally assured the owners of the King Ranch that all the characters would be just that, characters. Guarantees from Hollywood royalty such as Stevens seemed to assuage them.

The story treatments, however, began to evolve into a storyline that veered from Ferber's. The novel opens with a traditionally Ferberesque flash-forward. It is the future, and the bulk of the story has already transpired. We meet the older main characters en route to a gala in honor of Jett Rink, formerly a ranch hand, now a dissolute and desolate millionaire. In the treatment, Bick and Leslie are falling in love when Bick visits her family home in Maryland—Virginia in the novel—to buy the champion horse War Winds from her father, Dr. Lynnton. In the novel, the horse was called My Mistake. Ferber neither liked the new name nor understood why Stevens insisted on it. It was a small battle she allowed him to win.

In this treatment, Stevens saw exactly what he wanted for the fade on his opening sequence: "Leslie walks to the fence—War Winds comes galloping to her. Bick comes up and we fade out on B shot. Man, Woman and Horse nuzzling."

According to Stevens, alterations, cuts, and additions led to a collaborative first-draft script. "We had a terribly long script on *Giant*," he later reminisced. "Fred Guiol and I and Ivan Moffat . . . When we finished the script, it was 370 pages . . . I had talked with Edna and I took the script back to New York and had her read it. She was an exceptionally effective novelist and she liked the script very much. She said, 'You know I want to write this book once again. I wrote it twice and I want to write it the third time and fill it out.' She said, 'I think you've done it with the screenplay,' which is a surprise assessment to get from a lady whose novel you're massacring possibly."

Hindsight can be strange and wistful from every angle. Ferber volunteered extensive notes. True, she had at first complimented Stevens on his vision—possibly overtipping her hand at the thrill of this enormous entity that her original text had inspired. Ferber had manners. She had not wanted to offend her new partnership. She had complimented in haste, and now she drew back as the hardened pro she was. Moffat and Guiol, with Stevens's assistance, reduced the script to 240 pages and offered it to Ferber again.

———

History tends to gloss over what happened next, whipping through a portion that must have caused discomfort to everyone involved. Ferber had not approved of the first draft of the screenplay. This required a certain amount of diplomacy and finesse, because she knew that Stevens had been heavily involved in the process. Moffat and Guiol had stepped somewhat to the side to allow considerable room for the heft of Stevens's contribution. Never a person to be daunted by a difficult situation, Ferber confronted it pleasantly but firmly: "Curiously enough—or perhaps not so curiously—it is the LESLIE dialogue scenes that are faulty. The male characters are almost always right, except occasionally in the case of DR. LYNNTON. The LESLIES AND THE DR. LYNNTONS seem to lie outside the ken or the liking of the writers of the script."

Clearly, her nerves were on edge with the draft. She didn't like an early moonlight wooing scene with Leslie and Bick on the Lynntons' veranda in Maryland. She noted her distaste for a Leslie line that read, "It would be too touching," and another one when the couple is newly married and having a fight on the porch at Reata: "Elsewhere," Leslie says, "being gracious is acceptable."

"Pure Bronx" is what Ferber tagged the line. "It is Arthur Kober's Bella Gross. Leslie doesn't talk like that. I took it out once, but there it is, back again. I suggest leaving out the sick-making word 'gracious.'"

In the final scene of the draft when Leslie tells Bick that at last "the Benedict family is a real big success," Ferber had had it. The word "big" seemed the tipping point: no woman of breeding, she felt, would ever use it in this way, in this particular sentence, at the end of this particular story. She wrote to Stevens, upbraiding him and putting him on a certain kind of notice:

> I want only to say this: I know nothing about the making of motion pictures. I know about writing. I know dialogue, characterization, situation. I know how powerful words are to convey the meaning of a situation. The people who wrote this script know how to cut and shape a scene; transpose; visualize effects picture-wise; sense the impact of a scene of character . . . As a writer, I find some of these *Giant* speeches wooden, unvital, and uncharacteristic. A writer of proven talent and experience could not have written them. Also, I am sorry to say, some of them are ungrammatical. I say this not with a desire to offend or to be rude. This picture is a huge business venture. We cannot afford to use dialogue which is inept. I can't bear to read it, much less hear it.

Ferber certainly understood about leverage, knowing when to wield it and when to back off. As an equal partner in this venture, she was not in a scrap; all she had to do was to keep putting in her $33\frac{1}{3}$ percent.

During this key period, there were other events going on in Ferber's life that did not seem peripheral. She was beginning to feel the stirrings of a new book project. It had taken her such a long time to realize *Giant* that she was now a big timekeeper. At sixty-nine years old, she was eager to put on her parka and get herself to Alaska, where the air was chill and clean and the people were warm and accommodating. This was where the dawn of her new novel was rising.

Stage-door suitors were always buzzing around when she had a new best-seller. Luther Davis, a writer of plays and musicals (*Kismet* among others), was eager to convert *Giant* into a musical—an adaptation that would come to pass over a half a century later. He came to Ferber hat in hand, full of flattery and concrete plans—financially and artistically—and she was not uninterested in him, as she conveyed to Henry Ginsberg in a letter of May 4, 1954:

> . . . I had an unexpected letter from Luther Davis. It was about a possible musical based on *Giant* . . . but after reading it the idea came to me that Luther Davis would be an excellent choice as final writer for the picture. He is probably tied up with something else, but certainly he knows the book thoroughly, is enthusiastic about it, knows the characters and their meaning, and is an experienced and adroit writer for the screen, with excellent credits. I needn't tell you that I have never mentioned this idea to Mr. Davis, or to anyone else.

In this same letter, Ferber's muscularity is masked by blithe point making:

> Mitchum any good for Jett? Unknowns are all very well, and really exciting to present, but unless we have at least two Names I should think we'd be in trouble. By this time the people who naturally come to mind seem to be tied up for two or three years.
>
> By the way, I know absolutely nothing about the girl whose name Constance Collier happened to mention last week. She seems to be almost completely a novice and I doubt very much that an inexperienced unknown is the girl for the difficult and psychologically complicated role of Leslie . . . Connie says she's magnetic, attractive, talented. I don't know.
>
> I should think that Warners might begin to get pretty darn restive about their investment, but maybe that's something I wouldn't know, either.
>
> I sometimes wonder if Jett mightn't be effectively cast

against type, for a kind of sympathy. Smallish, compact, quick on his feet—a sort of Gene Kelly with a quick punch. This, by the way, was a suggestion of my niece, Janet Fox Goldsmith. Burt Lancaster Bick?

Ask George (I hope this won't make him hate me) if the two daughters mightn't be condensed into one, after all. Maybe that is a terribly wrong suggestion. But in the present form it seems to me young Les is sort of lost. Could she, as young Luz, be all for the ranch and its future (like her father) but fascinated by Jett's magnetism and power, and eventually drawn to young Dace when she is disillusioned by Jett. That may sound complicated. But in the present form Les seems to me somehow lost.

Ultimately Stevens would not only listen but adhere to many of Ferber's suggestions. But not at that time. Now that Jack Warner was his distributor—and boss of a sort—he was on a clock, propelling him to move forward with decisions.

His 1954 vision of Leslie was Audrey Hepburn. He approached Hepburn first with a synopsis of the latest version of the Ferber-disapproved screenplay, saying that "he hoped it would project the shape and temper of the film which will develop from it." He also sent her Ivan Moffat's profiles of Leslie, Bick, and Jett. She turned the project down rather readily as she was committed to preparing for *Funny Face*.

In the short meantime, Ferber had come to a decision. Because she continued to be displeased with the screenplay efforts, she would offer herself up at the altar. She did this in early June to a rather vacant reaction and so she stated her intentions in print:

> Forgive me, dear Henry and George, for sending you identical letters, one a carbon copy. Time is gnawing at my heels.
>
> You two lads baffle me, but perhaps I am easily baffled. In the year that has gone by since we tied *Giant* into an arrangement which was (and always will be, I hope) satisfactory to all concerned, I have tried to refrain from interfering with something about which I technically know very little, about which you both know practically everything.
>
> But I do know the characters in *Giant*, and I know what

they think, say and do under various circumstances. For this reason I volunteered to spend three or four weeks in Hollywood in the hope of attempting, at least, to be of some use in the matter of dialogue and character development. It may be that I shall not, after all, be able to carry through this hope or intention. We'll see and we'll soon know.

It may be, George, that your conception of a character, a situation, or of appropriate dialogue will differ from mine. I hope I'm flexible enough and reasonable enough to see another's viewpoint. I've had years of collaboration training with George S. Kaufman—and neither of us ever lost a spangle.

I want to work as an unsalaried writer. I'd like to do this little job, if it is done, for the fun of it. I think my main expenses should come out of the kitty—plane, hotel, etc. Don't you? My budget thus far in this picture has been zero on the company's expense or salary account, as you know. We might establish an expense limit so that I can feel free, privately, to go over it without a feeling of guilt. I'm rather a luxury-living person—or perhaps not too concerned with living costs, and the life, through these many years of work and work and work.

I'd like this only:

A reasonably quiet comfortable place in which to work.

A standard size Remington Noiseless typewriter.

A right-height desk or table or stand for the tv.

I'll proly have to have some sort of car and driver but as I'll be working most of the day perhaps we should talk about this when I arrive. I'm willing to cover this expense item myself.

No publicity, please.

Don't have me on your mind. Just let me work with someone who knows *Giant* and likes its basic idea. I'm hoping it will be you, George, unless you are swamped with other phases of the picture.

So, on June 20, 1954, she told them her flight numbers and arrival time and that she would be staying at the Hotel Bel-Air.

There was publicity anyway, despite Ferber's wishes. The deal that she had "pacted" with Stevens and Ginsberg was simply too big to go unnoticed by the press. In some ways it was similar to the merger of Mary Pickford, Douglas Fairbanks, Charlie Chaplin, and D. W. Griffith that formed United Artists back in 1919, relatively early in the evolution of motion pictures. Stevens, Ferber, and Ginsberg were not opening the gates of a formal studio but were at the gateway—certainly for Ferber—of some lavish opportunities. *Variety* trumpeted their propitious triumvirate:

> . . . *Giant* is a first on two scores. It will be the first time that Ginsberg, heretofore a studio production executive, will have billing as co-producer with Stevens (who will also direct) on the picture, and it's a first for Miss Ferber in such a co-partnership venture.
>
> She has had previous participation deals, and also a limited film leasing arrangement for *Saratoga Trunk*, but most of her stories (*Cimarron, So Big, Show Boat*, etc.) were essentially straight sales. In the Ginsberg-Stevens-Ferber setup she is a co-partner.
>
> The G-S-F setup will also embrace future filming of previous Ferber works, including remakes of some of her past film successes, rights to which have reverted . . .

When Ferber arrived in Los Angeles, she was greeted by reporters, and she gave them her best smile. She said that she felt the Texas reaction to her novel had cooled down and that no problems were expected with her new film venture. She kept smiling when reporters greeted her at the hotel along with Stevens and Ginsberg, saying that she was "as composed as a can of angle worms."

Stevens was the designated spokesperson for the actual film project, offering a blueprint: The film would be in color and shot for a wide screen; it would be either an all-star or a no-star project. "If we have to have stars," he said, "we have to have six of them at least."

Ferber feigned interest in the technical side of film development, but offered her usual succinct opinion about developing trends: "You can dredge up as many D's as you can call up out of the alphabet, but what matters is the story and the characters."

More than occasionally Ferber could seem schoolmarmish, but accompanied by a certain charm: the sensation was simultaneously forbidding and disarming. One could find oneself mixed up in her company. This was not the case with her newest collaborator. Stevens was a sensitive realist, straight talking, understanding the limits of a dream:

> . . . To produce and direct a movie today a man really ought to have two heads. It is like trying to be a traffic cop and write a poem at the same time. You need an executive head to handle all the vast paraphernalia of movie-making. You need another more sensitive head to get the delicate human emotional values you are trying to put on film. I try for reality. I like a story with enough drama in it the actors don't have to steam themselves up and start behaving like actors instead of normal people.

Ferber felt that Stevens was mishandling the character of Leslie, as well as that of the daughter then called young Leslie, and later called Judy. It was as if they were in battle for the soul of Leslie and her daughter. Wrote Stevens in a memo to Ginsberg:

> I note that Edna points out the lack of purpose the character of young Leslie has in the script . . . [Young] Leslie has a purpose. We are aware that the character has little to do and have examined the over-all value in discussion at some length. She participates only for the purpose of making it possible for TWO grandchildren to be present in the playpen at the finish: a blonde and a brunette. In contrast: one of pronounced Latin strain and one of the more Nordic, or if you please, "pure Arian [*sic*] strain" as I recollect a description of not so long ago.

Stevens then goes into quite an aria, defending some of the previous choices upon which he was still insistent:

> We felt the need for the development of young Luz's relationship with Jett Rink as it is, and as this development takes place almost at the finish of the story, it makes it impossible that Luz could be the one to be married and have the child that is going to be in the playpen with the new little Jordan at the finish. This necessitated a marriage somewhere around the time that the son Jordan married Juana, so that the two children could be born and be approximately the right age at the time that Jett Rink's party takes place.

Stevens still felt that despite Leslie's feminist views and declarations, her contribution was more to the story's dramatic tension than to any platform, and that she ended up—finally—with the marriage that she wanted.

Ferber was in Los Angeles working on the screenplay for eleven weeks. She ate the same farm breakfast every morning: freshly squeezed orange juice, oatmeal, poached eggs on whole wheat toast, strong coffee. For lunch she had developed a fondness for tuna melt—a West Coast specialty that she found exotic, noting that "it should be dreadful and if decadent is dreadful then it is. I simply love it." Her dinners were varied, as she accepted invitations and had some good friends living on the "coast," such as Garson Kanin (to whom she had often referred as "dear Gar," until at one point he pursued my mother romantically, and then it was simply "Gar") and his wife, Ruth Gordon; George Oppenheimer, who she always thought was "dependable as a Burberry raincoat"; Leland Hayward, her "clever boy" agent, and his current wife, Slim Keith. When she dined in, it was often in the hotel dining room, alone. She never minded being alone with a good book. She also enjoyed studying people. Bedtime was between ten thirty and eleven, giving her ample time to digest her food. She was as regulated and disciplined as she ever had been, while writing this, her first—and as it would turn out, her last—screenplay.

She captures a sense of her time in Los Angeles in a letter to her longtime favorite crony Noël Coward:

> I, to my astonishment and horror mingled, am working with George Stevens on *Giant*. I've never before worked in pictures, and my work agreement is, perhaps, somewhat a deviation from the normal. I came with the definite understanding that I was to have no publicity; that I was to receive no salary; and that my name was not to appear on the screen credits as writer of the script. I therefore am free and full of mischief and rather enjoying it. Henry Ginsberg, George Stevens and I own the picture, which will be released by Warner. I work from 9:30 to

6:30, and later, six days a week, and I don't know why I don't topple forward with my face in the Remington typewriter— but I don't. The face, in fact, isn't even wan.

The key word in this letter is "mischief," but with her work schedule such as it was, one wonders whether she just thought it was jaunty to write the word.

It is not surprising that in her version of the screenplay she restored the opening scene of the novel where the guests arrive for the Jett Rink Airport celebration. This then fades to a flashback of the young Leslie and Bick in the courting scene in Virginia, which Stevens later turned into Maryland due to potential defamation issues—Mrs. Kleberg, on whom Ferber reputedly based her character of Leslie, was not originally from Virginia but went to school there, and strongly identified with the state. To make for an even more complex situation in terms of locale, Ferber's three sisters in the novel were all born in Ohio prior to the family's move to Virginia.

When Leslie and Bick are on the train as newlyweds headed for Texas, there is more sexual repartee in Ferber's version than in the eventual shooting script, and certainly more than in her novel. Spicing things up was somewhat of an aberration for Ferber. It is curious and could make one wonder and reflect on an odd comment in a letter from Henry Ginsberg to Harriet Pilpel dated September 1953, while contracts were being finalized. Ginsberg was organizing a meeting in New York and wrote: "My plans at the moment are to come to New York the last week of the month. George Stevens will follow soon after for a conference with Miss Ferber. You have probably had Edna's report about her visit to Los Angeles and what might be construed as a romantic episode between herself and George Stevens at the Farmers Market." Nothing more about that has ever been alluded to, but once read, it's hard to forget. One might envision a more highly charged collaboration between the two—or was it one that Ferber only yearned for?

In her attempt at the screenplay, Ferber heightened Bick's love for Leslie and Luz's jealousy toward her new sister-in-law. For example, there was a larger struggle with Luz over running the household, leading to more of a general adjustment for Leslie at Reata.

Ferber ratchets up Jett's discomfort surrounding Leslie's first visit to the Mexican family's home and taking care of the baby, Angel Obregon.

She generally points up the story's racism, and certainly when pertaining to Bick. There is also more anger and escalated fighting between Leslie and Bick. They argue about Bick's running Reata and about his running everything in their lives. They argue about power. This last is very important to Ferber in her version.

In general Ferber gives more emphasis to the condition of Mexican Americans. She writes an exposition scene, not in the film, about Leslie's parents reading a letter from her about her helping Dr. Guerra tend the Mexican sick. There is considerably more emphasis on Dr. Guerra in Ferber's version, as he was based on one of her recently acquired heroes, Dr. Héctor García.

Then there is a moment that is new and strong. It occurs in the tea-drinking scene with Leslie and Jett at Jett's shack, snidely called Little Reata. The scene is in the movie, but there it doesn't include Dr. Guerra. In the Ferber script, Leslie comes in with the doctor; the two have been looking for Fidel Gomez, who has been working with Jett. Gomez and the doctor leave Leslie with Jett. As they chat, Ferber offers insight into Jett's bitterness and racist views. When Leslie asks him if he ever wants to do things for people, he scoffs, and then flings an answer back at her, saying that he thought she was too busy "loving up Bick" to do stuff to help Dr. Guerra. Leslie then flashes, "Does anything mean something to you?" and Jett answers, "You do." In the movie we see Jett's yearning, his near-obsession with Leslie, but Ferber's version shows his awkwardly sweet, deep feelings for her.

There is a new moment when Leslie leaves Bick, taking the children back to her family's home in Virginia for Thanksgiving. As she and her mother are making preparations, Mrs. Lynnton puts Texas down, saying, "Nothing but cows and dust and Mexicans," whereupon Leslie rallies to its defense with ". . . and hospitality, energy and life." Ferber wanted to show how her new home in Texas was beginning to invade Leslie. Now, she and her mother each had problems in their different lifestyles. They were no longer subtle variations of the same woman.

Ferber constantly emphasized the Mexican American characters, giving them as much to do as in her novel, and hoping to elevate their participation in the movie. Here, she has Jordy and Angel as boyhood friends, with Angel teaching Jordy how to work with the horses and

Jordy teaching Angel to speak better English. Ferber lays the ground-work for Jordy's later affinity for the Mexican community.

Ferber left in much of what Stevens, Moffat, and Guiol had laid down from here on until the last section of the story. However, she makes much more of Jett's passion for Leslie and later for her grown daughter Luz. His love proposal to Luz is more overt and plaintive, and he is much drunker.

Jett's banquet speech is considerably longer in Ferber's edition, and yet he still ends up passing out and slipping under the table.

The much-talked-about second-to last scene in the diner is the same in Ferber's version, which shows how she respected the process of evolution from novel to movie—when it worked. Earlier I pointed out how she fashioned this scene in her daybook, the instrument of change for the whole movie, which was pinpointed in this scene. Ferber saw this and knew it was right. There is, however, a slightly sour note in Ferber's version of the final scene. Bick calls the Benedict family a failure and Leslie calmly says no, they are a success at last, as they gaze at their grandchildren in the playpen: one dark-skinned baby and one white. Under Ferber's guidance we are to gather that, yes, a mountain has been moved . . . but Bick isn't so sure he doesn't want it back.

What happened next is vague in terms of exact wording, but it can be deduced that Ferber's screenplay was declined. On August 8, she delivered her script to Stevens, who regarded it as more of a treatment as it was so visually skimpy. Ferber's verbiage was her trademark, but not for a screenplay. This is where she fell woefully short. For instance, there is a shot where Jordy Benedict tries on a Stetson hat his father, Bick, has given him for Christmas. His head is drowning in the huge hat, and Ferber has Jordy say, "They never did fit me, did they, Dad?" In the margin Stevens wrote, "Let the picture say this—do all our jokes need explaining?"

Stevens was a master of the sight gag, perhaps stemming from the fact that his parents were both admired vaudeville actors. They'd launched their careers at the Hal Roach Studios in 1922, when Stevens was a lanky seventeen-year-old. Stevens defended silent slapstick and

Laurel and Hardy, saying about the duo, who became his dear friends, "By some artistic instinct they had this wonderful business of being in touch with the human spirit."

In Ferber's final Jett banquet scene, where he is falling-down drunk, she has him say, "Stand up . . . Ought to stand up," to which Stevens wrote: "NO! (The art is to tell what he is thinking—without having the actor leave his part and explain changes for the author—Bad as the Chinese stage hand that comes on and hands the dagger)."

If Ferber's pride was mashed, she took it like a trouper—albeit a verbal one. Stepping aside, she couldn't help coaching and correcting. Her pet peeves were not small and were never truly rectified. She felt that the "chosen writers"—this with a sniff—had demoted Leslie's dialogue and built up Bick's role with a certain grandeur at the expense of his wife's—*her* Leslie, the fulcrum of the piece, as Ferber saw it.

She was distressed, and in a final attempt before she abdicated, she stated her biggest reason to Stevens and Ginsberg: "I feel that Leslie has to quite a degree, faded into a somewhat pale character as the two leading male characters have taken on additional stature . . . When Bick takes that flag off the wall and drapes it around the casket of Angel, I reject that act. It is a thing Leslie might do; Bick would not. Not yet, at least. It is a tear-jerker, but it is not the truth."

She never withdrew, because contractually she didn't have to. Unlike Leslie with Bick, she was a total equal in her new marriage. It would not be long before she became harmonious, but while Stevens, Moffat, and Guiol were still hammering and sawing, she was voicing alarm, as in a letter to Ken McCormick:

> I got myself into something really grisly when, in my youth and innocence, I came out here to write the *Giant* dialogue . . . The script dialogue was beyond belief at that time. I never would have permitted it to be used. For eight weeks, at exactly nothing a week, I've been working with a young man named Ivan Moffat. He is 36, charming, talented, sensitive; he has taste, a feeling for words; he can't write worth a damn, he is indolent and can't do a real day's work. He knows as much about Texas as I know about Iran. Less. If I get out of this town without killing him it will be the greatest triumph of restraint against honest impulse.

Ferber took her hat in hand, but before she was out the door, she gave Stevens some useful tips about Mexican American civil rights. The first was advising him to contact an authentic Texas Ranger, Colonel William Sterling. She wrote:

> Sterling knows Texas. He's three-fourths genuine. Likes publicity. May resent me. He was a wonderful source of information. Speaks fluent Spanish, especially Mexican-Spanish (which certainly is not Castilian Spanish, and which should be the Spanish of *Giant*). Knows the Latin Americans through and through. Likes them, but "in their place" I should think he'd say. "Why do they have to come into a restaurant such as Whatshisname's when I'm eating there." I've heard him say that. Great charm, fairly gabby. Full of remarkable background stuff.
>
> Then, Dr. Hector Garcia. Wonderful man. Captain in the last war, served over-seas. Married to a lovely Italian Neapolitan woman (blonde, blue-eyed, serene, intelligent). Garcia's patients are Mexican. His office usually is jammed with them.
>
> Herbert L. Garlitz: Conservation and soil expert. AG College. Technical. Modern. May not talk to you because of *Giant*, but perhaps.
>
> I have, of course, many other names.

After these helpful hints, Ferber had more, about casting: "Yesterday Janet Fox Goldsmith (my niece, whom you met) spoke of a girl named Pat Neal. Whatever became of her? She made a great hit in a play of Lillian Hellman's. I think it was *The Other Side of the Forest*. She then went to Hollywood and sort of disappeared. Tall, attractive, convincing, good voice. Ever do anything about Jo Van Fleet?"

———

At the end of 1954, Ferber turned her interest in two directions: casting for *Giant* and revving up her new project about another American frontier. Alaska was the chosen one, but she seemed somewhat less excited about it, as she wrote to Stevens: "I'm tossing and turning over a new novel which I gladly (and I mean this) would temporarily put aside if I thought a few days or even weeks would clear anything in the path of *Giant*'s production. If the revised manuscript is coming east, or if you are coming east, or if you want me to come west for a couple of weeks, just say so."

She stayed where she was, and he stayed where he was, but in that same letter there is a rebuke, praise, and lots of chat. There is an intimate tone suggesting they'd been through a patch, survived it, and were now compadres:

It is now three-months-going-on-four, George, dear, since I flew from more or less sunny California to the hurricane coast of Massachusetts.

I've heard nothing from you. I wish you'd pull that leonine head of yours down from the Jovian clouds (don't tell me it's smog) that you inhabit, to give me your news, if any.

Occasionally I pick up a crumb from the newspaper columns. Last week Henry Ginsberg wrote me that a location scouting crew was headed for Texas.

My reasons for wanting news of *Giant* are, I think, legitimate, and, itemized, they are:

1) I am more interested in seeing *Giant* emerge as a motion picture than any novel, play, or short story I've written in all these years.

2) Your treatment of the book seemed to me to strengthen the book's weaknesses and clarify its theme. [This was an unusual admission for her. It indicates she respected Stevens's vision of her story to the point where, perhaps, she felt he could visually clarify and bolster some of her themes.]

3) That theme (I regret in a way, to say) is truer, more vital, more prevalent today in the United States than it was when I began to write the novel.

4) People, all the way from a glove-counter clerk at Saks Fifth Avenue to E. L. Bartlett, Delegate from Alaska, in Washington, daily ask me what's become of the picture and who's playing Leslie and who's playing Bick and who's playing Jett and who's playing Luz. I say I don't know, feeling foolish.

5) It is possible that ten years from now—of perhaps even five,
   though unlikely—unless our world is destroyed—which IS
   rather likely—oil and oil millionaires will be anachronisms
   like the dear old covered wagons and the California gold-rush
   boys. The atom is obsolete as a weapon, having given way
   to the hydrogen bomb and that other pretty thing. Cobalt,
   or something? Anyway, the atom will push and pull things,
   instead of oil. I'm not trying to be funny.

6) There is a partnership of sorts between you, Henry Ginsberg,
   and me. In the past, having sold a novel or play in pictures,
   I haven't cared very much, or I've told myself I didn't care.
   Now, in this case, I do care. This is true, I think, chiefly
   because the picture is in your hands, and therefore likely to be
   a really dimensional and arresting and courageous work.

7) I worked on this picture for eleven weeks, under conditions
   suggested by me, and which were unusual in the motion
   picture field. I find this experience enormously rewarding,
   personally.

8) My criticism of your original version was concerned with the
   dialogue, and a very few treatment incidents. I concentrated
   on dialogue and when I left Hollywood on August 31st I felt
   that the characters spoke in character, definitely. I hope that
   further work in revision, cutting, etc., has not blurred the
   characterizations. In the first script I had a real shock at sights
   of Bick Benedict's ain'ts and gonnas and was-es. There are,
   as you know, Texans who talk and behave like comic-strip
   Texans, and Texans who behave with taste and intelligence,
   even though their outlook may be narrow.

How are yo'all? Are Ivan and Fred still wrestling with the
Benedicts? I miss them and you.

My new novel certainly will be a year or more in the
making, but its theme and background and characters are
right up your alley, though you'll never say so, being a boy
chary of praise. I read of your new contract to do two pictures
in ten years, and I thought, well, I should live so long!

I love you, in a nice way.

Ferb

The confessional camaraderie that she offers is rare for her. Her feeling for Stevens seemed equal to the title that they would share forever.

There is a sentence in this letter that seems to contradict an outstanding issue: "Your treatment of the book seemed to me to strengthen the book's weaknesses." Depending on how one regards this admission it is either conciliatory or alarming. If she is suggesting that Stevens strengthened her own book in the conversion, it is disturbing. She had never deferred to a director's interpretation of one of her properties before. Of course they would be different, but never improved. Her deference suggests some kind of emotional attachment.

There were definite alterations made. Although Stevens was concerned about the treatment of Mexican Americans, he reduced them to symbols in the movie. None of them had more than a few lines to say. It is theorized that perhaps this was a statement of their weakness within the system, and had they been portrayed as physically and verbally more powerful, it would have been easier to overlook the racial injustice. In keeping them mostly weak and silent, was Stevens pointing to their vastly overlooked civil liberties?

Also, Ferber's novel—like all her novels—showed feminism evading suppression and then overcoming it. Stevens did not make a feminist Western. His Leslie will always be in a fight. She will learn how to better contour her heart and soul, and to maneuver what she must, but she will never be able to crow until the very end, when she glimpses a victory of sorts.

Another difference was in the way Stevens depicted Jett Rink in the script and in the casting. Ferber's Jett was pitch; he refracted no light whatsoever. Stevens's Jett was lost, and found, and lost again. In Stevens's notes on a line of Jett's in the novel, "Nobody's king in this country—no matter what they think," he wrote: "Memorable line. Should register on some people later on."

Three months had gone by since the work had started. What Stevens, Moffat, and Guiol hoped would be the final edition of the script was shown to Ferber. From the look of her notes, she wasn't entirely pleased. She addressed herself to Ginsberg, whom she designated as the most neutral one of the bunch: "I haven't, after all, finished this job or even covered the section I did attempt to do . . . I could, of course, spend weeks on this script. But I shan't. I have said to you before, and I now repeat, I think it is powerful, dramatic and often emotionally compelling."

And then she took quite a bit to task:

A slight matter; but WAR WINDS is difficult to enunciate, and hard to hear. I suppose MAN O' WAR suggested it. SWIFT WINDS, FOLLOW ME, CARE FREE (too much like Karfrey [Leslie's sister's married name]), HIGH BOY, GREEN LIGHT (anachronism?)

P. 2. You must have good reason repeating Dr. Lynnton's speech (That's my daughter riding him . . . Leslie's my daughter, etc.) but I don't get it.

P. 2. DR. LYNNTON says . . . We'll get with the horses, etc. I took this out last June, but it's back again. Perhaps this form of speech is used in certain parts of the country, but I never have heard it. Certainly Dr. Lynnton doesn't use it. He would say:
DR. LYNNTON
We'll go down to the stables first thing in the morning, have a good look at Swift Winds. Now, let's go up to the house, have a drink before dinner. Nice to have you here, Mr. Benedict.

P. 3. LACEY says—Leslie's going to have a fit. I took that out in June. It's an expression I hate and I don't think this girl would use it. Can't she say—Leslie won't let you.

P. 5. Bottom of page. Leslie suddenly calls him JORDAN. It's a bit sudden, isn't it? Perhaps on P. 3, where Bick speaks, he could say: Yes, Ma'am—Texas. Benedict's the name. Jordan Benedict.

Page 6. Top of page. Scene between Mrs. Lynnton and Dr. Lynnton. As written here the scene is pointless. The scene in the novel plainly shows that she is impressed with Bick's acreage. Why not indicate that here—otherwise it does for less than nothing.

And then Ferber actually writes the dialogue as she thinks it should be. She does this all the way through, but this is an example of her owning her own characters and knowing how they sound:

DR. LYNNTON (MILDLY DEFENSIVE)
    What have I done now, Nancy?

MRS. LYNNTON
    Never telling me a word about this Mr. Benedict. Millions of acres! Why, it's a kingdom!

I believe that these corrections come from a deep place. Ferber feels that injustice is being done and she truly can't help pointing it out. Some might consider her simply a tiresome old scold. That would be a grievous misunderstanding. Ferber is protecting her creation. What is seen in these notes is a passionate hovering.

P. 8. I don't understand the word YUS. I didn't understand it when I took it out and I don't understand it now. What does it mean? If it means a vigorous affirmative I've never heard it.

P. 9. Dr. Lynnton says,—We'll get and we'll get going. All through he seems to be a great "get" boy. We'll have breakfast and "get" going. A small matter, perhaps. But multiplied it becomes a big matter.

p. 11. SUGGESTION: Leslie says: Jordan, you would think someone had spoiled you, etc. Why not a simpler and better form: Jordan, someone must have spoiled you terribly—your wife, etc. (What a pity LESLIE'S bit p. 90 in the novel, beginning "the cactus—ending—"I'm in love with it"—isn't used in the picture. It's the heart of the scene.)

It might be a nice quarrel climax if, at the end of Bick's speech— get pampered and spoiled out of all reason. Add: The men ask the questions in Texas. LESLIE: (wistfully) All of them? or— All the questions?

P. 12. DR. LYNNTON: Gotta hurry. Oh, let's spell it: Got to. Can't we? Even in a rush Dr. Lynnton can be literate, can't he?

P. 16. Last line, bottom of page. INJUN-broke Obregon. This is a confusing term, to an audience. Besides, I have never heard it used in Texas. It probably may be used in other parts of the west. Indian country. Texas isn't Indian country. The term here is misleading and conveys to an audience the thought that Obregon (if they ever get the name here) is an Indian, not a Mexican. You may not think this is important. I do. "Beating on my Duesenberg." I don't understand that, either.

P. 20. SUGGESTION:

BICK

Some say she runs the ranch.

Would there be any value in adding—and me.

P. 22. LESLIE says, on meeting LUZ—"Of course." This seems to me a strange way in which to take an introduction, especially this one. Shouldn't she say, "rather"?

P. 24. LUZ (introducing JETT to LESLIE) says: "He works for us." I think it would sound less small-farmer if she could say, "He's a handy-man on the place."

BICK

When he's on the place.

Rock Hudson as Jordan "Bick" Benedict, 1955

P. 51. Dr. Walker says, "I wish't I could have made it for Luz."

Nowhere in the novel *Giant* is Dr. Walker portrayed as an illiterate. I don't know why he is written here as a hillbilly who says wish't instead of wish that. But won't you please take it out, unless he is to be pictured as an oaf.

P. 70. LESLIE: "About lover's quarrels—the best part is making up."

You can't seriously mean to use this tired old cliché. There isn't a critic or reviewer who won't pick it up and use it derisively, to the injury of the picture. Unless Leslie is suddenly a dull boring stodgy old mess she CAN'T say this.

P. 78. LESLIE says (and here is Bronx Bella Gross again, all clumsy coquetry) "May I pay you a rather personal compliment? . . . You make a very good cup of tea, Jett."

I can't bear to read it, much less to hear it.

P. 78. LESLIE: "When are you going to get married, etc. "—this kind of responsibility."

Leslie doesn't talk like that. No young woman talks like that.

LESLIE: "Money isn't all."

I took this out once. Here it is again. It's no use my telling you that this is the dullest kind of cliché. If you thought it was it wouldn't have been in in the first place.

Ferber knew her Leslie. However, "her" Leslie wasn't yet cast. She thought she very much wanted Grace Kelly, and Burt Lancaster for Bick, and Robert Mitchum for Jett. During this time of script versions and revisions, casting feelers had been put out and the search was definitely underway. In retrospect those three might have carried too much Hollywood varnish on them.

During the first month of 1955, offers had gone out and rejections had come in. Ferber was involved in all of it, as one can see in

James Dean screen-tests for the role of Jett
Rink, 1955

her telegram to Henry Ginsberg: "I AM RELIABLY TOLD GRACE
KELLY VERY ANXIOUS PLAY LESLIE BUT METRO WANTS
HER FOR SPENCER TRACY PICTURE WHICH SHE DEFI-
NITELY DOES NOT WANT TO DO. AS SHE NOW DOES
PRETTY MUCH AS SHE PLEASES, I THINK SHE MIGHT
DO 'GIANT' IF PROPERLY APPROACHED. THIS COMES
FROM SOMEONE HERE WHOM YOU KNOW VERY CLOSE
TO TRACY."

The connection to Tracy was Katharine Hepburn—dear friend of
Ferber's—who apparently could not influence Tracy to influence Kelly,
who was committed to making pictures hand over fist. After *To Catch
a Thief* in 1955, she went right into *High Society* in 1956. And, in fact,
neither of these had anything to do with Spencer Tracy.

Many actors were considered for the cast of *Giant*. Clark Gable
aggressively went after the role of Bick, but Stevens felt that his presence would not benefit the story as much as that of a younger actor who
could age over the required decades. He also turned down the agents of

James Dean's screen test

Charlton Heston, Gregory Peck, Sterling Hayden, Kirk Douglas, Burt Lancaster, Tyrone Power, Henry Fonda, and James Stewart.

The final choice of the twenty-nine-year-old Rock Hudson came abruptly, and as a "loaner" from Universal. His luck came about through an inside channel: a young woman named Joan McTavish, who was dating Stevens and would become the second Mrs. Stevens, worked at Universal, where Hudson had gotten her attention by aging twenty-five years in a movie called *The Lawless Breed* (1953). But it wasn't totally on McTavish's say-so, as Stevens had seen Hudson age with his own eyes in director Douglas Sirk's *Magnificent Obsession* (1954).

A Warner Bros. press release heralded the casting choice:

The prize acting plum of the year, and one which has often been reported in the grasp of a number of Hollywood's top male stars goes to a dark horse who has never once been mentioned in the spirited competition. ROCK HUDSON has

James Dean's screen test

been selected by George Stevens out of all of Hollywood's great
as the best to play Bick Benedict, the towering Texan.

Although both Stevens and Ferber agreed on Grace Kelly as the
best Leslie candidate, it was Stevens who zeroed in on Elizabeth Taylor.
This could have been tricky, knowing, as Stevens did, how proprietary
Ferber was about her heroine. Taylor won on one count. She had given
a stunning lead performance for Stevens in *A Place in the Sun* in 1951.

No one could dispute Taylor's ravishing looks, but Ferber had seen
her Leslie as "a tall slim girl, not pretty." This doesn't seem like type-
casting for Kelly, either; but it was Bick Benedict's first impression on
meeting (unbeknown to him) his future bride. And he had softened
and been won over the next time he saw her: "She was wearing the
disfiguring evening dress that was in vogue—the absurdly short skirt
and loose-hip-length waistline that so foreshortened the figure. Long
slim legs, lovely shoulders . . . he saw how exquisitely her head was set

James Dean as Jett Rink on the set of
Giant, 1955

on her throat, and how, in some mysterious way, she was really a beauty in disguise."

My mother recalled that when casting was set, Ferber had commented on Taylor, calling her short but somehow majestic. Years later, when my mother and I tried to dissect the mystery of the seemingly perfect cast, we would talk about how others might have done these roles. When we pictured Grace Kelly, we saw her in a bonnet. That simply wasn't Leslie.

In a quirky bit of potential casting, Richard Burton had been considered for, and had considered, the role of Jett Rink, but turned it down before he could be rejected. He wrote to Stevens from Spain, where he was filming *Alexander the Great,* "I have worked at the 'Texas' material. But to no avail. I just don't seem to drawl in the right places and my 'You-alls' don't quite come off. There are quite a few Texans staying at this hotel—Castellana Hilton—and my efforts totally fail to impress them."

Today Jett Rink is synonymous with James Dean. The two literally

Elizabeth Taylor as Leslie Lynnton
Benedict on the Warner Bros. set of
Giant, 1955

died together in a Porsche speeding along the Pacific Coast Highway
not quite before the filming of *Giant* was completed. But in early 1955,
they were only about to meet. In fact, Ferber's Jett wasn't physically
embodied by Dean: "Leslie glimpsed this Jett Rink in the doorway
now—a muscular young fellow with a curiously powerful bull-like
neck and shoulders. He wore the dust-colored canvas and the high-
heeled boots of the region, his big sweat-stained hat was pushed back
from his forehead and you saw his damp dark curls. His attitude, his
tone was belligerent. About twenty, Leslie decided. She decided, too,
that he was an unpleasant young man."

Great casting so often is accidental. Dean had not even been sub-
mitted for Jett. He had been filming his second picture, *Rebel Without
a Cause*, for Warner Bros. and had become friends with another Warner
employee, Fred Guiol, who was the writer on *Giant*. Guiol related to
Stevens that a boy, Jimmy Dean, used to hang around the back door to
Stevens's office. Dean, still relatively unknown—at least to Stevens—
hadn't remotely been considered for *Giant*. So, he would hang around,
twirling a rope, just twirling away, "making tricks out there," Stevens

Taylor and Rock Hudson during a break
on the set of *Giant* in Marfa, Texas, 1955

recalled. Then, through Guiol, Dean got to call on Stevens, and he continued to play with the rope. Stevens knew that he wasn't seeing Jett, but Dean intrigued him: "This guy was fascinating. He wasn't looking for a part in the film, but Freddie and I said, 'What would happen if he played this part? He's such a brilliant chap.' And so we engaged him."

Ferber balked when Stevens informed her—gently—that he was thinking hard about engaging Dean. Still ruffled about certain elements of the script, she tried to have some leverage, saying, "What about Mitchum? I hear he's free. You'll get value with Mitchum."

Stevens urged her to just meet Dean, who would be in Manhattan and could have lunch any day of her choosing. He would set up a screening of *Rebel Without a Cause* for her prior to the meeting. If she agreed, Stevens felt, she would be better off lunching alone with his leading candidate.

They met, and she fell hard for this compelling young, young man who flirted with her. She described him in *A Kind of*

Magic: . . . A young actor who was spectacularly talented; handsome in a fragile sort of way; and absolutely outrageous. He was an original. Impish, compelling, magnetic; utterly winning one moment, obnoxious the next. Definitely gifted. Frequently maddening. He was James Dean.

LESLIE/ELIZABETH

Elizabeth Taylor was young—twenty-three. She relished her role as a spirited yet refined woman, made tougher by her circumstances, telling Ferber that Leslie was who she aspired to be. Some of Leslie's traits were also hers: unpretentious, respectful, loyal, and caring.

As Leslie Lynnton Benedict, a precursor of a liberal feminist who pointed out sexism and racism, Taylor was Ferber's mouthpiece. Taking up the mantle of Leslie, in later years Taylor advocated inclusion. Interestingly, one of her major causes involved the real-life situation of Rock Hudson during his decline from AIDS. After his death in 1985 Taylor became an official activist, forming amfAR, the Foundation for AIDS Research.

In the summer of 1985, when Hudson was hospitalized at UCLA Medical Center, his life waning, Taylor made a clandestine visit. Michael Gottlieb, the immunologist who first brought AIDS into the light in 1981, took Taylor to his bedside. "She was a little nervous about seeing him for the first time because she knew how sick he was," Gottlieb recalled. "She asked me if it was okay to hug and kiss him. She was worried about his immune system. Not hers."

Giant had kept them together for decades. In a sense, they had melded into Bick and Leslie, a loving and accepting couple of friends. If you watch closely, you will see something magically collusive in one particular scene of *Giant*. Leslie has needed a separation from Bick. She feels shaky in their marriage, takes the three children, and decamps for her parents' home in Maryland. She arrives in time to see her younger sister getting married to an old beau of hers. During the wedding ceremony, Bick appears, looming in the background. Leslie "feels" his presence, turns, and by the look they exchange, we know they will reunite.

The night before the scene was shot, Taylor and Hudson had a lot to drink, and they had terrible hangovers the next day. They sail through the scene looking almost like their usual gorgeous selves.

———

Ferber was traveling to Alaska for research, but her pull toward what was happening in Hollywood was strong. The movie was the thing. However, because she had been so exacting about the screenplay, production was behind schedule. Filming was now slated to begin at the Warner Bros. Studios in Burbank at the end of May 1955. Although the production had its three leads, they were still finishing up casting and Ferber was still pointing out her grievances in the script:

> But how can I make someone in your outfit understand that LESLIE wouldn't say . . . a real big success. She wouldn't say it because it is not the way a woman of taste and education would phrase it. Perhaps a big bluff westerner might say "I hear you're a real big success"—but Leslie wouldn't. How can I make you understand that this is important. The word BIG weakens the whole thing, anyway. In the novel *Giant* (Page 447) Leslie says:
>
> LESLIE
> . . . after a hundred years the Benedict family is a real success at last.
>
> And that's what she'd say. Not just because it's in the book. That's what she'd say.
> Look, won't you tell Elizabeth Taylor this:
> LESLIE, the young girl, is educated but inexperienced; idealistic but impractical. She speaks of freedom without knowing what she means. Perhaps she thinks that wide spaces and vast skies and uncrowded lands mean freedom. As she grows older she learns that freedom dwells in the mind. That's why she says . . . the Benedict family is a real success at last.
> By the way (another small point) please don't have her say, as she does a few times, for example: I'll do LIKE you do—or

whatever the use of the word LIKE in a similar connection. She really wouldn't use the word this way. Perhaps these are small things in a big picture. JETT would talk that way, or PINKY or VASHTI.

On the heels of this final plea to Henry Ginsberg, the leading members of the cast gathered in New York. Rock Hudson came with his fiancée, Phyllis Gates; Elizabeth Taylor with her husband, Michael Wilding. James Dean was there, and Mercedes McCambridge (Luz the elder). There was to be a press conference, some luncheons, and a dinner given by Ferber. Stevens, Henry Ginsberg, Ivan Moffat, and Fred Guiol were also present.

My parents were invited to the dinner party. "Bring Julie along," Ferber had said, "she might enjoy it."

The day before it was to be, the fever came and then the spots. I was put to bed, too sick to go, and too feverish to understand that I really couldn't. I lay in the darkened room with all sorts of empty and full juice glasses around me and cried. The maid came in and turned on the desk lamp. She said that I had a visitor. Mr. Dean. He must have been right behind her, for he was suddenly in the room, mumbling, "Hihowareya?" He dragged over the blue desk chair and sat by my bed. He studied my pocks. "Bad case," he said. I asked him if he'd ever had them. He shrugged and said that he didn't remember. I told him not to get too close or he might catch them. He shrugged again and said that everybody should have chicken pox at least once in their lives. Then he gave a funny little squawk. He asked how many chicken pox I had. I said I didn't know.

"Ya mean ya haven't counted 'em?"

"Uh-uh."

So he counted the ones on my face. He asked me if I'd read *Giant*. I said no, I was only nine. He said, "So?" Then he asked me if I liked Ferber. I told him I loved her. He nodded, as if in approval, and then said, "If ya do, ya better read her stuff."

Then he drank some of my juice and was gone.

On May 17, 1955, the entire cast and crew gathered in LA at the Warner Bros. Studios, sans Ferber. She was preparing for a research trip to

Alaska in early June and felt that much traveling would prove too tiring. It brings to mind what her friend Louis Bromfield said about her underlying dislike of travel. She had offered to send a cable, to which Henry Ginsberg responded by cable, half understanding and half making her feel that she was missing something special:

GEORGE AND I UNDERSTAND CIRCUMSTANCES WITH REGARD YOUR ALASKA PLANS. WE WILL MISS HAVING YOU WITH US NOW BUT ARE HOPEFUL YOU WILL PLAN VISIT ON YOUR RETURN FROM ALASKA.

OUR LUNCHEON FOR ENTIRE CAST AND NATION WIDE PRESS REPRESENTATIVES WILL TAKE PLACE AT STUDIO WEDNESDAY NOON. A WIRE FROM YOU TO GEORGE, MYSELF AND ASSEMBLED GROUP IS IN ORDER AND WILL BE APPRECIATED.

Ferber wrote a very long cable back:

DEAR HENRY AND GEORGE AND ALL YOU BOYS AND GIRLS GATHERED TODAY AT THE WARNER STUDIO:

PLEASE BELIEVE ME WHEN I SAY THAT I'D RATHER BE THERE WITH YOU THIS MINUTE THAN ANY OTHER PLACE IN THE WORLD. I DON'T QUITE KNOW WHY THE MOTION PICTURE PRESENTATION OF "GIANT" INTERESTS AND FASCINATES ME MUCH MORE THAN THE SCREEN CAREER OF ANY OF MY OTHER NOVELS OR PLAYS. THAT GOES FOR "SHOW BOAT," "SO BIG," "CIMARRON," AND MANY OTHERS. PERHAPS IT IS BECAUSE BEHIND THE CHARACTERS AND EVENTS IN "GIANT" THERE STANDS A DEFINITE MEANING, A PURPOSE. THIS WILL, I AM SURE, THROUGH YOU, SUSTAIN IT AND GIVE IT DIMENSIONS QUITE APART FROM ANY CINESCOPIC GADGETS. IF THIS SOUNDS SORT OF SOLEMN AND POMPOUS IT ISN'T MEANT TO BE. UNDER GEORGE STEVENS' MAGIC DIRECTION THE

STONE AND MORTAR AND BEAMS THAT HOLD THE STRUCTURE WILL NOT SHOW AT ALL BUT THEY'LL BE THERE. HOW I WISH I COULD SOMEHOW MANAGE TO COME AND SEE THE THOUGHTS AND THE CHARACTERIZATIONS EMERGE THROUGH THE TALENTED EFFORTS OF ALL OF YOU. GOOD LUCK TO YOU ALL, WHICH IS REALLY JUST SLANG FOR HARD WORK.

She then must have phoned and spoken to all, to which Ginsberg responded, with news, in a day letter:

DEAR EDNA: EVERYONE WAS VERY THRILLED SPEAKING WITH YOU YESTERDAY. DIMITRI TIOMKIN WHOM YOU HAVE MET HAS BEEN ENGAGED TO DO THE MUSICAL SCORE, THE COMPOSING AND CONDUCTING OF "GIANT." DIMITRI LEAVING HERE TONIGHT AND WILL BE IN NEW YORK TOMORROW. GEORGE AND I MOST ANXIOUS THAT YOU AND HE GET TOGETHER DURING HIS VISIT. HE WILL TELL YOU ALL ABOUT OUR LUNCHEON, AND SOME OF THE IDEAS HE HAS IN MIND ABOUT THE PICTURE. GEORGE JOINS IN VERY BEST TO YOU.

Three days before she left for Seattle, the first stop en route to Anchorage, she had a few more things on her mind—and shared them with Ginsberg in a letter of May 27, at first sweetening them with praise of Dimitri Tiomkin: "I found him most discerning and amusing, too. I feel sure that he will do some fine things for *Giant*." And

Dennis Hopper, age nineteen (left), as Jordy Benedict, and Sal Mineo, age seventeen, as Angel Obregon then, her last licks—for a while—and they are powerful—certainly about Leslie and Jett:

I have, as you know, a number of dialogue and situation res-ervations, but I don't think anyone wants particularly to hear them. Nevertheless, very briefly, here they are:

1. I feel that Leslie has, to quite a great degree, faded into a somewhat pale character as the two leading male characters have taken on additional stature. In many places, too, her dialogue is that of a Texan, not a woman born and reared as Leslie was.

2. The tea-drinking scene between Leslie and Jett is not clearly defined and is not—to me, at least—anything but dull. This boy is in love with Leslie, as much as he can be in love with anyone outside himself. She is no fool. She knows this and tactfully puts the boy off, though she herself is attracted to him and might be the last to admit it. This should have been brought out in the scene.

3. The attempted fight scene between Bick and Jett in the pantry of the banquet hall—the fight which does not come off because Jett is too far gone in drink to stand up, much less fight—doubtless will be staged believably by you (George), but I somehow cannot see him meekly following Bick into the pantry simply because Bick has said, "Do you want to fight here or do you want to come off alone with me?"—or whatever it is. I just don't believe that, drunk or sober, he would walk meekly along with Bick.

I mention these things only because they are a few among many. As I've said to you before, I think the over-all script is powerful and dramatic and effective. And that Jett Rink ban-quet speech scene seems superb.

It is difficult to give you any information as to my sched-ule, because I can't be sure that such information will be of any use to you. During the next few days it will be impossible to reach me because I shall be at remote Alaskan spots that are not even towns. However, as I'm going up around the Arctic Circle following that and mail should not be sent to me during that period, it would be best perhaps to continue sending mail to Fairbanks, if necessary, until June 26th or 27th. It will be there for my return. In the meantime, if there is any change, I will try to let you know.

I am delighted to learn that things went well during the first week of work. I met Judith Anderson on the street yesterday, and she said she would have been so happy to be in the picture, particularly because of George's direction.

Affectionate regards to you all.

Although Ferber had a say in the casting, she became uncharacteristically demure, leaving the ultimate decisions to the far more knowledgeable director. Not being a big moviegoer, she was unfamiliar with the cast, who were young and thrilled to be working with Stevens.

Carroll Baker, cast as Leslie and Bick's daughter young Luz, was a twenty-four-year-old New York actress, reverently studying with Lee Strasberg at the Actors Studio—where she knew and had worked with James Dean. She describes her elation but also trepidation at the prospect of "going Hollywood":

> I was offered a starring part in a television show . . . called *The Web* . . . George Stevens, the great film director . . . saw *The Web* the night it was shown. George was preparing to make *Giant*, and he asked to screen-test me for the part of Luz Benedict II . . . Warner Bros. was anxious to have me if I agreed to a seven-year contract.
>
> Jack [Garfein, her husband] and I sat up all night discussing the *Giant* offer, and whether or not I should go to Hollywood. I felt completely insecure about myself as an actress in the film medium, but Jack maintained that the best way to learn was to put myself in the capable hands of one of the greatest film directors, George Stevens. And it was Jack who persuaded me not to pass up this splendid opportunity.

Dennis Hopper was also young but a bit more movie savvy, having just filmed *Rebel Without a Cause* with Dean. He was a big believer in the message that *Giant* carried about ethnic and racial justice. *Giant* offered him his breakthrough role, as young Jordy Benedict, son of

Elizabeth Taylor, Rock Hudson (center), and George Stevens filming in Marfa, Texas, 1955

Bick, but conscientiously not a chip off his father's block. Jordy was his
own person, marrying a Mexican woman and becoming a doctor, and
both he and Hopper were mindful that the struggle for civil rights went
farther than for African Americans only.

Hopper was excited just short of worshipful about working with
Stevens, having heard how meticulous he was and that he "shot every
corner of the room." In his early publicity interviews, he spoke about
working again with "Jimmy" and their notion about Method acting.
Dean had asked Hopper why he wanted to be an actor, and Hopper,
not entirely sure, turned the question back to Dean, who was ready
with his answer. His mother had died when he was young. He used to
go to her grave and lament, "Why did you leave me?"—which turned
into "I'm going to show you!" Hopper was clearly impressed. "He was
working with his subconscious," he said, speaking for both of them.

Sal Mineo, who was cast as Angel Obregon II, had also worked
with Dean in *Rebel Without a Cause*. He was playing an important
"symbolic" role, which had far more resonance in the novel. However,
Mineo's slight, almost feline demeanor and large, plaintive brown eyes

Rock Hudson and Elizabeth Taylor filming

gave his brief presence a memorable appeal. Mineo, who later became one of the first openly gay actors in Hollywood, somehow reflected this by living outside the margins of his relatively whittled down role.

When Earl Holliman made *Giant* at twenty-seven, he was already a veteran Hollywood character actor, with about fourteen films under his belt. One of them was *Broken Lance* (1954), playing one of Spencer Tracy's four sons. Stevens was watching on the set as it was filming one day to scout for possible locations for *Giant*, saw Holliman, and was known to have said, "I want to use that boy." Holliman's agent was emphatic about Holliman's getting the role of Bob Dace: it was not large, but to work with Stevens would be a coup. "Just go and meet with him," said the agent. So, Holliman interviewed for the role, which Stevens saw as "a kind of Booth Tarkington character"—like "a whisper going by." Holliman was cast, and recalls that "Stevens took liberties with the screenplay and built up the part."

Elsa Cárdenas was cast in the small but pivotal role of Juana, Jordy's Mexican bride. She is key to the emotions stirred up by racial intolerance. There is a heart-stopper of a scene toward the end of the movie where Juana goes downstairs to the beauty salon in the Conquistador

Rod Taylor (left), Hudson, and Taylor on a
break from filming

Hotel in Dallas, where Jett Rink's gala is to take place that evening. She
has already called for an appointment, but when they see her color,
they tell her there's no room to take her, that they're fully booked. The
look on her face is the story of everyone who has ever been made to feel
inadequate.

Cárdenas was twenty when she was chosen for *Giant*, which was
her first Hollywood movie. Her later films of note included *Fun in
Acapulco* (1963) with Elvis Presley and Sam Peckinpah's *The Wild Bunch*
(1969).

Ferber already knew about the qualities of character actress Mercedes McCambridge. She had no real comment, having put some
weight behind Patricia Neal, Jo Van Fleet, and Judith Anderson for the
role of Luz.

━━━━━━━

Ferber came home from Alaska at the end of June to difficulties, which
had begun to brew as far back as mid-1955. Henry Ginsberg was already

Taylor and Dean filming the tea scene

alerting Harriet Pilpel about trouble ahead due to being behind sched-ule. He did not specifically blame Ferber for the myriad critiques, rewrites, and notes on rewrites. He took the messenger role. Harriet troubleshot back on June 30, diagnosing and pointing out contractual incongruities even though filming had already begun. This issue would present itself to Stevens many times over, but Ginsberg always handled Ferber & Co. when it came to business. Pilpel wrote to Ginsberg in measured tones:

> According to our calculations, it would seem, however, that even if all had gone as planned, Warners would still have had 19 months less than a full ten years from the release date. Even if production had commenced by June 14, 1954, it would cer-tainly not have been completed in less than six months. War-ners would then have had until June, 1955 to release the film, but it's right under the story purchase agreement would have expiration November 16, 1963. In any event, therefore, Warner, when it accepted the limitations of the story purchase agree-ment, was agreeing to a less than ten year period . . . Warner's argument is that as a result of the various delays, not its fault, it has lost two years of its grant.

Filming Where?

Although *Giant* initially began filming with an interior scene at the Warner Bros. Studios in Burbank, and then for a short time in Virginia—subbing as Maryland in the movie—the cast and crew had moved for the long haul to Marfa, Texas, in early June 1955 to shoot the Texas landscapes and scenes outside Reata. Marfa was a minuscule town on US-90 in the West Texas desert between El Paso and Del Rio. One legend has it that the wife of a railroad executive named the town Marfa after a Dostoevsky character in *The Brothers Karamazov*. It was an authentic ranching town, dependent on ranching even after the Texas oil boom. Authenticity was precisely what Stevens sought for the central locale of his movie. He had been concerned about setting down filming stakes anywhere in Texas, saying, "The story's so hot and Texans object so hotly, we'll have to shoot it with a telephoto lens across the border from Oklahoma."

The Ryan Ranch, in the middle of nowhere seventeen miles west of Marfa, was renamed Reata, or some referred to it as Little Reata for the movie. This private property, on which Stevens erected a whale of a ranch-house spread, now crumbled to a skeleton, can still be seen on the right of US-90. It is not uncommon for necks to crane, not wanting to miss the spectral landmark.

Clay Evans was nineteen when the cast and crew settled for six weeks on his family's Ryan Ranch. Taking a backward glance at the $20,000 his family was paid for the use of their ranch and cattle and horses, it truly was "the times they are a-changing." In 2011, Evans's asking price for the ranch he couldn't tend anymore was just under $29 million.

Much has been written about those magical yet turbulent six weeks. I am not sure how much was reported to Ferber, who had removed herself to another forsaken landscape. And as she had told Henry Ginsberg, there would be white-out days where she could not be reached. True, it was an ideal time to stride around Alaska, but I also think she literally wanted to be far from the *Giant* picture for a while. Whenever she had a play produced, she rarely attended the early rehearsals, so perhaps this was her rationale for being physically absent during the gestation time in Marfa. She was kept extremely well informed by letter and cable and responded promptly to both.

After Grace Kelly had turned down the role, Ferber was happy with the eventual choice of Elizabeth Taylor to play Leslie. She was actually chosen not by the director but by Rock Hudson. Stevens, who had been gratified by Taylor's performance in his first Oscar-winning movie, *A Place in the Sun*, had given Hudson several choices of who was to play opposite him, with Taylor being one of them. Stevens wanted Hudson happy, and Hudson, who had formed an affinity for Ferber, wanted her to be pleased with his "new wife." I'm not sure that Ferber was ever told about Stevens's deferral to Hudson in selecting the role of her prized heroine.

Ferber had little to say about the casting of either of them, or about the slightly unorthodox way it was done. Her focus was mainly on the choice of Dean, and how "dazzled" she was by him, as she writes in a letter to her sister, Fannie: "Authentic, upsetting, dazzling. Wot a boy!"

At the start of the shoot, Taylor was less than sunny in the deadly heat of Marfa. The only aspect she liked was her accommodation—a little private house away from most of the cast members, who were staying at the Hotel Paisano in town. Stevens stayed there, and Ginsberg—shuttling between Marfa and LA—stayed there as well.

Taylor was suffering from postpartum depression following the birth of her second child in February. Her marriage to British actor Michael Wilding was also in a depression—as was the state of Texas, which was experiencing the seventh year of a drought. The phrase "the time it never rained" stood for much of Taylor's experience there. When she had signed on for the role, being loaned out by MGM to work with Stevens again had seemed like it would be a warm bath. Meanwhile, her body had changed and she was not comfortable with long hours of exterior work in more-than-one-hundred-degree heat.

There was another curious and disconcerting aspect, which she thought was marvelous in theory but in practice made her somewhat grumpy at times. Stevens determined that the exterior set in Marfa be an open one—meaning that everyone and anyone from the town could watch the day's filming. At first this was a difficult concept for Taylor, but because she was innately a good, gracious sport, and an instinctive actor, she only radiated charm and friendliness.

As soon as Stevens would shout "Cut!" the onlooking fans would rush up to her, wanting to snap photos and have her sign autographs. She went somewhat overboard in the graciousness department when she agreed to star in a short 8mm film shot on the set by one Bill Christopher, owner of the sole department store in Marfa.

Clay Evans recalled the cowpokes gawking at Taylor: "She cussed a lot and we thought she was good lookin' but we didn't pay much attention to her." But Taylor was a huge hit with cast, crew, and townsfolk. There was a caterer named Wally Cech who served her in the lunch line and recalled wondering how someone so ravishing could have such a tame ego. And she was thoughtful as well, keeping a bowl of dimes by her front door to tip anyone who might help her with anything. A dime stretched quite a ways in the fifties.

Taylor and Hudson were an immediate duo, more intimate and affectionate off camera than their roles in the movie dictated. Their bond had solidified during the first week or so in Marfa, prior to James Dean reporting to the set. They both had easygoing temperaments and loved to laugh and to flirt innocently. They were both married unhappily. At that time no one was openly gay.

In 1976, when I interviewed Rock Hudson for my biography of

Ferber, he looked back on that precious time when he had "Elizabeth" all to himself. They would always take lunch together, both having big appetites despite the heat and gossiping behind their hands, laughing uproariously at everything and everyone.

In the evenings after dinner—usually at the Hotel Paisano—the cast would go drinking; they often would go off campus to Ojinaga, Mexico, for many rounds of margaritas. Earl Holliman reminisced, "We all learned to drink tequila real good."

The jolly life became compromised with the entrance of James Dean, or "Jimmy" to pretty much everyone. In most stories of Dean filming *Giant*, he was a tricky combination of irascible and elusive. Although there is much talk and debate about him personally, there is no dispute about his indelible performance as Jett Rink. Hudson mused that "the longer he's gone, the bigger it grows."

Dean altered the dynamic of the shoot as well as zeroing in on the bond between Hudson and Taylor. He refused to be the third wheel, and taking advantage of Taylor's kindness, he began actually repositioning their chairs so that she was angled away from Hudson and toward him, where he would fret about things, gossip, and make her laugh at clownish antics. Hudson became the disgruntled odd man out, forcing him to either drop Taylor or vie for her—which he chose to do. To invoke another big Western movie, theirs was a "duel in the sun."

Although originally *Giant* was known as a Western epic focusing on the travails of a Texas ranch family battling the prospect of oil mega-millions, and Marfa was no more than a water stop for steam trains, the one made the other legendary. The movie has a lasting legacy, having been added to the United States National Film Registry as "culturally, historically or aesthetically significant," and visitors come to Marfa from all over the world to see where *Giant* was filmed. A relatively new piece of art installation by John Cerney is helping to boost the legacy. It

Mercedes McCambridge as Luz Benedict

includes several huge pop art pieces of James Dean and Elizabeth Taylor and set pieces from the movie that line a side of the highway. They are so large they are visible five miles west of Marfa.

Today the Hotel Paisano thrives because of *Giant* and the actors who were guests there for those six weeks. There are the James Dean Room, the Rock Hudson Suite, the Dennis Hopper Suite, the Elizabeth Taylor Suite. Taylor and Hudson both had their own private houses away from the hotel, but lore changed that fact. There is also a restaurant called Jett's Grill, with a full bar and a garden patio with a fountain.

Memories of that shoot stand tall today. There are two vocal ambassadors whose recall is hypnotic. Earl Holliman, now in his nineties, had the best time playing Bob Dace as well as a "high ole extra-curricular time." He knew he was in something special, and having been part of what is now a historic cinematic event, he is a responsible spokesman, setting the scene:

> George was a character and loved actors. He was tough on crew because he demanded perfection, but there was never a cross word to an actor. He just loved them. I went direct to Marfa for my part in things. Dennis Hopper was my roommate at the Paisano Hotel, where we took all of our meals. Supporting actors were always roommates. Luckily, we became quite good friends. Marfa was like a dying town, and then the circus arrived. Stevens invited the whole town to watch the filming. On the first night after a long day of shooting, we all watched the rushes—the whole town of Marfa! I had no idea that all that bigotry was going on. [Until Stevens took over the town and had everyone do-si-do, it had been deeply segregated.]
>
> We were the "second unit"—Fran Bennett [who played the Benedicts' older daughter, Judy], Dennis, Carroll Baker and myself. We were there for almost a whole month before we filmed our scenes. The town really welcomed us and treated us wonderfully. Taylor and Hudson had their own houses, of course, but were in on most every event . . . The presses were constantly flying in from all over the world. Most everyone

was happy to give interviews . . . Carroll Baker, Jane Withers [Vashti] and Fran Bennett had their own house. They built a lasting relationship.

Dennis and Jimmy and I used to go out late at night hunting rabbits, or something. There were complaints that Jimmy was aloof. He and I would walk around town for hours, and I said, "Why are you rude to press and crew?" And he said, "Why am I rude? I don't have to make the crew like me. All I'm concerned about is my part."

Some went back to Hollywood when they were finished, but I was kept there. Fran Bennett was sent back. She was so upset. We were all eating and she left the restaurant crying. We were about to go after her but Jimmy said, "Hold up—don't go after her." Perhaps they'd had a little something.

It seemed that most everyone either had or wanted a little something from or with Jimmy.

Carroll Baker, about to become a full-fledged movie star, was still part of the second unit during *Giant*:

. . . Everything was of an age gone by, with the exception of a movie house, a gas station, and the paved road.

The hotel had perhaps fifteen rooms, so private accommodations had to be found for our enormous cast and crew. But the housing shortage around Marfa was also acute and oh, dear, oh, dear, did that create problems!

In assigning us our living space, the sole consideration— aside from gender, of course—was billing. Elizabeth, who was terrified of living alone, was the only one to get a house all to herself. The dodo in charge even made the grave mistake of attempting to put those diametrically opposed personalities, Rock and Jimmy, under the same roof! With fourth billing, I was made to share a house with (in order of billing) Mercedes McCambridge, Jane Withers, and Fran Bennett. Fortunately, we got along well together, but the stickler was being stuck in Marfa for six weeks or more without the privacy to invite out our boyfriends or husbands to join us.

Our lonely clapboard house was off the San Antonio highway in the middle of nowhere. Only Mercedes was brave enough to sleep in the downstairs den next to the kitchen with its broken, whining refrigerator, and the living room with its naked picture windows and flimsy excuse for a front door. Jane and Fran shared one of the upstairs bedrooms and I had the other smaller bedroom for myself. Also upstairs was the only bathroom—to accommodate four working actresses!

Meanwhile the business of *Giant* was raising Cain in Hollywood. There were many ground-out cigars as the initial budget of $1.5 million swelled to $3.2 million. With Stevens's vast and meticulous shooting schedule, it was predicted that the film might, with luck, come in at $5 million.

Jack Warner was becoming upset. His list of demands was being refuted. He had wanted the running time of the movie under two hours, which was not meant to be—not with Stevens at the helm. Holliman recalls that "George would end up with thousands of feet of footage that never appeared in the final cut." Far from a one-take director, Stevens bulged over budget daily.

Warner's penchant for CinemaScope would not be realized, although it had been favorably discussed when the terms of the contract were being hammered out. Stevens later was known to have said that it was the perfect process if you were a boa constrictor. Eventually everyone settled on what Stevens wanted, which was a ratio of 1.66 to 1. This made the characters seem taller, which was not all bad for a movie about Texans.

Stevens, who was thoughtful, fair, and tough on occasion, made amends to Warner in certain ways. For instance, in order to cut the budget, he hired locals as extras, guards, and custodians. He also induced Texas millionaires to be extras in the party and banquet scenes.

While Stevens was filming in Marfa, the "heavies" were out of the way. Jack Warner was vacationing in France, and Ferber was mostly out of reach in the tundra. An ally, twenty-three-year-old George Stevens Jr., was at his father's elbow as a temporary assistant director. This Marfa period was considered "peacetime" and he enjoyed it thoroughly. "That's kind of a favorite picture," he said. "I worked with my dad on the script and then went in the Air Force for two years and came back and worked with him on the editing. That was the pace he was moving at."

Stevens Jr. felt that the picture was certainly the most socially significant his father had made, just as it was, in its way, technically advanced in its storytelling. For instance, he noted the subtly shifting light between Rock Hudson and Elizabeth Taylor that subconsciously shifted the audience's feelings toward Bick and Leslie's marriage: Taylor's shots are well lit while Hudson's are in shadow. Other times, Stevens Jr. noted, his father's technique was more blatant, as when he cut from an extremely wide shot of a horse in the distance to a tight close-up of a spur digging into the horse's side until it bucks off its rider, Mercedes McCambridge's Luz. "He used to say he made his films in the editing room," Stevens Jr. recalled. "He'd shoot a lot of film and then he'd look for the best way to tell the story."

According to Ivan Moffat, the shooting script was altered daily—at times a scene was still being rewritten at dawn of the day it would be shot. Carroll Baker writes about how chaotic and stressful the situation could get:

> It is traditional for film companies to issue each afternoon a call sheet which lists the scenes to be filmed the following day, and the equipment and actors required for those proposed scenes. It is also expedient, because the cost of moving a crane to location, for example, runs to thousands of dollars. George Stevens, however, refused to be bound by this tradition and insisted upon everything from props to horses to cranes being ready and waiting at all times, with each and every actor standing by in full makeup and costume—including the stars. Even though Elizabeth and Rock had by far the largest roles, not even their parts demanded that they be on the set continuously; but they too were made to follow this strenuous and inconsiderate schedule.

Offsetting the young, slightly green, but very opinionated actors were the veterans. Mercedes McCambridge led the pack of the tried-and-true. Her looks and voice were pure flint, so right for the reigning but about-to-be-deposed queen of Reata. She usually played characters of strength and intensity, to which she applied her own "method":

> . . . It's a cookbook and you have the recipe . . . All you do is follow the ingredients to make the soufflé that the playwright or the author has put into the script for the character. And if you have a pretty good mixture, all you have to do is put it into the oven and know when to take it out . . . You have to identify with the soul of the character or you shouldn't play it. I don't believe you should play anything until you realize that you are the defense attorney for that character.

McCambridge and Ferber already had shared a devoted support of Adlai Stevenson during his 1952 run for president and would work arduously for him again in his 1956 campaign. They were both women of conviction and character, differing more in their personal habits than in their beliefs. Ferber was meticulous, fastidious, somewhat girlish in her choice of colors, shapes, and fabrics, and with no messy habits. McCambridge was far more bohemian, favoring drapes and shawls and long, wide skirts and trousers. She was a drinker, a smoker, and a turbulent presence. Their styles may have been opposites, but their work ethic and humane approach to life were shared.

Ferber had a special fondness for character actors—evidenced by the fact that she and George S. Kaufman wrote for them with such depth, humor, and compassion. Also, Ferber would have done character work had she realized her early dream of being on the stage: her forte would have been the sister or the aunt. So, she felt warm toward Chill Wills and McCambridge—but not so much toward Jane Withers, who, although she was a native Georgian, reportedly had a script condition that Texans not be framed as harshly as they were in Ferber's novel.

Wills, as Uncle Bawley, Bick's bachelor uncle, gave no one trouble, was a favorite of everyone's, and was given some very choice lines, such as this one referring to Jett Rink's striking oil: "Bick, you shoulda shot that fella a long time ago. Now he's too rich to kill." A born Texan, a big, brawny six-footer with a mustache and a thunderlike drawl, he had worked the movie gamut from musical comedies to plain comedies to Westerns to dramas, including such A-pictures as *Meet Me in St. Louis*, *The Harvey Girls*, and *The Yearling*. In *Giant*, his character—with

Carroll Baker as Luz Benedict II and James Dean
as Jett Rink, oil baron

a shoulder for everybody in the Benedict family—is soulful and somewhat secretive. Television and film critic Bobby Rivers has an unusual
take on Wills's interpretation of Uncle Bawley:

> I think if Uncle Bawley did fall in love, it would be a same-sex
> attraction and affection. It's just not talked about there in Texas
> at that time. Not that a big, burly, bourbon-drinking cowhand
> who plays Debussy's Clair de Lune on an organ automatically
> means he's heterosexually challenged, but it's an inspired detail.
> Early in the film, we see that he has a foot in the groom's life
> and a foot in the bride's life. Both love him and he loves them.
> He's got to be "one o' the guys" with Bick and his chauvinist
> macho posse when they're sitting around talking "men's stuff."
> But he also respects and understands the outspoken Leslie, a

woman with a fine mind of her own . . . Could Bawley have once been secretly in love with Jett . . . the way Jett was in love with Leslie? Chill Wills gives an expert dimension to the role. It's not a large part but it's constant throughout this epic American tale. Chill Wills' understated performance and his big sweet bear of a character are worth another look.

Another "sport" among the character-actor crew was Jane Withers, who was everyone's big sis in the early days of filming in Marfa. She had been a child star during the Great Depression, when kiddies on the screen were known as the "blue plate special." In *Giant*, she plays Vashti Snythe, ex–lady friend but continuing neighbor of Bick's, and for most of the film one of Leslie's champions. In a latter-day interview, reflecting on the Marfa days, Withers said more than once, "I love Marfa!" Her enthusiasm and recall don't seem to have diminished with time: "It was such a terrific cast of sweet people. I made good friends and there's nothing better in the world than to have good friends."

Withers held frequent parties while in Marfa, with food, Monopoly, and bridge, and most everybody from the cast and crew would cram into the house she shared with Baker, Bennett, and McCambridge. Rock Hudson, another friend to all, came by often. Taylor preferred to go to a country club way outside of town. She once had come over for Withers's hospitality, thought it was a great deal of fun, and never went again. Dean seemed drawn to Withers's motherly spirit. One night, when most of the cast and crew had left, she went into her bedroom to find him lying on her bed with his hat covering his face. He hadn't come through the front door because he wanted to see only her. He had considered himself homeless for a while as his small period of sharing a house with Rock Hudson had ended with hostility on both sides. He later moved into the Hotel Paisano—hence the James Dean Room and Jett's Grill.

There were versions about what happened between the two stars when they were assigned to be housemates. One was Hudson's—that there was antipathy from the start because of Dean's horning in on Taylor's time with him, always acting the charming brat. According to Hudson, their flare-up was over what Hudson termed the "girl." The other concerned Hudson's attraction to Dean, who had some sexual ambivalence anyway. The situation offered some heat; at the time—a term for it was "forbidden fruit." Dean shrunk from it, bolting away so fast that he left some toiletries behind.

Dean was impossible. One couldn't get close to him or turn away from him. He seemed to have been a legend wherever he went, and at twenty-four years old, in the last year of his life, he was indelible. Nobody, it appeared, could turn down being fascinated by him. Ferber was riveted: "Occasionally—rarely—one encounters a dazzling human being who is obviously marked for destruction. Such a one was this young Jimmy Dean. Only two or three times have I encountered an example of the brilliant and ill-fated."

When she wrote to my parents from Alaska, she would always mention him, wondering how he was getting along and how much trouble he had already caused. She had told my mother early on, when he was first cast, that she had a premonition, based on another young life she had known and cared about decades earlier:

> The fundamental lack, possibly, is the complete absence of the sense of caution. By this I do not mean fear, but the quality that prevents them from observing ordinary precaution; the

Dean as Jett Rink, having just struck oil

common sense, really, of everyday physical behavior. William Allen White's brilliant young daughter, Mary White, was one such. Bill White used to say that if, when a child of twelve or thirteen, she had managed to climb up to the roof of a shed or barn on their place in Emporia, Kansas she would not only walk about on the roof but seemingly with deliberation walk right off it into space. When she drove a car downhill she landed it in the ditch with the car on top of her. She died at sixteen after having been struck on the head by an overhanging tree-branch as she rode her horse on the town parkway. At a pell-mell gallop she had stood up in the saddle, her head turned over her shoulder, to wave to a friend passing by. The over-hanging branch struck full force.

"Jimmy" lore rose up and out of Marfa during the memorable filming. Everyone seemed to have a story and a perspective. Elizabeth Taylor, surprisingly private for all the hoopla, and loyal, divulged a key to Dean that remained locked until after her death. She said: "When Jimmy was 11 and his mother passed away, he began to be molested by his minister. I think that haunted him for the rest of his life. In fact, I know it did. We talked about it a lot. During *Giant* we'd stay up nights and talk and talk, and that was one of the things he confessed to me."

Dean had an acting style that was organic. He devised it using portions of his own life, his experiences, dreams, and wishes. He was able to excavate the deepest of internal material and funnel it into whatever part he was playing. It was startling because it was so direct and visceral. He had studied the craft of acting, but by importing his own quirky, mournful material, he branded it. This was his own version of the Method, which he had elaborated upon before the time in the mid-forties when he studied with Stella Adler, the prestigious teacher who espoused the Stanislavski Method.

The year before the filming of *Giant* began, Dean shot a television drama called *The Dark, Dark Hours*, which starred future US president Ronald Reagan. The irascible spontaneity of Dean did not mesh with Reagan's straightforward approach to acting. Dean, who had done live television previously, had enjoyed the liberty of ad-libbing. Reagan was strictly by-the-script—and anti–James Dean.

. . .

As the weeks went by in Marfa, Dean's errant behavior seemed almost involuntary. Carroll Baker, close to him at times and then spurned at others, recalled the effect of the grueling schedule on him:

> Elizabeth and Rock took this seemingly senseless routine in their stride, but after three days of doing nothing Jimmy blew his stack and refused to report [to the set] for a fourth. Stevens claimed that Jimmy's behavior cost the company a day of lost production. As no one knew what George intended to film, this claim could have been either genuine or simply meant to teach Jimmy a lesson . . . George was a very intelligent man, and he must have realized that Jimmy's behavior was prompted by insecurity and jealousy. But he refused to cater to Jimmy and demanded of him that he act like a grown-up and a professional . . . The severe scolding George gave Jimmy came on the fifth day of filming, before work began, and took place in front of the entire cast and crew. It was a lesson to all of us . . . Jimmy was prompt from then on, and George's honesty and just punishment must have worked: Jimmy's brilliant performance is now recorded movie history.

A muffled fact is that Dean was not yet a star when *Giant* was filming. He had only come before the public in one film, *East of Eden*, as *Rebel Without a Cause* had yet to be released and was slated for October of 1955. So that June in Marfa revealed more of a troubled and vexing young actor than a major box-office property. One can only surmise what he might have been like on a set five years from then. However, there was always more Jimmy and Jett lore emanating from that dot of a Texas town.

There was intrigue during the day, in the evening, and after hours under the wide, burning Marfa skies. The Elizabeth-Rock-Jimmy triangle became a shifting quartet about two weeks into the shoot. Carroll Baker was a busy ingénue:

> At first . . . it was Jimmy and I as a couple "versus" Elizabeth and Rock; but when Jimmy began stealing scenes, that

changed. (Dean could steal focus by simply running his fingers around the brim of his hat while another actor was talking.) Elizabeth and Rock wanted revenge, so they arranged to meet me secretly after work and enlist my friendship and support. The appointment was set—it was so exciting and clandestine! I hurriedly changed out of my costume and slipped out of the hotel, by the back stairs so that Jimmy wouldn't see me. I went around to the rear of the building where Elizabeth's chauffeur was waiting for me beside her limousine, all the time thinking of myself as Mata Hari! He drove me to Elizabeth's house, where Rock was already waiting with a pitcher of martinis and a glorious big welcome. Elizabeth called out for us to bring the drinks and join her in her dressing room while she did her face. I was so thrilled to be in intimate contact with Elizabeth, so stunned by her extraordinary beauty without makeup, so star-struck, so honored to be taken into Elizabeth Taylor's confidence, that had she asked me to poison Jimmy, I probably would have, willingly.

And then, as Baker tells it, the scene with the three began to resemble a Shakespearean coven:

Suddenly those violet eyes flashed and that perfectly shaped mouth puckered in anger. "Dean is an outrageous scene-stealer."
     "Yes," Rock added, "and we can't handle him, but you can."
     "Yes," Elizabeth hissed . . . "Rock and I aren't good enough to get back at him, but you're from the Actors Studio, and you're as good as he is."
     "That's right," Rock interrupted. "He doesn't get away with anything in your scenes. He can't steal scenes from you."
     "So we want you to join us—be on our side, and get even with him for us."

At this point, according to Baker, there was an unexpected plot twist—this time more commedia dell'arte than classical. Just when Baker had settled into being part of a chaste but merry threesome, Jimmy "stole Elizabeth away from us . . ." Literally, Taylor went off with Dean every evening. This "infidelity" was corroborated by Hudson, who said that Dean was quite a "sob sister" where Taylor was concerned. He poured out his soul to her and she, being extremely sympathetic, clucked over him, dispensing soothing advice. So, Baker and Hudson were left deprived of the divine Elizabeth.

The plot thickened. One day during a photo shoot, Dean playfully upended Taylor so that her skirt fell over her head, exposing her thighs, panties, etc. The shutter clicked away, leaving her mortified. Then, at lunch, which the whole cast and crew had together, Baker said to George Stevens, "Gee, George, do you think you could get the negatives of that photo the photographer took this morning and destroy it—the one where Jimmy held Elizabeth upside down?" And Stevens said, addressing Taylor, "It certainly was undignified, Liz. Why do you allow Jimmy to do things like that?"

Baker had her victory. Taylor stopped speaking to Dean for a while. It is a wonder that Stevens tolerated these shenanigans for as long as he did.

The tight little island in Marfa got tighter. The combination of the extreme heat, the star wattage, the mercurial, demanding, and gifted director, and the rigorous work schedule under the constant gaze of the entire community made for an indelible experience that is still ruminated over today.

Ferber commented on Dean's behavior even though she never set foot in Marfa. She had asked for and got cable reports that awaited her at each hotel stop. And it seemed like everyone was buzzing with Jimmy Dean anecdotes at all times. In her account of these reports, her tone is part doting, part scolding:

> During the shooting of the picture, and particularly when on location in open ranch country, this behavior was often intolerable; his performance always brilliant. There were times when he would absent himself for days, no one knew where. This is the unforgivable crime in the process of filming a picture. It means one of two things; work must cease if the sequence immediately requires the presence of the absent actor, thus creating a really gigantic financial loss to the company; or the filming may proceed, if possible, by the process known as "shooting around him"; that is, shooting scenes in which he is not immediately involved, while waiting for the missing actor's return.

This lad performed like a gifted angel and behaved like a juvenile delinquent. Everybody loved him including the Mexican extras on the set and George Stevens, the harassed and patient director, Elizabeth Taylor and Rock Hudson, the leading players.

In their last scene together, in the wine cellar of the Conquistador Hotel, Bick has challenged the drunken Jett to a fight but reconsiders. "You aint even worth hitting!" he says. "Jett, you want to know something true? You're all through." Hudson enjoyed saying these lines; he felt they served both the character and the actor. How could he have known that they were so prophetic? But in one way Dean was hardly "all through": he would live large on celluloid to this day.

The two actors were fascinated with each other, circling like hombres in an old-time Western. A man named Robert Hinkle—"Texas Bob"—recalls some of what went on between them in Marfa. A former rodeo cowboy and movie actor hopeful Hinkle auditioned for Stevens. When he got a call from the director, his sky-high hopes deduced it was for the role of Jett Rink. No, he was told, the role had already been cast. Stevens wanted to hire him as a dialect coach for the leads and other actors to learn to "talk Texan." An enthusiastic Hinkle was added to the payroll. He recalls his initial Dean encounter in the early days while the cast was still in LA:

> He said, "You Bob Hinkle? I seen you over at the studio restaurant a couple of times." Well, I'd seen him, but I never had met him. He was kind of a loner, quiet. He ate by himself. He said, "I'd like to work with you in playing Jett Rink. I'd like you to help me create that character . . . I'd like for you to make a Texan out of me where I can be a Texan twenty-four hours a day." And that is what we really tried to do. Two or three times while we were down in Texas I had people ask me, "What part of Texas is he from?" and I thought that was a compliment, because he talked like a Texan down there, he wore Levi boots and a hat, and rolled his own cigarettes just like them old timers did and things like that . . . First night I met him he offered to pay me out of his own pocket but I said that's not necessary.

I asked him when he wanted to start. He told me, "I'd like to start today." So we went to dinner that night at Barney's Beanery over on La Cienega . . .

Giant was really something. I was on the picture seven or eight months. It was a wonderful experience. Everybody bonded, except maybe Rock and Jimmy were a bit jealous of each other. Jimmy was jealous of Rock because Rock had all the good dialogue . . . and was getting all the attention from the media. They never had words, but you could feel the jealousy. It would come out when Rock would say, "How is Jimmy to work with?" or Dean would say, "How do you like working with old Rock? You know, has he ever come on to you?" We all knew about Rock, but on the set he was as straight as could be. There never was an inkling. He was a very nice guy, very easy going, always prepared.

Ferber had some weeks to think about her next project, although geographically she was already in it. She seemed to be taking stock of past proclivities in her work—especially in her character depictions, which, of course, included Leslie Benedict and how she, Ferber, still felt forced to defend her to George Stevens.

The major women in all of my novels, plays and short stories written in these past fifty years and more have been delineated as possessed of strength, ingenuity, perception, initiative. This is because I think that women in general—and certainly the American female of the United States—is stronger in character, more ingenious, more perceptive and more power-possessing (potentially) than the American male.

How can it be denied that the vast majority of women in the United States have failed to claim their legal rights; to use their inherent powers; and to fulfill in any degree at all their great potentialities?

. . . I mean that women are inherently tougher than men; they know this; and potentially they could rule the world if they wanted to. They may even have to, eventually . . . The feminine in the man is the sugar in the whiskey. The masculine in the woman is the yeast in the bread. Without these ingredients the result is flat, without tang or flavor.

During my preliminary visits to Alaska I met and talked with many women . . . some of these were full-time workers, some part-time. I do not recall having met any woman who did not have some sort of job or constructive working interest outside her own daily home interests and responsibilities.

These Alaska women seemed to me to be alert, healthy, outgoing, and certainly as happy as any of the more idle women I had encountered elsewhere . . .

If Ferber had had the time and focus for a different vein of writing, these thoughts could have fueled a sociological study. She had so many opinions about so much, and mostly in terms of women. I think she fought so hard for the correct depiction of Leslie in the screenplay

Edna Ferber learns a rope trick from James Dean
on the set.

because, in a sense, she felt threatened by the overwhelmingly male interpretation. It had been four against one—five counting Jack Warner. And indeed, when it came time to shoot the final scene between Leslie and Bick, reflecting on their lives as their baby grandchildren study them from their playpen, one Mexican American and one Caucasian, Leslie says, "Well, after one hundred years the Benedict family is a real big success." How Ferber had fought against that "big"! She wrote:

> Fighting as a sport, or as a means of attack or defense is supposed to be a manly performance. It is actually merely male . . . Most adults have seen hysterical women, boisterous women drunken women, angry resentful unreasonable women. One can go through a lifetime without ever seeing a fighting woman . . . Innately they hate fighting and are opposed to war. In this characteristic they are more civilized than men.
>
> Perhaps it can be argued that a woman, confronted with what would be, for a man, a fighting situation, resorts instead to tears. If true, it still can be said that tears do not result in broken bones or broken countries.

Toward the end of her trip, upon arriving in Fairbanks, a June 28, 1955, letter from Henry Ginsberg was waiting for her. She understood "feel good" letters and the underlying truth of them. All it took was one word such as "unfortunately":

> My dear Edna—
>
> Please excuse my neglect. Have been spending a good deal of time at Marfa, Texas. The film shot thus far is indeed outstanding. Unfortunately however, we have been losing time and at this writing we are about eight days behind schedule, due to various circumstances. The company will return from Texas next week and will resume shooting at the studio.
>
> Our reception by the newspapers in Texas was really wonderful. A great deal of space was devoted to our activities at Marfa throughout the State, and in Marfa alone, which is a very small community, many hundreds of paperback editions

of *Giant* were sold, and I suppose this was repeated many times over in other parts of the State.

I hope you will be able to arrange your schedule so as to visit with us on your return to the East. This would permit you to see much of the film shot to date.

Ginsberg was in on everything, so much so that it would land him in the hospital for an undisclosed reason at the end of the summer. Until then, he was keeping the plates twirling, all the while knowing exactly what to convey to Ferber and when. He sent her a positive schedule of the final editing and scoring, which were planned for late June through August. Dimitri Tiomkin would have seven weeks, until August 17, to write and record the score. By August they would have what was called a "first answer print" and a final preview. During the week of August 27, they would have "Final cutting changes, if necessary. Re-dubbing, if necessary, print corrections, etc." And by August 31: "Completion."

It all sounded rosy, but it wasn't. Complications were sprouting. A major one was with Elizabeth Taylor, who was not well and had to prove it. This interoffice communication was sent out in mid-July:

It was reported . . . by Mr. Stevens that we might have to release Miss Taylor for 2 days rest (Sat. and Sun.). I questioned her husband, Michael Wilding, re. this and he told me that this came from her doctor . . . her doctor said that he would give no answer until he came into the studio and examined her. Following this examination he told me that she had previously, while in Marfa, been treated for an infection of the throat—which she still has. He also stated that this infection had gone to her bladder, causing acute pain, and that she was very tired—and that her resistance was very low. He further stated that she must have medication and go to bed for 48 hours. At the end of this time he said that he would let me know if she would need an additional 24 hours to correct her condition.

He also said that if we did not give her these 2 or 3 days rest there was a good possibility that we might lose her in the picture for 2 or 3 weeks later on . . .

Hudson, Ferber, and Taylor on the Warner
Bros. set

In the midst of this, Ferber arrived in Los Angeles on July 26 and checked into her suite at the Bel-Air Hotel, eager to witness a nearly completed movie.

This "ideal" of the completed movie was grounded by a serious situation, as stated in this July 27 memo from Roy Obringer, head of the legal department at Warner Bros., to Stevens and Ginsberg:

> As you know, the final approved budget for *Giant* was set at $2,549,000. The daily production report indicates that at present time you are close to three weeks behind schedule.
>
> I just talked to Mr. J. L. Warner and he asked me to remind you of the necessity of making up this lost time, as he states the company does not want to spend more than the budget price to bring in the picture. Also, he desires that I again remind you that overages beyond the guaranteed periods of the two stars in your picture and possibly on other members

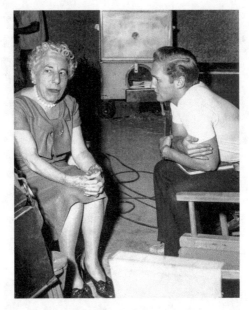

Ferber and Dennis Hopper on the Warner
Bros. set

of the cast would be a very serious problem and this he does
not want to happen.

In early August came more rain from Taylor's doctor. It now
seemed she had an infection under her left leg, was hospital-bound,
and would be unable to resume filming until August 5 at the earliest. It
was also reported that because of a first-unit schedule change they had
lost another whole day of filming.

—————

Backtracking on "the best laid plans": Ferber had planned to get home
from Alaska toward the end of June. By then the filming in Marfa
would be over, so she would head out to Los Angeles and visit the set
a bit. She would stay at her hotel of choice, the Bel-Air, and looked
forward to being greeted effusively.

I remember her return from Alaska, the Inuit doll she brought me along with a small woodcut to hang in my room. It was an Ahgupuk, she told me, a leading Alaskan artist whom she had met. I remember her vigor as she described a working trip where she loaded up on research. I remember the name Ernest Gruening (not yet Senator), who had become a friend and would steer Alaska toward American statehood. I remember how youthful she seemed in her anticipation of this major movie that was really all because of her.

She had been kept up to date on Marfa doings, but it is curious that she avoided being on-site for at least one visit. Perhaps she felt that her presence would be disruptive or distracting in some way. It is unlikely that she sensed a loss of bearings in the forsaken little town. As a diehard reporter, she knew how to cope with any and all conditions. True, she was already invested in her next novel, but as a producing partner of *Giant*, she obviously had ground to stand on. Why didn't she go? Could she have felt that the proximity of Stevens would have been uncomfortable? Could she have anticipated feeling old in the youthful company of Taylor, Hudson, and especially Dean, and that a visit to a

Ferber and Dean on the Warner Bros. set

studio set had a more protective, dignified sense about it? There is no one to ask anymore.

The Marfa filming was one of a kind and ultimately draining for those involved, as are all high-wire performances. Once safely on the ground, it proved worth the effort for having stayed up so long and achieving the desired results. The citizens of Marfa relive that time to this day, some identifying it as their crowning event—not unlike a personal best. It bestowed on Marfa an unexpectedly large identity.

The filming was also a racial marker for the town. In certain ways it emancipated the Marfans from a lockdown of segregation. The story in the movie showed a rising consciousness leading to an interracial marriage; it showed a woman quietly steering her family toward a new day; it showed a husband able to finally accept change; it showed a proper funeral for a Mexican American war hero; and in the last moment of screen time it showed a Mexican American baby and a Caucasian baby side by side looking at their shared world. Alongside them were a white lamb and a brown lamb. What could be more peaceful than lambs?

Every evening Stevens provided the best public relations possible by screening the daily rushes for the whole town in Marfa's only movie

Edna with "Jimmy," made up as the
middle-aged tycoon Jett

theater. Everyone was in on the movie's progress; the development of the performances; the deepening of the impact. The movie belonged to Marfa first, and then to the world.

Although the director is often thought responsible for delivering a movie—hit or otherwise—that is a fallacy. They call movies "the director's medium," and indeed the overall look of the film is dictated by the director. Whether his vision will be realized is always the lurking question. One of the ways in which it can be is in the choice of an editor. Stevens chose William Hornbeck, whom Frank Capra referred to as "the greatest film editor in the history of motion pictures." Hornbeck was there in Marfa to absorb the job requirements prior to when he was literally needed. "If you had rules for editing, you could put it in a book and anyone could become an editor," he said. He had rules of his own: he served the story and the intent of the director, employed craftsmanship, instilled humanism.

Bill Hornbeck had worked with Stevens editing *Shane* and *A Place in the Sun*. He used rapid cutting in *Shane*, which emphasized the boy's point of view, and in *A Place in the Sun* he used tight close-ups and slow dissolves, lingering on Elizabeth Taylor's and Montgomery Clift's love-drunk faces.

Hornbeck learned what *Giant* needed through patience. Because Stevens would often bring the script pages to the set the morning of the shoot, there didn't seem to be an overall look for some time. There were scenes that extended out, talky and slow, and there were startling, active interludes. Hornbeck devised a theory for Stevens's vision where he was able to employ three levels: sweeping, heart-pumping panoramic shots of the dusty Texas prairie and rugged plains; the personal and emotional impact of the fundamental story; and the message Stevens intended to impart.

Hornbeck had heard and read a lot about *Giant* and its original creator. He had yet to meet Ferber. He said it was "like having been exposed to the in-laws prior to meeting the girl." When I interviewed him, he never mentioned that he had read the novel, and I never thought to ask.

Ferber on the Set

Everyone was waiting for Ferber to visit the set once they got back to Los Angeles, and she had seemed eager to be there. However, in a letter to Joe Linz she wrote, "Tomorrow I'm leaving for trouble and Hollywood. They want me to see some of the *Giant* rushes, which are, I'm told, very good." Perhaps her ambivalence was why she was stricken with the Face, brought about by the dreaded trigeminal neuralgia. It was bad enough for several trips to Dr. Alvin Steiner, her longtime physician, who then sent her to various specialists. We had to hold off making dates with her while she was being treated. My mother would say "Not yet" when I asked to call. Usually, she had to prod me to reach out to relatives with a polite "Thank you" and "How are you?" It was different with Aunt Edna, who always had some penetrating and wondrous question for me.

This time the Face was severe enough to have hushed talk of an extreme measure for a condition with no known cure. A nerve along the side of the face could be severed. No more pain, but a frozen side of the face. This was not an option for Ferber. She would endure.

The proof is in the photos of Ferber's joy at being in L.A. for the wrapping up of the filming. All had been smoothed over with Elizabeth Taylor in terms of her health, and her contract was extended for an extra month. Ferber was fond of her and was able to see how deft she was in those last scenes of the movie. This was Leslie, her champion, and she was gratified.

Ferber and Taylor might have had Leslie as their bond during *Giant*, but they had good personal reviews of each other beforehand through Noël Coward, among other English and Anglophile friends. Michael Wilding, Taylor's British husband, had friends on both sides of the pond, who also socialized with Ferber. So, the two women had met, admiringly, at various exclusive gatherings. Taylor was well-read and knew a Magnolia (*Show Boat*) from a Selina (*So Big*).

Ferber was driven daily to the Warner Bros. set from the Hotel Bel-Air and then back again when the filming wrapped to dress for dinner either with friends or occasionally alone in the hotel dining room. Very occasionally she dined with James Dean alone, but it was usually in a trio with Mercedes McCambridge. Dean liked Mexican food; McCambridge didn't seem to have a preference; Ferber liked La Scala. They went to La Scala. A few dinners were with Hudson and his fiancée, Phyllis Gates. There is no indication that she took any meals with George Stevens during those final days of the shoot. Her gaze, maternal though it might have been, seemed reserved only for Dean.

Edna Ferber and George Stevens, Warner Bros. set

There were certain photos taken of Dean by Roy Schatt in late 1954 known as "The Torn Sweater Series." These had a Greenwich Village Sunday-morning-hair look that when pointed out to Ferber made her sniff. She much preferred the Dean-the-intellect photos taken of him wearing ordinary black-framed grade-school glasses. These were taken later by Dennis Stock and yet revealed a younger, boyish, touch-of-the-nerd Dean. By the time Dean was living in Manhattan, his black-framed glasses were a bit more urbane. Dean's last photographer was Sanford Roth, who captured him on the set of *Giant* and off. Roth's photos show Dean goofing around. In some he plays with a lariat, tying it in a knotted masklike structure, or putting it as a noose around his head. In some he twirls it, wearing a vest over a bare chest, a Stetson perched back on his head. In a few, he is trussing up Elizabeth Taylor, who is laughing on the ground. Ferber, who saw all these phases of Dean, seemed to look beyond them to a day of maturation, when he would be integrated. However, never one for blind faith, she knew better.

Something else occurred on and around the set at the end of July or early August. A mutual attraction sprung up between Ferber and James Dean. They seemed to come from equidistant positions to meet in the middle. Dean certainly had enough mother figures with McCambridge and Withers; this was of another color. It was based on fun. Not allowed to drive his car around the Warner Bros. lot, he would ride a motorcycle instead. And he would take Ferber for spins. Here was a septuagenarian, with freshly done Elizabeth Arden hair, a pretty polished-cotton dress, Ferragamo shoes, and a large pocketbook, speeding around the lot holding on to the waist of twenty-four-year-old Jimmy Dean.

He taught her how to twirl a lasso. They laughed and talked. One can see the look on her face when they are together in photos. She was happy. It seemed he could easily play the snake charmer with others, but Ferber could be hardened to and wary of easy charm. However temporarily blinded by him she might have been, though, whatever he offered her did not seem ersatz.

Ferber wrote around her feelings in trying to capture his wildness:

There was a pattern that was characteristic of the James Dean behavior. Aware of this, and knowing, too, of his passion for driving racing cars, the motion picture company had included

Dean as the older Jett Rink

in the Dean contract a clause to the effect that he was not to own or drive a racing car or to enter any automobile race of any description until the conclusion of the filming of *Giant*. Cast against type by the astute director, George Stevens, Dean was playing the part of the ruthless unpredictable young ranch hand Jett Rink, who became the even more ruthless—and the doomed—wildcatter oil millionaire. He was, perhaps, miscast; yet enthralling.

Ferber had never been average in any way but this one; she was drawn toward the Dean magnet just like everyone else. Mercedes McCambridge was similar to Ferber in outline: strong-featured, forthright, accomplished—and also a Deanite. He took McCambridge into his confidence during their time in Marfa—especially when Taylor had other concerns—and they openly adored each other. If this caused a prick of envy in Ferber, she would never have admitted it—quite the contrary: "Mercedes McCambridge talented character actress, was playing the difficult part of Luz Benedict. In her kindness and warm-heartedness she tried to be of help to this gifted and insecure young fellow-actor. He frequently turned to her for advice as one would to an older sister or a mother. She did not fail him. Usually he rejected any other counsel."

When Katharine Hepburn called herself and Ferber "unicorn women," I assumed the term meant that they were unique. It sounded original and right on target. They both had singular heads on their shoulders.

For much of my life people have been inquiring about my great aunt's proclivities. Now, in the time of variety-pack sexuality, I am finally grasping what a "unicorn woman" is all about. It is a woman who grazes with couples. I think back. While doing my research for the biography of Ferber, I came across a multitude of correspondence with well-known couples: Alfred Lunt and Lynn Fontanne (however devoted they were to each other, both allegedly preferred their own gender); Moss (with longtime homosexual leanings) and Kitty Carlisle Hart; Katharine Cornell (allegedly bisexual) and Guthrie McClintic; the Louis Bromfields and the William Allen Whites—Ferber had deep friendships with both men. Spending long weekends and protracted visits in one another's country homes was the custom. Lavish parties were planned day and night.

Their correspondence was full of fun and gossip. In reading deeply, I cannot say I ever saw any innuendo. This crowd was as sophisticated as one can get, however, and knew that whatever is put in print stays in print. The only allusion, extremely vague, to anything carnal came from Blanche Knopf in her letter praising Ferber for the novel *Giant*. And then there was the George Stevens alleged incident at the Farmers Market in Los Angeles.

When I think of Hepburn's statement now, the curtain parts on Ferber, Dean, and McCambridge in Los Angeles during those final weeks filming *Giant*. They spent a good deal of time together on the set and off. Ferber and Dean became close, but McCambridge was never far. Perhaps there was a liaison. McCambridge was married, but did say "I love you" in a letter to Ferber; and Dean was so young and arbitrary, it seemed he would try anything. The curtain closes. Maybe this was part of the "everything" Ferber had promised to tell my mother some-day. I will never know if there was any lover for Ferber other than fame.

In her words: "Life can't ever really defeat a writer who is in love with writing, for life itself is a writer's lover until death—fascinating, cruel, lavish, warm, cold, treacherous, constant."

My family talked about Dean. My mother wondered at the sparkle when Ferber mentioned him. Even when she was recovering from the bad attack of the Face, she would worry about Jimmy and his errant ways. "Stranger things . . ." my mother said, leaving off finishing the sentence. My mother's sister, Mina, agreed that there was something ineffable in the air. My father, a confirmed realist, thought it was a fabrication, and that Ferber had her feet too solidly planted for anything remotely transporting. Then my mother reminded him of the carpet.

Every family has its ghosts, and Ferber and her mother, Julia, had theirs. They were at Treasure Hill one summer. It was after dinner and they were enjoying a card game and a glass of port when Julia jumped and port splashed. "Edna, look at the rug!" she had commanded. As they both stared, the carpet lifted, floated, and rearranged itself in a different place. As we all know, ghosts are not consistent, so the next night and for many after the rug stayed put. But it did happen again and again at various intervals. "Edna was matter-of-fact about the flying carpet," my grandmother had told me. "She and Mother definitely had company."

While Ferber was on the West Coast, she decided to go up to San Francisco prior to visiting the production in Los Angeles, staying at her favorite hotel there, the Mark Hopkins. She was used to traveling alone. And since she knew no one there—no friends, no relatives, no business associates—she treated herself to a lovely solo summer sojourn.

Harriet Pilpel addressed a letter to her there. She began with the niceties of weather talk, graduating into business news—Lerner and Loewe were interested in working on a musical version of *Saratoga Trunk*—and then on to *Giant* business. There had been a request for an extension because the production schedule was so far in arrears. This was soon to blow up very large at Warner Bros., but Harriet was keeping it contained: "We haven't heard from Henry [Ginsberg] in answer to our letter about the requested *Giant* extension and the next move is up to him. It is disturbing to learn that 'George is still mooning around' though I am not surprised and I still think that it will be a superb picture."

If the "mooning around" reference was originally reported by Ferber to Pilpel, it is provocative. Usually, we think of mooning as being associated with cow-eyed affection. From all reports Stevens was in an energetic fever while directing *Giant*, demanding excellence in every inch of it. There was much disturbance happening all around him—with Dean's indulgent, prankish behavior, Taylor's vapors, budget ballooning, and schedule extensions. The word "still" is also curious, implying that the mooning happened earlier. It might have been possible that Stevens didn't think he was getting the picture he wanted and was often listless, mistaken for mooning. Or, a stretch, would be that he did have a real feeling for Ferber, who had turned her attentions to Dean.

When she was not at Warner Bros., she walked a good deal, which was considered an oddity in LA. She also shopped at I. Magnin and some of the other Beverly Hills emporiums. Luckily there was an Elizabeth Arden, where she had her hair done more frequently than usual. She wrote to her friend the actress Margalo Gillmore that she had "smog locks."

A ruckus was going on behind the scenes while Ferber visited the set daily, behaving in a lighthearted fashion, mostly chatting and laughing with Dean and McCambridge. The dailies were going well, but there was still no continuous footage, per Stevens's method of waiting until the picture was entirely shot and then assembling, cutting, and pasting. On August 11, Jack Warner sent a cable to Steve Trilling, a Hollywood executive and Warner's longtime second-in-command: "Stevens now has two hours forty minutes / Have you explained to him that first cut will be upwards five hours, can't use more than two and a half hours. He must not squander dollars / certainly make eliminations now / Is he using more than one camera? / They have now exceeded ten percent maybe can frighten Stevens / We may take legal position protect our investment."

Roy Obringer, general counsel for Warner Bros., had studied Warners' contract with Giant Productions, advising Jack Warner to stay calm and carry on for the moment in order to preserve peace. Rocking the boat might generate bad feelings from Stevens, which might put the picture in jeopardy. Scary news lay behind this calm advice: "Contract provides Giant required within four months after completion principal photography delivered to Warners the negative and a final cut positive print including the sound track fully cut, titled, edited and scored. If fails to do Warners must notify then Giant has ten days to cure failure after which they are in default and we can take over."

A takeover would be the worst action ever for the Stevens-Ferber-Ginsberg triumvirate. Not only would it be humiliating and expensive, it would seriously damage the artistry of the picture. Ginsberg knew what could happen—perhaps was imminent, even inevitable. He sheltered Stevens, as Harriet Pilpel sheltered Ferber.

There were about two weeks in mid-August when exciting artistry was taking place despite the ticking clock. The cast had disassembled, again living separately, but the bonds forged in Marfa continued to hold. Any romantic leanings were perhaps over or dwindling in the semi-reality of the Warners lot.

Carroll Baker had experienced a growth spurt over those weeks. She had become close not only to Hudson, Taylor, and Dean but also to the affable Earl Holliman, with whom she admits to having had a near-romantic call: "Earl and I had come close to a serious involvement, but we had made a mature decision, of which I was very proud, not to let ourselves get carried away." There had been rumors of Taylor's infidelities with both Hudson and Dean, as it became obvious to most that her marriage to Wilding was fading.

There was also talk in the Wilding camp about the ruckus Taylor had made of their marriage and household. What had begun as a calm and cozy home became—in Wilding's term—"an animal shelter," with dogs, cats, and a duck relieving themselves all over the place. The bond that was left between Taylor and Wilding was liquor. Later, Taylor would learn that all the while, Wilding had Marlene Dietrich on the side. She was thirty years older than Taylor.

Carroll Baker had a key scene shot in Hollywood on the lot. It was late in the story's chronology. Baker's recall expresses the longing and pride of her character:

> It was the one in which the older Jett Rink proposes marriage to the now grown-up Luz Benedict II. We did that one scene, take after take, for three entire days! It was incredible. George Stevens believed in extensive coverage, but no other scene had gone on that long. The repetition wasn't because of the mistakes, because as far as I could see, there were none. Jimmy and I had rehearsed and were both word perfect. Because we were competitive, there wasn't one take in which either of us was anything less than concentrated and intense; there were no technical hitches because the camera set-ups were simple (the action of the scene took place in a booth of a deserted restaurant in Jett's about-to-be inaugurated hotel). Later I discovered that George Stevens had deliberately allowed can after can of film to be used to record what he was quoted as having called "a great boxing match between actors." George kept the outtakes and played them at home for his friends . . .
>
> We were well into the third day of this acting marathon when Jimmy suddenly made a foul play. He hit me below the belt, so to speak. He slid one of his hands under the table. He clamped that hand right up between my legs and squeezed with all his mighty strength.
>
> He didn't remove his hand or loosen his grip. He also didn't miss a beat of the scene.
>
> And what did I do? I was so shocked and embarrassed I didn't know what to do. I gasped. I wiped the tears of pain and humiliation from my glazed eyes. I looked at George Stevens for his help as referee, and when he made no sign to intercede, I finished the scene.

Apparently, Dean knew what he had put her through, and minutes afterward drew her into a big, childlike hug, his head buried in her shoulder, unwilling to let her go, repentant for being so result-oriented. As it turned out, Baker was the one who earned Stevens's praise for the well-played scene.

Then, there was another acting challenge that Baker met. It was Jett Rink's "drunken downfall" scene, where he is alone with only a few busboys in his vast dining hall after he has spoiled his own banquet. He is in the middle of a sloshed rant, which Baker/Luz watches from the doorway. She has been steered there by Uncle Bawley to study the pitiful man she thinks she loves. Baker recalls: "The evening we watched the first rushes of that scene, Jimmy came up to George Stevens and me with tears in his eyes. 'I'll never do that scene the way it should be done,' he said, 'but just keep cutting to the close-up of Carroll. Everything that has to be expressed is right there on her face.' Jimmy had often said marvelous things about my ability, but that was the finest compliment he or any great actor could possibly have given me."

When one thinks of the salary disparity among the three leads, and that Dean, posthumously, could have outdistanced everyone in worth, it is stupefying. Taylor was at the top of the pay scale, receiving $177,430; Hudson got $101,667—and Dean got $18,500. Toward the end of production on *Giant*, *Rebel Without a Cause* was released (October 27, 1955) and the late James Dean emerged a full-fledged star.

As shocked and saddened as some of the *Giant* cast was at Dean's premature death, there was a strain of cynicism running throughout as well. A lack of surprise from some: Dennis Hopper was used to Dean quoting from a movie he had seen—"Live fast, die young and have a good-looking corpse." Hopper, who had appeared with Dean in *Rebel Without a Cause*, seemed to enjoy telling the story of Dean's Method preparation for one of the scenes he had with Elizabeth Taylor: "He walked halfway between where we were shooting and where the people were, unfastened his pants, peed, and then walked back into the scene and got it in one take." Hopper asked him why. "Well, I was really nervous," Dean said sheepishly. "I figured if I could go and pee in front of all those people I could get back and do anything on film." In retrospect some years later, Rock Hudson still insisted, "He was hard to be around. Full of contempt." Dean had made it known throughout the shoot that he thought Hudson was a lousy actor.

Ferber's life had been upended by *Giant*, the movie. A dervish of emotions and on the brink of caring too much, she would then pull back and become flinty at relatively small upsets. In a little-known character profile of Leslie Benedict that Stevens himself had drafted in light of his association with Ferber, he treads softly on the natures of both women—the fictional and the real: "Leslie romanticized truth, without necessarily understanding it. She idealized it, and made it a possession, as something defined and objective, like her conception of beauty . . . She simply reacted with a direct . . . impulsiveness to whatever stirred her—be it the sure awareness of beauty or the certain apprehension of evil . . ."

There was a flap ahead concerning publicity, about which Ferber had mostly negative feelings. She always thought it reeked of ineptitude: they got it wrong; they didn't care that it was wrong; they didn't bother to correct it. I came across an example of what made her cross in an archive of *Giant* housed at the University of Pennsylvania, listed under "Henry Ginsberg": "Summary: Bick Benedict, his society-gilded wife . . ." After all the fuss about getting Leslie right, this la-di-da description, which doesn't even name her, was what was derived. Ferber was virtually helpless in protecting her own creation for posterity.

Henry Ginsberg shouldered the continuing legal worry of skimming too close to the characters Ferber might have used as models; Stevens worried about bringing the picture in on time; and Ferber worried about her characters being betrayed. Warners' interoffice communications voiced all the worries, especially addressing Ferber's. She was in the peculiar role of being culpable for writing the thing in the first place and now having to be protected. These were some of the points brought out in a memo dated December 14, 1954, from Carl Milliken Jr. to Henry Ginsberg that Ferber luckily never saw.

> A) LESLIE BENEDICT. This character, portrayed as the first lady of the Reata Ranch, is a very close prototype of Helen Kleberg, wife of Robert Kleberg, who is the present owner, manager of the King Ranch. In the script Leslie Benedict is shown as the daughter of Dr. Horace Lynnton, who lives in the state of Virginia . . . Most telling similarity of all, perhaps, is the fact that Helen Kleberg married Bob after a whirlwind 17-day courtship, which is, of course, closely similar to the situation of this story.
>
> B) BICK BENEDICT. Owner-manager of the Reata Ranch in the story, is a close prototype for Bob Kleberg, owner-manager of the King Ranch. There is, to begin with, the similarity already noted regarding his courtship and marriage

of a girl from Virginia . . . Benedict also mentions that his father built the tremendous ranch home. It was Robert Kleberg, senior, the father of the present Kleberg, who built the Santa Gertrudis Main House, which is an almost exact replica of the house described in Edna Ferber's novel . . . To be sure, Bick Benedict is shown in the script as undergoing a regeneration which is not apparent in the novel. At the end of the story he is actually shown doing battle for a Mexican-American; but whether or not the character traits are true of him as well, Bob Kleberg can sue for heavy damages if he chooses. In the same way, Glenn McCarthy can take violent issue with us if he can prove himself to have been the prototype of Jett Rink, for we portray Rink as a thoroughly obnoxious character, one who is licentious, habitually drunk, and dedicated to the false principles of racial discrimination.

Then there were worries about the lengthy 218 pages of the possibly litigious script. George Stevens was well aware of *Giant*'s excesses, cabling Jack Warner at the end of the Marfa filming: "DEAR JACK: DEEPLY AWARE OF THE URGENCY EXPRESSED . . . DOING UTMOST, REPEAT UTMOST, TO PICK UP TIME. RETURNING TO STUDIO THIS WEEKEND AND WILL CONTINUE EFFORTS . . . REGARDS AND THANKS."

Ginsberg perhaps more than Stevens knew the seriousness of a breach of contract. Blessedly, Ferber did not know—or knew but felt it less than either of her partners, who were directly in the breach. In the original structuring of the Warners' deal, she hardly exists. For example, a clause about budget reads: "Budget $1,500,000 direct. No compensation Ginsberg, Stevens and novel to be included."

It was not that Ferber was unaware of the complicated-cum-fraught business side of *Giant*. It just didn't seem to vex her as terribly as it might have in the past. It was obvious that she was enjoying herself to the hilt every minute on the set with the cast, and especially with Dean. One can see from the photos and know from her letters home that she was having a ball. To my parents she wrote: "No brooding that I can see from the young Mr. Dean," and to sister Fan: "I am restored to a pink-cheeked, cherry-lipped colleen."

Ferber got back from her elevated time in LA to stifling late August in Manhattan—and unpleasantness. Joe Hyams, a columnist at the *New York Herald Tribune*, had written an extended interview with Ferber, which the paper had run as a feature. The piece was titled "*Giant* a Film Story of Small Things." The trouble was, the interview never happened, as she makes abundantly clear in a letter to Henry Ginsberg:

> I never have been interviewed by Joe Hyams, so far as I know. You will recall that I cancelled the proposed interview with him for the perfectly good reason that I didn't want to be interviewed at that time. You then arranged an interview with ten or fifteen foreign correspondents. I went through with this simply because I didn't know how to get out of it without seeming rude to you. This I certainly would have regretted.
>
> The Hyams alleged interview was regrettable. A number of people called me about it today, expressing surprise. It was, I explained, patched together from things I had said here and there about the studio, to friends, to acquaintances, etc.
>
> Henry, I can't and won't have this sort of thing. You must remember that my position is not that of a Hollywood writer or actor. No studio owns me. No nobody owns me. No one has the authority to send out an interview in my name without my permission.
>
> I not only must ask you not to allow this to be done in the future, I must tell you that if it ever is done again I shall refute the publicity in the most certain terms and I shall go even beyond that.
>
> I came to Hollywood on my own. I stayed there under the same conditions. I am as keenly concerned as you are in the possible success of *Giant* and I, too, wish to God it could be finished and stowed away in the pantry. But I won't be used as a piece of studio property because that I am not, never have been, and never shall be.

It seemed clear to Ginsberg—who gently relayed it to Stevens, and then to Ferber—that an extension of their producing partnership was necessary at the request of Warner Bros. in order to remain under their roof. This would mean a financial alteration for the three of them. He had a calming way of delivering difficult news, as in this to Harriet Pilpel on August 25:

> George and I feel we should comply with Warners' request for extension of the Story Purchase Agreement. Roy Obringer, Warners' attorney, prepared the attached. If it meets with your approval, please obtain the necessary signatures, following which George and I will sign and turn over two copies to Warners.
>
> Edna has probably made a full report of her visit here. At this writing I have nothing further to say about the picture other than it continues to look exceptionally fine. I am hopeful that shooting will be completed in about three weeks . . .

Ferber retreated to Elizabeth Arden's Maine Chance spa over a long Labor Day that extended into the second week of September. She went in hopes of physical restoration. She liked a young woman there named Judy Shorey, who was secretary to the manager and saw to Ferber's every comfort. Shorey, a down-east native with so many years between them, seemed to have just the right touch. "This little Maine girl," as Ferber would call her, had real intuition about the protective, sometimes persnickety writer:

> I think in my eleven years at Maine Chance there were fifteen different managers. Miss Ferber used to bypass them and correspond with me because I guess she felt I could handle her requests.
>
> She was on her own a "Giant" of a woman . . . truly. A demanding woman, but nicely. She wanted her schedule exactly as she wanted it and as long as she got it her way her stay went well. When she was writing in Maine, she always took her morning walk. Seldom was there a morning she didn't stop into the office just to say hi and leave mail or discuss travel plans or banking business or something she needed in town. But mostly she came to sit and chat . . . Maids, trays, clients and problems were constantly going back and forth in front of my desk and between Miss Ferber and me. She used

to comment, "How do you ever get anything done with these continual interruptions?" I'd smile and say, "It sometimes isn't easy." She would always smile back with some little reply . . . Sometimes she forewent her treatments in order to write. Those mornings her walks would be earlier and sometimes she would only look in and wave as she passed. On her walk she never wore the Maine Chance dress of the day. She always wore a pastel shade of a simple linen sleeveless dress with a sweater, white bobby socks, and white wedge-type sensible walking shoes. She always walked softly and spoke in a low soft tone except when upset by something. Then, she spoke slightly louder.

. . . I found her personally to be a kind, generous, thoughtful and to me, a very considerate person. For all her fame and fortune she was a lonely lady . . . not something she dwelled on or that many people ever knew or realized . . . but I know this from our many personal visits. She'd sometimes talk about her childhood . . . how she used to read to her ailing father . . . how she had never been a pretty child . . . things of this nature. I remember telling her one day that each person has their own beauty . . . some of face, some of body, some of mind, some of personality . . . just like each person has their own God given talent and ability . . . you, Miss Ferber for your brilliant mind, imagination and ability to create so much pleasure for so many people in your writings . . . Tears came to her eyes as she said something like, "My for such a young girl you have so much adult wisdom."

I honestly believe she was a very lonely lady . . . lonely within, a sad sort of thing.

There were compensations for being a lonely celebrity. Her work—past, present, even future—was always generating interest. The contract for a Lerner and Loewe musical version of *Saratoga Trunk* was being drawn up. The motion-picture rights for Kaufman and Ferber's play *The Royal Family* were being revised. The original 1930 pre-Code film was called *The Royal Family of Broadway*, directed by George Cukor and Cyril Gardner from a screenplay by Herman J. Mankiewicz and Gertrude Purcell and starred Fredric March and Ina Claire. Ferber thought it hardly needed an update and wanted to ensure there was no remake. And a call had been received from a story editor for 20th Century–Fox wondering whether she would consider writing the screenplay for a remake of *Jane Eyre*, which was to star James Mason. She said no. The project never materialized.

At the end of September another brouhaha arose, concerning billing for *Giant*. According to Ferber, someone got it all wrong, and she counted on Harriet Pilpel to fix it.

> . . . When I talked to you at 3:30 this afternoon . . . I must confess that I didn't grasp what you said about the *Giant* billing. It was something about the names of the cast coming first. At least, that's all I remember. I really don't know much about that, if anything. I don't know that I've ever made a fuss about billing of any description. It always—like that song in *Annie Get Your Gun*—came naturally.
>
> If, however, this is some special arrangement or some unusual stunt, or some idea of George Stevens', I'd like at least to know clearly what it is.
>
> I wrote Henry Ginsberg that I definitely did not want the line—EDNA FERBER'S GIANT. I have no Giant. I want my billing, wherever it comes, to read:
>
> > From The Novel
> > GIANT
> > By Edna Ferber
>
> That is, I want the name, which is my trademark, clear of apostrophes and s's.

Then there is a postscript that is classic Ferber: stalwart and therefore endearing, like a head girl at boarding school who will take the brunt: "THE GIANT CONTRACT IS ALL UNKNOWN TERRITORY TO ME. BUT IF IT SAYS 'EDNA FERBER'S GIANT' they can hold me to it, I suppose."

September 30, 1955, would prove to be an agonizing day for everyone connected with *Giant*, as well as for the motion picture industry into posterity. Because Los Angeles is three hours behind Eastern Standard Time, Henry Ginsberg was busy first thing in the morning trying to set the billing straight, as he wrote to Harriet: "I will ask Warners to amend the credit reference from—'Edna Ferber's *Giant*' to 'George Stevens' Production *Giant* from the novel by Edna Ferber'—if this is agreeable to Edna. From a standpoint of proper presentation the title should follow the Stevens credit. The name 'Edna Ferber' would be 50% and the title *Giant* 100%, as presently provided for in the distribution agreement."

Ginsberg mentions in this same letter that they were hoping for a closing date of the picture on the following Tuesday or Wednesday, October 4 or 5, when the production of *Giant* would finally wrap up filming. All that was left to do prior to editing was some dubbing— particularly in the Jett Rink banquet scene. Dean had finished his on-camera work for the entire picture. All he needed to do was to reappear to voice-over his drunken rant, which was virtually inaudible. Other than that, he was free. He could take his new Porsche 550 Spyder for a spin.

Ferber had been concerned about Jimmy, probably from the time she had met him, but her concern seemed to grow along with their acquaintance. He had become synonymous with *Giant*. In *A Kind of Magic* she recalled how zany he had been toward the finish of this taxing work period:

> The day following the finish of the main scheduled filming Jimmy Dean bought his Porsche racing car. It was capable of a speed of more than one hundred and twenty miles an hour. He brought it round to the Warner studio and invited Henry Ginsberg to have a ride. The Warner lot in Burbank, California is, in size and architectural planning, like a neat white cement town in itself, with wide paved streets and solid buildings. Up and down those streets one might in those days encounter anything from a truck towing Cleopatra's barge to an Alaska false-front saloon. To drive any vehicle on these streets was precarious. Jimmy Dean stepped on the gas and drove Henry Ginsberg up and down and in and out and around corners at Porsche speed.

It was a ghastly experience. After a few minutes of this Henry stepped out of the car, his knees turned to liquid, staggered into the studio building on whose stage a scene was being shot, and clutched George Stevens' arm.

"Shoot those extra Jimmy Dean scenes. Quick! He's going to kill himself in that car."

ROLF

It was Friday, September 30, just after noon. Dean was near Cholame, California, on Route 41. He was headed to an auto rally in Salinas, traveling with his mechanic and pal, Rudolf Karl Wütherich, known as Rolf. German-born, Rolf had worked for Porsche and was sent by them to the US as a field engineer for a competition in LA. Arriving in April of 1955, he met Dean at the Bakersfield races. They became buddies while he worked on Dean's old Speedster for race competitions. In mid-September, a sale was being held of five new Porsche 500 Spyders to select racers. Dean wanted one badly and traded in his old car. However, the company's manager agreed to sell Dean the 550 Spyder only if Rolf accompanied him to the races as his mechanic, whereupon Dean entered himself, Rolf, and the car into the Salinas Road Races booked for October 1 and 2.

On the morning of Friday September 30, the two men were diligently preparing the Spyder for the weekend races. Originally Dean had intended to put the Porsche on a trailer behind his station wagon, which would be driven by Bill Hickman, a friend and stuntman, and accompanied by the photographer Sanford Roth, who was going to shoot a photo story on Dean at the races for *Collier's* magazine. So, it was to be a quartet heading for Salinas in the sturdy station wagon. But the Porsche, new and untried and not yet fully "optimized," needed to be broken in, deemed the expert Wütherich, suggesting that Dean drive the Spyder to Salinas. And so it was decided.

The four had coffee and doughnuts at the Hollywood Ranch Market, across the street from Competition Motors. Joining them there was Dean's father, Winton, who had always had a somewhat strained relationship with his son but felt it was worth the drive from Indiana for an attempted rendezvous. The remnant of an olive branch was extended during what was to be their last meal together.

Dean, Wütherich, Hickman, and Roth left for Salinas around 1:15 Pacific Standard Time. Wütherich recalled: "Jimmy's and my nerves were pretty frayed when we finally pulled away from Competition Motors. Our first stop was at a service station on Ventura Blvd." They all piled out of both cars, and it was at that Mobil station on Ventura and Beverly Glen Blvd. in Sherman Oaks that Roth snapped a photo taken with Dean standing beside the Spyder, which they had already nicknamed "Little Bastard." They left the station around 2:00 p.m., headed north on Route 99, and then over the "Grapevine" toward Bakersfield.

They had been driving for about an hour and a half and were just south of Bakersfield when they were stopped and ticketed by Patrolman O. V. Hunter for driving 65 mph in a 55 mph zone. Bill Hickman, accompanied by Sanford Roth in the station wagon behind the Spyder, was also given a ticket for driving 20 mph over the 45 mph limit for what were considered trailer vehicles. Dean and Hickman conferred and decided to avoid going through Bakersfield's pokey 25 mph downtown district and instead opt for a well-known shortcut known as "the racer's road," which took them to the Blackwells Corner rest stop at Route 46—a site now known as James Dean's Last Stop. The two cars pulled up there briefly for Cokes and snacks, meeting up with two other racers—Lance Reventlow (only child of Barbara Hutton and heir to the Woolworth dynasty) and Bruce Kessler—also headed for Salinas. As they parted, they agreed to meet for dinner in Paso Robles.

It was after 5:00 p.m., close to dusk, when Dean and Hickman began to drive west on Route 46 toward Paso Robles, about sixty miles away. This was where Dean revved up the Porsche and left Hickman way behind. Dean was heading down toward the junction floor at Routes 46 and 41 when he saw a black-and-white car heading toward the junction in the opposite direction.

The other car was driven by a twenty-three-year-old student, who made a left turn in front of Dean in order to take the left fork onto Route 41. Suddenly, he hesitated, spiking the brakes as he crossed over the center line. Dean then tried to "power steer," a "sidestepping" racing maneuver with his new car. It was too late to avoid an almost head-on crash. Dean's car flipped into the air, jettisoning into a gully, where it landed back on its wheels. The other car slid thirty-nine feet down Route 46 in the westbound lane.

The first witnesses were brothers-in-law driving behind the student, who later claimed in a court hearing that it had been Rolf behind the wheel with Dean as his passenger. For the rest of his life, Tom Frederick, one of the pair, maintained that this was true—that in fact Rolf was lying in the road on the driver's side after the accident.

A severely injured Dean was extricated from the crushed cockpit and placed into an ambulance. Loaded in next was a barely conscious Rolf. They traveled for twenty-eight miles to the Paso Robles War Memorial Hospital, where Dean was pronounced dead on arrival.

Rolf was transferred to a Los Angeles hospital for immediate surgery, with a double-fractured jaw and serious hip and femur injuries. His hip was so badly torn it required several surgeries over the following months, during which time he began to develop severe depression and suicidal tendencies. He soon became an alcoholic.

In the following decade, having returned to Germany in 1959, Rolf married three more times, as his first one had ended in 1954. During the last marriage, he stabbed his wife several times in her sleep after previously attempting suicide. He was found guilty of attempted manslaughter but sent to a psych ward in lieu of prison. Released in 1970, he began to freelance as a Porsche mechanic, but his problems ran interference. In 1979, he got a job working for a Honda dealer.

In July of 1981, he signed a contract to do a television show featuring him discussing the death of James Dean, for which he would be paid handsomely. However, it never happened. Later that month, he went on a drinking bender, lost control of his red Honda Civic, and crashed into the wall of a private home. He had to be extricated from the car just like his buddy Jimmy. He died at the scene at age fifty-three.

TURNUPSEED

There are varying versions of what happened on that day, turning it into one of the enduringly lurid American mysteries. Who was driving? Were there other deaths? Who was at fault? How fast was the car going? Who was the other driver, Donald Turnupseed? What ever happened to him? Did he live?

Donald Gene Turnupseed could be considered an American folk figure; one can almost hear the ballad. He was a college student at Cal Poly State University when attempting to make his fatal left turn. Standard procedure would indicate that he was at fault by making a left in front of Dean, but then there was Dean's excessive speed and the near-blinding sun as Dean was driving west as the sun was sinking.

Turnupseed was cut and bruised but walked away from his Ford Custom coupe. He was not charged. He lived almost forty years after the accident, ran a successful electrical contracting business, kept a low profile, and died of lung cancer in 1995 at age sixty-three, leaving a wife and two children.

He gave one interview, to the *Tulare Advance-Register* hours after the crash. He said he'd been going home to Tulare from California Polytechnic State College in San Luis Obispo. "I looked but didn't see him coming," he said.

On September 17, 1955, slightly under two weeks before the crash, Dean filmed a two-minute public service announcement for the National Highway Safety Bureau, the last line of which was: "Take it easy driving—the life you might save might be mine."

True Grief

There was shock and disbelief at first, of course, but George Stevens had a movie to finish. Elizabeth Taylor had a marriage that was over. Because of *Giant*, Rock Hudson's days of being merely a handsome hunk of studio hype were about to end. The fledgling careers of Earl Holliman, Carroll Baker, and Dennis Hopper were about to take flight. And Edna Ferber was pursuing Alaska. These people were already moving on when the news of James Dean's death came to them. News took time to travel. Carroll Baker writes:

> . . . Around 6:00, Elizabeth, Rock and I and a small group were watching the rushes. George Stevens was behind us at his desk by the controls. The projection room was dark. The phone rang. The soundtrack screamed to a halt. The picture froze. The lights shot up. We turned and looked at George. The phone dangled in his hand. He was white and motionless. Death was present in that room.
>
> Slowly and with great effort, his voice coming from a long and distant tunnel, George said, "There's been a car crash. Jimmy Dean has been killed."

"Crash Kills Film Star James Dean" was the headline of the *San Francisco Chronicle*. "Film Star James Dean Killed in Auto Crash" led the news for the *Los Angeles Times*. And in bold type on the front of the *Fairmont News* the headline read, "James Dean Killed as Result of California Car Accident."

Some on the West Coast saw or received the news first thing Saturday morning. Others, somewhat later. Around midday, Mercedes McCambridge, whose work on *Giant* was completed, was driving to San Francisco with her husband, Fletcher Markle, for a much-needed holiday. This is what happened, as she wrote in a letter to Ferber:

> . . . Fletcher and I started out for San Francisco where we had reserved the Fairmont's fanciest suite overlooking the bay. We were off for a week of rest and riches . . . Next morning, Saturday Oct. 1, we started out on a short-cut route . . . for Pebble Beach, where we would spend the night. So we had gone about 60 miles, I guess, on this isolated highway—straight and solid and deserted. As a matter of fact, I told Fletcher the country was very like the *Giant* country in Texas. So, Fletcher said we should watch for a gas station because the tank was low and pretty soon, on our right, there it was—a beaten-up old station with a lean-to tin-roofed garage—nothing else—just hot space.
>
> A great slovenly peasant girl came out to fill the tank and while Fletcher was with her, I went inside to the grubby little cigarette stand for a couple of cokes. Then the fat lady said to Fletcher. "We have James Dean's sports car in the garage." And Fletcher, knowing that Jimmy was always racing up in that area said rather calmly: "Oh, is that so?" thinking Jimmy was having it repaired or something. Then he heard me call: "Oh my God" and he thought I had seen Jimmy coming out of the men's room and we were wildly glad to see each other. But what had happened was this—another cow-like lady inside the station told me that Jimmy's car was there and then pointed to it through the open door leading to the garage. I shrieked Oh my God when I saw it because it was a crumpled mechano-set and the blood was everywhere. By that time Fletcher had come inside and they told us. It had happened one-half mile down the road we had just travelled.
>
> I will never understand what devilish fate made us stop at that particular place—of all the stations in central California.

The lady said she had never seen any body so limp and broken and she kept saying things like that, in the morbid way strangers do—she didn't know who we were—or Jimmy. They had told her "the kid was some kind of movie star." We drove stunned on into Paso Robles to the funeral home, but there were so many cars there, and we didn't want to be in the way, so we circled the block a few times and then went on. Talk about your small stifling world. So, we spent three days in SF and I broke out in a fever so they flew me home and off to St. John's Hospital. I got home this morning.

As you said in your thoughtful letter which I have just read, it IS like the solution of a puzzle. Jimmy could never have died in any other way. The people up there seem to feel it was the local boy's fault, because his turn-off has always been a dangerous corner, and in the dusk, with its deceptive light, he may not have seen Jimmy's streaking low grey bullet. The boy's name is Turnupseed.

If Jimmy knows, I'm sure it would make him laugh to know it was a man named Turnupseed who did it.

Please keep in touch with me. I feel a little bewildered, but I love you.

The mourning for Dean was widespread. There were those who felt it more keenly than most; these were the people of Marfa, who had been with him day after day. They had "witnessed this extraordinary confluence of fantasy and real life. Many were kids . . . their lives mirroring the controversial themes in the film." Until being a part of *Giant*, many of them were not treated as equals. That a barbed-wire fence was the line of demarcation for burials at the local cemetery said everything.

The Marfa community of Mexican Americans saw Dean daily. Sometimes they served him, and at other times ate alongside him. He horsed around with the children. He was a tease to the young and older women. He was a cool temporary buddy to some of the young men—sometimes not so cool as he sniggered at the behinds of some of the females. He was the idealized kid brother who was the most brashly fun person, but who also needed protecting. For a fleeting time, he was theirs.

That was the way Ferber must have felt—that he was hers, because he had the ability to get so personal in such a short time. I can only imagine how strongly she reacted when she heard the news late on September 30. Her story that came out was a loaded one:

> Just a few days before this I, in New York, had received in the mail a large photograph which he had sent me. It was inscribed and it showed him in character and in costume as Jett Rink, the ranch hand. It was not characteristic of him to send his photograph unasked. I was happy to have it and I wrote to thank him. ". . . when it arrived I was interested to notice for the first time how much your profile resembles that of John Barrymore. You're too young ever to have seen him, I suppose. It really is startlingly similar. But then, your automobile racing will probably soon take care of that."
>
> I was told that the letter came the day of his death. He never saw it.

After Ferber died (on April 16, 1968), my mother allowed me to select some items from her apartment before her estate went into probate. I chose a mahogany secretary, which I still honor; it houses copies of all her books, a set of Limoges china, several art deco pins customized with her initials, and an eight-by-ten-inch photo of James Dean—high hat of wild, thick hair, cigarette dangling, shirt open to mid-chest, lounging, insolent, untouchable. He is posing in character as Jett Rink. The photo was inscribed: "To Edna, Gentleness is respected and remembered in the cruel man." It was signed "Jett Rink."

Shortly after I was permitted to take my treasured items, I was cast in a touring company that was to perform in Houston, Dallas, and Fort Worth. In my youthful stupidity, I decided to pack the Dean photo as a kind of reverent lark. That way, Ferber would be with me, fittingly, in Texas, along with Jimmy/Jett. It would inspire my cast and comfort me. And there the photo stayed, somewhere in Houston, Dallas, or Fort Worth. It must have slipped behind a desk or . . . I still curse my callow self. The photo that Dean sent to Ferber, personally and enigmatically signed, is lost forever. Or somebody treasures it. Or perhaps somebody has sold it for a good deal of money on eBay.

Improbable as it may sound, Stevens and company planned to work on Sunday, October 2, two days after the tragedy. Elizabeth Taylor balked, unable to function. She had plunged into despair at the news, literally taking to her bed. There are various versions of this episode: Taylor collapsed upon hearing of the crash; Taylor was so distraught that she had to be hospitalized; Stevens was "furious at Taylor's histrionics"; Taylor either could not or would not continue working because of, as her internist wrote, "the extreme mental duress she was put under by the director."

There were actually several confluences. Stevens's reaction to Dean's death was strong and mournful. He and the young actor had difficulties that could never be resolved. He had tried to wrangle Dean into respecting himself as part of a whole endeavor. He wanted him to recognize the astonishing artist he was becoming. Dean's reaction was bratty, as if toward an overbearing parent. He deliberately did things that scratched at Stevens's nature. He was late to the set, causing Stevens to fall even farther behind schedule, which meant that the leading cast members had to be paid extra salary. These delays also meant further displeasure in Jack Warner's corner. Told that Stevens had 875,000 feet of film to edit, he didn't want to hear about a troublesome twenty-four-year-old who occasionally urinated in front of everyone.

Taylor's extreme reaction to Dean's death caused a permanent rift between her and Stevens. Perhaps this would not have been so if Stevens hadn't been under such pressure to get onto a faster time clock, which Dean had so badly disrupted. One report chronicles the dialogue between Taylor and Stevens on October 1, 1955: "I can't believe it, George; I can't believe it," Taylor was to have said, to which Stevens replied, "I believe it. He had it coming to him. The way he drove, he had it coming."

Supposedly, Taylor's face and eyes were badly swollen from crying through the night, which evoked a stern reaction from Stevens, who said that Dean was "not worth the self-indulgent tears that had sent her spinning into hysteria." Rock Hudson corroborated this version of the "break-up" between Taylor and Stevens: "George was not very kind to her . . . Elizabeth is very extreme in her likes and dislikes. If she

Ferber and Stevens at Warner Bros.

likes, she loves. If she doesn't like, she loathes. And she has a temper, an incredible temper which she loses at any injustice. George forced her to come to work after Dean's death. He hadn't finished the film. And she could not stop crying." Reportedly the climax came when Taylor unleashed, "You are a callous bastard! I hope you rot in hell!"

Stevens had required Taylor to complete reaction shots in a scene she had already played with Dean. So, it wasn't reciprocal acting. It was reacting in character to someone freshly deceased whom she had loved and revered. Despite the eventual tremendous success of the movie, from that day forward, Taylor and Stevens kept their distance from each other. She never forgave him.

It seems that Dean had affected everyone working on *Giant*, and Hudson was far from impartial to his presence or his death. There were many versions of what happened between the three stars during the filming. It depends on whom you talked to.

In talking to Hudson, he was so sorrowful when recounting the death of Dean, and so honest about how he disliked the younger actor, that I believed him. Taylor seemed entirely transparent about Dean and her abiding affection for him and for Hudson, who called her "Bessie," which she loved. She later confessed that she would have slept with Hudson if he had asked her.

Perhaps Hudson had more of an agenda or backstory with Dean than it would have seemed. Certain truths were not spoken of back in the mid-fifties. Hudson had a good deal on the back burner. He was a closeted gay man embarking on a heterosexual marriage of convenience. His stardom was hitched to a studio-planned personal life. He was to be married to a woman and entirely discreet about everything else.

According to various sources, Hudson fell deeply into a platonic love with Taylor but was also attracted to Dean. In the beginning of filming in Marfa, when Hudson and Dean shared a house, Hudson purportedly enjoyed dressing in drag in the privacy of this rented home. Dean deplored this as well as the overtures that Hudson made toward him, hastily moving out and into a room at the Hotel Paisano. It has also been mentioned that Dean was seeking rougher trade than what Hudson could offer and that each actor struggled with his sexuality. What is fact is that both men came close to despising each other, which worked just fine for their characters. "I had been wishing him dead ever since we were in Texas" was Hudson's rueful epitaph.

What Ferber knew about a "deeper Dean" was kept to herself. She had heard about his destructive side, but with her he was playful and charming. No one will ever know what they talked about when they were alone. The photos always show them on the set with others either circling them or in the background. Dean did take her for rides on his motorcycle, but there the story ends. She told our family only that she had ridden on the back of his "chariot" and that it was "enough for many lifetimes." On the face of it, their intimacy was that they both had given birth to Jett Rink. And Ferber knew just how seriously Dean took her invention. He had read up on Texas history, as she had, and studied a volume devoted to cattle raising, as she had. He admitted that playing Jett Rink was the hardest challenge he had ever had to face. Ferber took this as high praise.

She had also enjoyed Dean's ode to Stevens, albeit early on and before their Marfa debacle. He had been as high on Stevens as she was, and she fully supported his assertion that "George Stevens is the greatest director of them all—even greater than Kazan. Stevens was born for the movies. You know, when it wants to, Hollywood can accomplish tremendous things. And this movie might be one of them."

In *The James Dean Story*, author Ronald Martinetti, a former writer for *The Wall Street Journal* among other publications, intrepidly tracked down important figures in Dean's life. These included Liz (Dizzy) Sheridan, a young dancer with whom Dean lived in New York, and who years later played Jerry Seinfeld's mother on *Seinfeld;* Rogers Brackett, a thirty-five-year-old radio director and television producer with whom he lived in Hollywood and New York; the actors Julie Harris, who played opposite him in *East of Eden,* and Sal Mineo, who played John "Plato" Crawford so affectingly in *Rebel Without a Cause;* Elia Kazan; and many other intimates.

Bob Hinkle, the native Texan who had been hired by George Stevens as a dialect coach, offered more intense insight into the young star's chameleon ways. Apparently, aside from Hudson, Hinkle also coached Dennis Hopper and Carroll Baker, but was eventually monopolized by Dean. He and Dean stayed together all the time. Dean's pet name for him was "Double Buckle." According to Hinkle:

> We just became real good buddies . . . He spent a lot of time over at our house, eating . . . We went rabbit hunting and at night we went to the bullfights down in Del Rio . . . We only had one room with one bed. A double bed, so I said, "Well, I don't mind if you don't mind." He said, "Hell, no," So, we go to bed. Now, if he'd been gay, he would have at least given me a look when we were undressing. We get into bed with just our shorts on—not even a T-shirt—and we sleep. I guarantee that. He would have touched me or something. I know he wasn't gay. I'll guarantee that . . . We spent about seven and a half months, nearly every day together. I can't even think of a day that we missed, on weekends and everything . . . He wasn't really a celebrity as such when he died. Because he died so young, he actually only had one movie out. He had *East of Eden,* and then *Rebel* was released after that, and that is the movie that really kicked him upstairs until *Giant* came out and then it was all over and he was a top star. But he never thought of himself as a star.

Hinkle seemed to keep a paternalistic eye on Dean, certainly more so than Stevens, who, despite Dean's swearing early on that he was an even greater director than Elia Kazan, lost favor with him in Marfa—and vice versa. According to Hinkle, the two were at odds, calling for Stevens to use reverse psychology, which revealed itself in the "windmill" scene:

It was Jimmy and I, George and the cameraman. George said, "I just want you to walk right straight for that fence post. What you are doing is walking off your deal." Jimmy says, "Okay," and starts walking out there. Stevens yells cut. He takes a page from the back of the script and starts tearing it up into little pieces. Never saying a word. Then he throws a little piece of paper down, puts a rock on it. Walks ten feet, does the same thing, until he makes a path to the post. Stevens then asks Jimmy, "Do you think you could follow that line?" Dean says, "Yeah, I think I can," and they roll the camera. Jimmy walks out there, picks up the rock, tosses it away, and wads up a little piece of paper. Stevens yells cut, but Dean picks up every one of those pieces of paper, walks back to Stevens and drops them in his lap. He told the director, "Look, if I need marks, I'll put down my own marks. All you need to do is tell me what you want me to do, like a director is supposed to. Then, I'll do it. Otherwise, I'm going to get my ass on a plane and go back to California."

Stevens said, "Well, okay. Let's just do it." So, the cameraman begins rolling again.

This time Dean is pissed off. He rears back and begins strutting over to this windmill. None of this is in the script, but Stevens tells the cameraman, "Now, stay on him, Bill. Stay with him." Meanwhile Dean climbs up on the windmill, crosses his legs, and sets up there like that. All the time, Stevens is asking the cameraman, "You got him? Stay with him. That's perfect. Perfect." That was George's reverse psychology. He just set Jimmy up. He wanted him to do that. But nothing was ever said about the matter after that.

There was another incident between Dean and Stevens late into the Marfa filming. This time Stevens was more taciturn.

It was toward the end of the picture. Jimmy was having some problems. They called him in at seven o'clock in the morning, and come 9:30 Jimmy wasn't working, and then Jimmy wasn't working at eleven o'clock. It got to be about twelve-thirty and we went to lunch . . . We came back and Jimmy says: "I'm not going to sit around here all goddamn day. This is a bunch of shit. You know I come in here prepared this morning, and you know I'm tired now . . . I can't give a good performance when I come in like this. You know that they're wearing my ass out all morning waiting and I'm tired now. I'm going home. Just tell 'em I've gone home, or gone fishing, or something, and I'll see them in the morning if they want to do that scene, to call me and I'll be here in the morning."

As good as his word, Dean took off, leaving the production up a creek. Stevens raised hell with the assistant director for not stopping him, whereupon Hinkle got Dean on the phone, imploring him to come back, and receiving a "Fuck 'em" from Dean. Eventually, according to Hinkle, Dean's diva behavior brought forth fawning results. Elizabeth Taylor got on the phone and said, "Jimmy, please do me a favor and come back over here. We have that one scene; it's with me and we can knock it out. It would be a real easy deal to do. Come on and do it. Bob and I will come over and get you." Dean acquiesced, but still grumbled about waiting so long that his makeup was coming off. According to Hinkle, Stevens seemed fed up with Dean and didn't talk much to him after that.

In the Ferber archive as well as the George Stevens archive there is a surprising dearth of personal correspondence between the two. There is much business interaction delivered by "their people," but little having to do with any issues between them for almost half a decade. There is nothing mentioning the catastrophe of Dean's death, no word of condolence. This epistolary silence is somewhat strange. Perhaps after an embarrassing spark between them, or from one of them toward the other, most of their would-be interactions were left for others to carry out.

In the summer and early fall of 1955, Stevens was still filming, leaving Henry Ginsberg to be the official messenger. Ginsberg developed a warm relationship with Harriet Pilpel, also a messenger. They troubleshot together as Jack Warner's people kept sending "confidential bulletins of impending disaster": "The preliminary estimate for *Giant* has come out at $3,367,750, based on a 72-day schedule. I do not believe this picture can be made for this figure. We know that Mr. Stevens is very meticulous and will demand perfection . . . causing expenditures that are impossible to foretell . . ."

Jack Warner was also receiving dire reports, about which Stevens attempted to calm him while asserting himself and protecting his picture. Stevens wrote:

> . . . You made inquiry . . . if *Giant* could be made for the budget figure. Original budget, plus added cost, came to $2,912,500. This was $412,500 over our agreed-to $2,500,000 figure. Since this date, no commitment to an expenditure has been made without regard to necessary reduction. Following is the summary of expenditures so far:
>
> Three stars for cast, carried in budget at $350,000, have been pared to $296,000—
>
> Taylor—$175,000
> Hudson—$100,000
> Dean—$21,000
> Reduction here—$54,000 . . .

Stevens continues to report his dutiful budget shavings, but includes a polite reproach:

> We have been too busy cutting these dollars before they were spent to work out the cut script requested, but now having this other work behind us we are getting out the pared final version. But let me say that I do not believe it is wise to put the burden of saving production money entirely on the writer's shoulders. This is a prime function of production management. Along with reducing the *Giant* script we do want to eliminate budget fat and production sloth.

There was a technical and emotional concern with wrapping up the movie. Although Dean's final scene was physically completed, the audio part had yet to be looped; his lines were close to inaudible. Jett was supposed to be a drunken mess, but Dean as a Method actor had taken it several steps farther. It has been said that he did this on purpose as an act of spite against his director. Stevens solved this problem by hiring a close buddy of Dean's, the actor Nick Adams, to dub in a facsimile of Dean's voice. What is heard in the film the last time Dean was ever seen on screen is not his voice. The process was referred to as "the late looping."

How to handle Dean's death prior to the movie's release was initially thought to be a publicist's nightmare. It turned out to be a huge selling point, grim as that may seem. In her diary Ferber was reflective in her grieving: "Poor Jimmy Dean! They are now trying to play him down in the publicity. He has grown into a kind of dreadful cult. But nothing, I should think, can hurt his magnificent performance. Poor crazy boy, you knew when you met him that he was starcrossed. And such brilliant talent, so winning and at the same time so terrible . . ."

After his death, she said little about him ever again—at least not to us. She was a realist, and as such, she preserved her health. No matter how dire the present situation, she was able to look to her future, which was always in another book. Even when she was dying and knew it, she was mapping out a book on the American Indian—another oppressed people in America. She had an instinctive feel for the underdog—hence her deep attachment to Dean.

One might say that it was directly because of Dean's chronic lateness that Jack Warner got close to pulling the plug and taking over the project. In fact, toward the end of the shoot in Marfa, Warner sent a cable to his second-in-command, Steve Trilling: "WORRIED GIANT ONLY FIVE REELS SCORED." He had planned on completion in late September, but in late August only nine reels had been shot. He cabled Trilling again a few days later, "Did you correctly legally record Stevens 26th will take over positively?" Letting no grass grow, the first week of September he cabled again: "Will positively 26th take over *Giant*; fed up [with] this genius remove all from *Giant* other payrolls [as] soon [as] possible."

Legally, a takeover would have been a quagmire; Warner knew that, but although the threat was pyrrhic, his ire didn't die down until he had seen an early preview: "GIANT REVIEWS HERE UNANIMOUS ONE HUNDRED PERCENT GREAT. AUDIENCE LOVED PICTURE. CONFIDENTIALLY PICTURE NEEDS TWO OR THREE

GOOD CUTS DOWN AT END. GOING OVER THIS THOR-
OUGHLY WITH STEVENS THIS AFTERNOON."

Mid-October of 1955 heralded the final touches of the shoot. It was
announced that principal photography had been completed, although
a second unit would still be tinkering with retakes, such as one with
Elsa Cárdenas, who played Juana: she would have to work with a different baby during the Sarge's Diner scene.

And they were still fussing with the credits—or, rather, Ferber was.
Henry Ginsberg thought he had gotten it straight in a cable to Har-
riet Pilpel: "EDNA ADVISES HER PREFERENCE IS SECOND
CREDIT READING QUOTE: GEORGE STEVENS' PRODUC-
TION OF GIANT FROM NOVEL BY EDNA FERBER."

Ferber was waspish when it came to credits and what she considered perverse publicity. The credits situation was somewhat mysterious.
Her ego was substantial, but she would rather not have been billed than
billed inaccurately. She had an ingrained sense of proper sequencing.
At the start of a meal, napkins belonged in napkin rings. For the rest
of the meal the napkin remained in the lap and only upon rising at the
end of the meal should the napkin reappear on the table. A Ferber rule.

Stevens shared her fastidious ways. During his next period of editing the movie, he catalogued it within fourteen books. Each take had
a number and a description, so when it came time to put the whole
picture together, he could immediately refer to what he wanted. He
included frames within the take so he could easily recall what he had
used and whether that was what he eventually would want. His film
editor, William Hornbeck, recalled: ". . . Sometimes after we have
worked on a scene till it has become substantially different, we go back
to the book and pick out a take that we had rejected before, because
now it fits better with what we've got."

Stevens understood cinematically that there could be no skimping
or stinting. Just as Ferber had the urge to convey her process, so did he,
in an interview with Philip K. Scheuer of the *Los Angeles Times*:

I want height and I want to be able to edit freely. Height because
the movie is a world of upright things and tall men. Freedom to
edit because, in the case of *Giant*, I am telling a story that goes
through three generations and it has to roll right along . . . I've
never seen anyone who can cut CinemaScope yet . . . why not?

because it's too inclusive: the wide picture is just all there. It doesn't put the demand on the filmmaker or editor for selectivity and it makes it difficult for him to eliminate things—things that he could save for the next shot.

If either Stevens or Ferber was nervous about libel or a racial backlash, there is no record of it. Worry about the outcome of the work was left to the publisher and the studio. The two creators were myopic; they only cared about process and result as the noose of anticipation tightened.

No one could refute the gargantuan impact that Dean's death had on the cast and creators of *Giant* or the movie industry at large, and no one could predict the ticket buyers' zeal at seeing a dead man, or the critics' evaluation of a final performance. So many variables accompanied this tragedy. Everyone was affected in different ways.

Perhaps the one who was the most underestimated in terms of being impacted was George Stevens. I think he knew he had a legacy to shape. He and Dean had had a complicated time of it, bringing out an almost paternal anger in Stevens. Dean's unpredictability was infuriating to a man who believed in controlled, professional behavior. Now, in the editing phase of the picture, he could control the problem-child actor and by doing so, immortalize him.

Waiting for George Stevens's *Giant*

Ferber was certainly not at loose ends during the period between October 1955 and October 1956. She was working steadily on her new novel, although she always felt it was inferior to *Giant*, which might have subconsciously hexed her work on it.

The idea of a minor Edna Ferber novel was unthinkable to Ken McCormick. Her market value after *Giant* was way up, but curiously enough she was working without a contract.

There was, however, a trust between her and McCormick that verged on a proper Victorian romance. By the spring of 1955 he really wanted to cement a contract, but he knew not to put too much pressure on her, although he was undoubtedly under the gun from Doubleday. One can see how hard he worked on just the right tone:

> . . . I want to offer you a contract for the Alaska novel. I haven't
> brought up the subject of contract before because I knew you
> were wrestling with enough problems concerned with the book
> not to want to brood over the terms of a contract. But I do
> want you to know that there is tremendous enthusiasm here for
> the book. As evidence we'd like to offer a $10,000 advance and
> 15% royalty on the retail price. Against your ultimate earnings
> of this book, this is modest indeed, but it is a tangible evidence

of our interest. May I discuss this with you and later with the Ernst office?

The idea of this novel is so right, so timely, and such a challenge to your magnificent talents because of its very complexity . . . I know it will be a wonderful book.

Ferber continued to have an unusual relationship with McCormick that should not be underestimated. He knew how to read her text as well as her personality and asked occasionally in return that he might seek solace from her when he felt low. She readily gave it, as he confirms: "You have been most generous in understanding my problems and helping me cope with them. I have a deep and abiding love for you which is unlike any relationship I've ever had with anyone. I cherish it and only wish that I could spend more time with you . . . Love to you, dear Edna. You are a very important part of my life."

She was more social than she had been in a while, chatting about her doings in a letter to her friend the playwright and screenwriter George Oppenheimer: "I had ten people to dinner last Wednesday: the [Rouben] Mamoulians, [the Robert] Sherwoods, Vinegar Nell, Backers, among others . . . George [Kaufman] and Leueen [his wife, the actress Leueen MacGrath] are in town. I haven't seen them. . . ."

And in between bouts of the Face, she answered reams of correspondence, campaigned strenuously for the second presidential run of Adlai Stevenson, feuded with her neighbor Richard Rodgers and with her very old and dear friend Moss Hart, and became closer to her fellow novelist Rebecca West.

Ferber was loyal to her friends and loyal to her feuds with them. It is interesting to note that she mainly had lengthy feuds with men—like love affairs off the track and then eventually righted again. If there was a problem with a dear woman friend, it would be resolved quickly.

An example of this was her relationship on equal but separate terms with Moss Hart and Kitty Carlisle Hart. When Ferber was youngish and Moss Hart was younger by a considerable nineteen years, their relationship was officially that of knowing woman and protégé. She was a literary and theatrical success and he was destined for success in the theater—which they both revered as the ultimate pantheon. And at one point, Hart's feelings of love of theater turned toward love of Ferber. The bud was nipped before full bloom, but he had proposed to her.

Respect and friendship for each other won out, and Hart went on to other pursuits and eventually, in 1946, married the musical theater and film actress Kitty Carlisle. Shortly thereafter, Ferber was introduced to Kitty and the two women developed an enduring bond.

Around this time, Rodgers and Hammerstein expressed interest in creating a musical based on Ferber's 1941 novel, *Saratoga Trunk*. In fact, they were extremely keen about it and hotly pursuant. And wouldn't it be something if Moss Hart were to write the libretto? These jolly friends could all share in making a substantial hit! But at some point Rodgers and Hammerstein's interest lessened until eventually they bowed out.

Meantime, something sour took place that Ferber professed never to fathom. It seemed to evolve out of an earlier attempt by Hart and Ferber to develop an outline together. It came at the end of 1954, and it was clear that their year had gone badly, as is evidenced in this letter she wrote to him in December:

> Again, *Saratoga Trunk* seems to be raising its hydra head, Moss. Apparently it dies hard. I have told the interested people that as you and I worked seven days on our outline I definitely would want to clear with you your position in the matter, following your withdrawal. Naturally, if there is a production (and I couldn't care less) the book would follow the story of the novel.
>
> All this sounds somewhat stilted, but as you and I did work on the original structure anything that you would want considered would, of course, be necessarily cleared if there's a play in the future.

This was the beginning of a feud. Hart took Ferber's attitude and tone badly, as did Ferber's usual ally, Kitty.

The postscript to this is that all, or most, was forgiven, and when Hart died, in 1961, Ferber delivered the most stirring eulogy anyone could ever want. She and Kitty remained devoted friends until Ferber's final day. "I've been around for the good times," Kitty had said. "I might as well be around for the bad."

Ferber was planning another Alaska trip in May. Although deep into her research and beginning to write, she had yet to sign her contract with Doubleday. There are no clues pointing to why; perhaps she was still mired in the peregrinations of her *Giant* deal with Stevens and Ginsberg vs. Jack Warner and Warner Bros. Whatever the case, she was evading Ken McCormick's entreaties, which were coming late into 1955. Finally, at the door of 1956, the contractual papers were signed, whereupon McCormick wrote with amusing candor:

> I have signed that contract which I at first mistook for the manuscript itself because of the bulk . . . Now that this preliminary fencing is over, we can get down to the only important thing which is THE BOOK. I am so sorry if the bickering over the contract distracted you. Please put the whole business out of your mind and do that one most important job which is to write THIS WONDERFUL BOOK. I really feel that book, Edna; I know it's there and I can't wait to see its fulfillment.

Planning ahead for the summer of 1956, Ferber decided to rent a house in Westport, Connecticut, during the standard season of Memorial Day through Labor Day. She chose to be near her favorite short-term sparring partner, her sister, Fannie. There was often a shared comfort; it wasn't always acrimony, which could have stemmed from a deep-seated, unexpressed rivalry: the pretty one vs. the successful one. The backbone of their relationship held firm. In a letter to the Lunts, Ferber was certainly able to acknowledge the merits of her sister: "She is an unusual and talented person who never has really utilized her considerable equipment."

The house was "suitable," as she reported to the family, a place where she could work without distractions. When in deep work mode, she seemed less easily agitated. But no matter where she was, obligations and entreaties always found her. Some met with a stony heart, others did not. In June she received a plea from something called the James Dean Memorial Foundation, Inc., extending an invitation to join the board of directors, and explaining itself to her and ending with flattery: ". . . It is particularly fitting that you should have a place on this board, not only for the invaluable assistance that you can render, but because Jimmy held you in such high personal regard. I'm sure that it would make him very happy to see you a part of such a worthwhile effort made in his name."

She wrote a huge "NO" across the top of this letter.

Another letter arrived with the stationery letterhead reading "The American National Red Cross." It was from Kurt Hollander, the refugee and distant relative whom, along with his family, she had sponsored during World War II. She had thought a great deal of him when he was a boy. He had a Mensa IQ and was a talented musician. He wrote to her of fulfilling the destiny that she had provided: "Just a few words to let you know that I am now an American citizen, having obtained my final papers . . . I hope you will not mind my having taken the liberty of writing, but since you did issue the affidavit I felt that you would be interested in my citizenship."

Her good deed had come full circle.

All in all, it was not a bad waiting period for the movie to come out.

Final Cut

The arduous final phase of *Giant* was helped enormously by the shrewd expertise of editor Bill Hornbeck. He had been nominated for an Academy Award twice for his editing and had won for *A Place in the Sun*. Having also worked with Stevens on *Shane*, the two were simpatico in vision and in nature. He, too, was a benign fussbudget when it came to good film etiquette. As Frank Capra recalled, "He had a great love for film and what it could do. It was amazing to him that on a piece of celluloid there was such great drama. He always used white gloves on both hands when handling film. If it ever fell on the floor, he'd scream because it would get dirty."

His work on *Giant* cannot be underestimated. Not only did he handle the Nick Adams dubbing flawlessly, but he gave *Giant* its magisterial look through its vast, shimmering close-ups accompanied by intensely held dissolves.

Because Hornbeck had worked so well with Stevens before, they'd developed a shorthand, and both attempted to be oblivious to any pressure by the studio, although "the studio was getting very irritated with us for taking so much time cutting the film. They said, 'Look, you fellows can play with the film after it's released' . . . They wanted to start getting some money out of it."

Jack Warner was not accepting artistry above timetable and found nothing humorous about the situation. In January of 1956, he wrote to Stevens:

> After reading . . . your completion schedule showing the final preview to take place about July 31, 1956, I would say from our Company's standpoint such arrangements are unsatisfactory . . .
>
> . . . You must keep in mind, George, that the Giant Productions agreement, as are all our agreements with independent producers, was passed by the Board of Directors of the Company who naturally expect the agreement to be fully complied with.
>
> . . . It is obvious that you will not be able to deliver the picture by February 12, 1956; however we cannot accept a delivery of around July 31, 1956. Therefore, prompt steps must be taken by you to make an earlier delivery, and in this connection I am willing to compromise with you and fix the date of May 7, 1956 for delivery, which we will insist upon your meeting . . .

Stevens and Ginsberg had no choice but to comply or be sued—dragging Ferber along with them. However, Stevens was determined to deliver his movie at his pace and dimensions. He was a stickler for getting the right height on the screen. He had seen his *Shane* cropped at the top and bottom by projectionists. In *Giant*, he figured out how to mask the top and bottom of his camera, so that projectionists had to comply with the proportioned image.

He reflected on the matter of an intermission. "I had organized it for a very big theatre," Stevens had said. "The film ran about three hours and nineteen minutes. I didn't see how we could keep an audience sitting for three hours and nineteen minutes without an intermission. We had previewed it with an intermission. We had also worked to cut to move it along as fast as possible. So we went into the theatre where people were going to sit for three hours and nineteen minutes. Hopefully we could get by. Well, somehow or other the pace of the picture let the audience get along without an intermission . . . the picture went straight through and has always been run that way."

Even though Stevens is talking in retrospect, he gives no inkling of pressure from being shoehorned into an absolute deadline by Jack Warner. He never compromised his message: "The character development herein is the story of the change of Texas. Leslie is the agent of this." Nor would he compromise his structure, which backed up his intention: "The structural development of the picture, I believe, is what saves it. It has an excellent structure design, which has to do with the audience anticipating and looking some distance ahead all the way to the finish, which is a reversal of how this kind of story would normally end—the hero is heroic. Here the hero is beaten, but his gal likes him. It's the first time she's ever really respected him because he's developed a kind of humility—not instinctive but beaten into him."

This last sentence could apply to Jack Warner's mandated compromise. Instinctively, Stevens might have needed more time for his *Giant* to be totally fulfilled, but he was not going to contribute to his own undoing. Having filmed the treacherous scene where Luz meets her destiny, he understood what not to do with Warner:

Long beforehand, I wanted to see this dowager woman, Mercedes McCambridge, on a bucking horse from a great distance— beautiful landscape, straight horizon line, blue sky, and distant

Giant opens in Los Angeles, October 18, 1956

image of this contest between a woman and a horse—skirts flying and the horse really breaking it in two. I wanted to go from the extreme long shot to the spur going right into the horse's flank—which, if you had sympathy for the woman—gave validity for the horse bucking like that. In two cuts there's a story—how we contribute to our own undoing.

Despite the tensions arising from Warner's extension-without-benefits (in fact, not only were there no benefits; the three partners were to take a deficit of $140,000), the relationship between Ferber and Stevens seemed to remain warmly cordial. She had created a distance by keeping busy researching and drafting her new novel, but *Giant* still seemed more chimera than reality. However, at last, by October of 1956, *Giant* was looking like a certainty. Stevens was beginning to preview the film for select audiences. He was excited to discuss it with Ferber at the beginning of October, but farcically they kept missing each other, as she mentions in a letter:

> George dear, when you telephoned me the second time (before 3 o'clock) I really was out. It wasn't until about five this afternoon that Molly [her housekeeper] told me you had again telephoned. How annoying for you! In the meantime I had talked to you at just about that time from a telephone booth.
>
> I can't convey to you what it will mean to me to see *Giant*. I never before have felt this way about a picture made from one of my books or plays. Please believe me when I say that it has nothing to do with its financial possibilities. The theme, the characters, the background mean a lot to me. I can't quite explain why this is true. I am genuinely emotional about it. Remember that I've seen only a few unrelated (or at least not connected) scenes. I know you will understand and not be offended when I say that I couldn't see it for the first time at the Thursday night preview with all those people around. I want to see it quietly, clearly, and almost coldly set, if possible. Then if I should see it again Thursday night I'll be able to feel composed, inside.
>
> I wonder if I'll ever be able to tell you and Henry how grateful I am for your patience, your courage, your talents, your honesty of purpose.

They had gone through a lot together. The last shambles had come a few months earlier. It had been about her old foe, publicity. Especially with the death of Dean as tabloid fodder, she had been placed even farther behind on the bandwagon. Technically, her name was supposed to go above the title along with Stevens's, but more than occasionally it simply didn't appear at all. She would rage to Harriet and Harriet would point it out to Ginsberg, who would attempt to rectify any similar situation in advance. But as everyone knows, publicity can be a behemoth, sucking up facts.

No one would point sharp fingers, but it was indicated that the "publicity team" for the movie occasionally demoted Ferber's ranking, leaving off her name in the credits above the title. And then there was an odious article in the *New York Post* by Hollywood gossip columnist Sidney Skolsky, who reported on August 16, that "Edna Ferber, after seeing *Giant*, told George Stevens, 'Thanks—that's the story I wanted to write.'"

Ferber was sent into one of her spirals. She addressed her legal team, Morris Ernst and Harriet Pilpel, that the "plant" had originated "in an organization devoted to the George Stevens publicity campaign in connection with *Giant*. I have not even seen *Giant* yet and I will not stand for this sort of publicity which is beneficial to someone else while it breaks me down." She demanded a retraction, and soon. Then—out of character even for a woman of considerable vituperation—she made a threat, saying she would take action that "will work against the picture's career." She ended with a flourish: "I wrote the novel *Giant*. I wrote it as I wanted to write it . . . It was not written with the idea of a motion picture sale in mind. I never have written with the idea of a motion picture sale in mind. A statement such as the one quoted at the beginning of this letter amounts to madness on the part of its instigator."

She never did get legal about the issue, as there was always a new battle waiting around her corner.

―――――

Ferber's initial reaction to the movie was euphoric. It was a full-hearted "all is forgiven, please come home" endorsement. Practically dizzy with its success, she wrote in a letter to Joe Linz: "After all these years and years of endless work and shooting and picking and turning this way and that it is due to be released in October. It will not, I am rather sorry to say, open in Texas . . . They have tried to cut as much as possible, but it still will be a long picture. But all this brouhaha has resulted, in my opinion, in a superb picture—rich, vital, humorous and compassionate. There is, really, no star performance. It seems to me that they are all good and dimensional."

Either I was not allowed to attend the premiere of *Giant* at the Roxy Theatre in New York City on October 10—it was a school night—or I was not invited. I only remember my mother's long black velvet coat with the emerald-green satin lining floating on her as she went out the door.

George Stevens's Production of *Giant*

(Based on the novel by Edna Ferber)

As far as the general public was concerned, there were only four names that counted in connection to *Giant*. Probably forevermore there will only be those four names: George Stevens, Elizabeth Taylor, Rock Hudson, and James Dean. For some older movie buffs, Chill Wills, Mercedes McCambridge, Jane Withers, and Earl Holliman might be included, and others might add Carroll Baker, Dennis Hopper, and Sal Mineo.

The night of the premiere, in front of New York City's Roxy Theatre, the red-carpet arrivals were being filmed for a half-hour television special, greeted by hosts Chill Wills and TV personality Jayne Meadows (wife of *The Tonight Show*'s creator, Steve Allen). The two do the best they can amid an excitement bordering on chaos. After Wills introduces himself and cites Stevens, Ferber (obeying the contractual stipulation that her name must follow Stevens's wherever *Giant* goes), and the three top stars, he introduces Meadows, and the pair bring up to the microphones George Stevens and George Stevens Jr., who smilingly say little amid the handshakes. Meadows, ever the gracious hostess, mentions that Wills called Stevens "the sweetest director in the world, and if you have anything at all he will get it out of you—and then some." Chuckles all around and the two men exit. Rock Hudson and his wife, Phyllis Gates, are ushered in—both genial, tall, and handsome. Next up is Jack Warner, who allows that it is such an important night that he is wearing a dickey—indicating the starched shirt piece under his black tie. He then commends Wills on his great performance as "Uncle Wally." "Uncle *Bawley*," Wills corrects him.

At one point there is a break for a commercial in between greetings. When they returned, an announcer's voice reintroduces *Giant* as "a big story of big things and big feelings." Next, Jane Withers is ushered in, sweet and bubbly, and accommodatingly says, "Working with George Stevens was about the biggest thrill I've ever had in my whole life." The introductions dwindle from there.

Everyone wanted to see Elizabeth Taylor, who arrived too late for an interview. James Dean, who arguably would emerge the biggest sensation of the evening, would never arrive. And Ferber would spend her evening about thirty blocks away from the Roxy Theatre, in her apartment with the ritual dinner on a tray.

━━━━━━━

The movie, which opened on September 26th, at Grauman's Chinese Theatre in Los Angeles, was a critical success and a box-office sensation on both coasts. Then came the opening at the Majestic Theatre in Houston. Stranger than Ferber's original fiction was the Texas embrace of it. Four years earlier the book had quite literally been an enemy of the state, and now this former pariah had become the high priestess of the Lone Star. There were plaudits such as "the national movie of Texas," "the archetypal Texas movie," and even "the state religion."

There have been many examinations of this geographical reconfiguration. It could boil down to a Ferber line of Leslie's, when she says to her new husband, Bick, upon glimpsing her new home, "Why, you talk about Texas as if it were a state of mind." Bingo. It is. And to paraphrase the old Hollywood trope, "Gable's back and Garson's got him," *Giant* was back and Texas had her.

Whereas Ferber's look was an unforgiving excavation of the greedy Texas soul, Stevens met the task of filming a hated novel in its birthplace. He was truly a maverick director performing a feat of changing the lens. In his previous movie, *Shane*, he held more to the tradition of the cowboy Western, although under the face of it there were similarities to *Giant* in their theme of a changing West. In *Shane* he had portrayed the shift from a cattleman's land to a farmer's. Now, in *Giant*, he was examining the transformative effects of oil, as exemplified by James Dean as ranch hand Jett Rink, arriving at Reata covered head to toe in oil slick, crowing, "I'm rich, Bick. I'm a rich boy. Yes, sir, I'm a richie!"

Stevens's seduction of Texas grew stronger when he chose to direct most of the picture in a location that would best capture the "true" Texas. His stroke of genius came when he hit on Marfa, a location so remote that they couldn't pick up a signal to watch television. Not only did he boost the profile, ego, and economy of Marfa, he immortalized the place.

There is another alchemizing factor connected to Stevens's choice of locale that resonated with Texans. West Texas had been in a seven-year drought, which crippled an economy dependent on agriculture. Now, in Marfa, anyone who needed work could find it on the movie set that had taken over the town. The movie literally saved the town.

The notion of filming on location is a common one today, but it was not then. Most feature films were shot on the back lots of the monopolizing studios: Warner Bros., MGM, Paramount, and 20th Century–Fox. These were still considered the days of the studio system, where power was wielded over every aspect of production, from who the extras were to what the stars ate for lunch.

There was something more threatening than any King Kong monster the studios could have manufactured, and that was television, which would erode the absolute power of the "major motion picture." The way the studios fought back was to produce epics packed with the hottest stars they could find or manufacture. *Giant* filled this bill with a budget of more than $5 million.

It made Texans proud to constantly read articles about the filming of *Giant* in their newly discovered backyard—little Marfa.

There were native Texans all over the place, helping to create a national monument. Billy Lee Brammer, who would later become one of the most promising indigenous writers with his novel *The Gay Place*, wrote an article about the filming called "A Circus Breaks Down on the

Prairie." He wrote, "It's the sheer magnitude of the operation that does it. It seems they came equipped for anything."

It was impressive that when there were no tumbleweeds to be found around the area, a truckload of them was brought in from California. There didn't seem to be any oil-producing wells around, so a mock rig was erected for the scene where Jett Rink strikes oil. And the estate that Ferber had conceived in the middle of the vast lands of Reata was a $250,000 expense to be constructed by the Warner Bros. crew, shipped to Marfa, and assembled by another crew imported for just that task. When a scene was depicted featuring Christmas at the Benedicts', a Douglas fir was cut down in the Sequoia National Forest and transported to the set. When it was discovered that Marfa had no lab in which to process film, the dailies were flown overnight to LA, processed, and flown back the following morning—in time for Stevens to show the rushes to the whole town that evening.

All these feats contributed to the glory days connected with the movie and to the proud reaction of Texans. There were also diplomatic factors: The movie cast dozens of actors who were Texans by birth. There were Fran Bennett, who played the "other" Benedict daughter, Judy, and was an authentic Fort Worth oil heiress; Chill Wills, playing Uncle Bawley, originated from Seagoville, Texas; and "Texas Bob" Hinkle, coach of the rolling walk and drawling speech of his home state.

Texas pride is thematic through the movie, often swerving away from its source, which told an unvarnished version of the Mexican situation. Until *Giant*, Mexicans in movies had been portrayed as either silent, poor, and subservient or as banditos. The sight of a Hispanic war hero, played by Sal Mineo, being given a ceremonial burial was something new and victorious. *Giant* showed a moving scene that Texans could claim for themselves. The larger screen victory was in the now-fabled diner scene. The movie version is harsh but colorful, and although it makes its point, the sign that is thrown on Bick's chest at the end says, "We Reserve the Right to Refuse Service to Anyone." It is a milder version of "No dogs, No Negros, No Mexicans."

In the novel Ferber writes the scene in almost the same way—save for one critical point: Bick Benedict does not appear, and so there is no climactic fight with Sarge, the bigoted owner of the diner. This was a "lesson" scene for Bick, and perhaps for some audience members as well. In it, for having stood up to prejudice against his family, Bick gets the living daylights beat out of him. And in this scene, as never before in the whole story, we see Leslie holding her Bick's head adoringly, amid broken crockery all around them. We see her being deeply in love with her fallen husband.

This scene made a huge impact on audiences, on critics, and on a fourteen-year-old Mexican American boy named Tino Villanueva from San Marcos, Texas. Sitting alone in one of the back two rows of his local movie theater, he watched the lengthy movie but *witnessed* the scene that directly frames anti-Mexican prejudice: the diner scene.

When I interviewed him, he knew all about being a hard worker. He was born in 1941 into a family of farmworkers: "not the most cheerful of circumstances for a young Chicano boy growing up in the 1940s and 1950s in Texas. Picking cotton around the state was our livelihood, so this meant being away each year from my hometown, engaged in this type of migrant work six to seven months at a time. Sometimes we even chopped cotton, a period right before the cotton began to blossom." How interesting that he says this, as it jibes perfectly with a phrase heard in the musical of *Show Boat*. A lyric goes "Cotton Blossom, Cotton Blossom . . . ," coincidentally what Ferber had named the boat.

A sure way to accelerate prejudice and to keep Hispanics picking cotton was the posting of signs in front of Texas restaurants such as "No Dogs Negroes Mexicans"—one that in fact was sponsored by the Lonestar Restaurant Association in 1942. In East Texas in the 1950s it got worse: "We Do Not Serve Mexicans, Niggers, or Dogs."

These signs relate to the diner scene in *Giant*, which relates to Villanueva as a young boy who witnessed it in the back rows of the theater: "I had no idea what the movie was about, really, but how could I not notice the host of Hollywood stars appearing in it—Rock Hudson, Elizabeth Taylor, James Dean, Dennis Hopper, Sal Mineo (the latter three had a remarkable screen presence the year before in *Rebel Without a Cause*). I saw *Giant* by myself that afternoon and reached home later than usual. No family member, that I know of, went to see the film."

At first, Villanueva went about his life as usual, simply having absorbed an extra-long movie: "It was an engaging film, no doubt, which I had just seen; but I don't see where it influenced me one way or another. I didn't particularly want to see the roadside café scene, that's true, for it reminded me of reality, meaning that that part of the film was documentary-like and I preferred not to be reminded of the way people that looked like me were treated at some restaurants in Texas. I wanted to see a more positive image of my community. I soon forgot the film and went back into the gladsome world of baseball."

The viewing of *Giant* must have stayed buried in his psyche for quite a while until one scene—the diner scene—sprang to life in the form of a crisis, manifesting in a work by Villanueva comprised of twenty-one poems. It is called *Scene from the Movie "Giant."*

Published in 1993, it is intended to be read in one sitting. The focus is the fight scene in Sarge's Diner. The narrator is a fourteen-year-old boy who is retelling the effect on him of witnessing the scene. The reader witnesses not only the boy's trauma but the poet's realization that he, as a Mexican American, is vulnerable to the same prejudice as his narrator. It unfolds like a fever dream, penetrating the one scene from multiple angles. Villanueva writes in the volume's foreword:

> . . . *I climbed out of bed and in my head*
> *Was a roaring of light—words spoken and unspoken*
> *Had brought the obliterated back. Not again (I said,*
> *From my second-floor room) . . . let this not be happening.*
> *Three and-a-half hours had flicked by. As the sound*
> *Trailed off into nothing, memory would not dissolve.*

In 1994, *Scene from the Movie "Giant"* won the American Book Award.

———————

In Hollywood-speak, the movie opened big. Rock Hudson remembered that prior to the Texas premiere, there were threats of shooting holes in the screen, but by the time it was released, the Texans either had mellowed or had gotten curious; they turned out in droves. John Rosenfield, film critic for *The Dallas Morning News*, wrote a piece discussing the unexpected turnabout called "Texans Can Take It." In *Variety*, the last line of the review stated, "At the b.o., it can't do anything but collect Texas-size chunks of coin."

The movie was pronounced an unqualified smash. Ferber was not so quickly dazzled. She suffered a bruise from a hometown movie critic that wouldn't go away. Bosley Crowther bashed her in the *Times*: "Mr. Stevens has made a heap of film. Hewing pretty closely to the content of Miss Ferber's agitating tale of contemporary Texas cattle barons and nouveau riche oil tycoons, Mr. Stevens and his able screenplay writers, Fred Guiol and Ivan Moffat, have contrived a tremendously vivid picture-drama that gushes a tawdry tragedy . . ."

"Agitating"! "Tawdry"! Although the two words pertained more to the screenplay than her novel, they seemed to coincide with a bad attack of trigeminal neuralgia. We were not to disturb her for weeks. Her housekeeper, Molly Hennessy, kept us informed of her condition. I can hear her thick Irish brogue: "Miss Ferber is not so good. The pain makes her a fairy." That's what we thought she'd said until we puzzled it out. What she had said was "The pain makes her afraid."

The Face seemed to strike most savagely when Ferber was at home. She was making consistent and sometimes lengthy trips to Alaska between 1955 and 1957 and seemed quite hardy in photos and in her letters.

Although *Giant* had demanded more brutal and often contradictory research, and keener writing, Ferber felt more alive in Alaska while preparing her new book. "Alaska air was my non-alcoholic martini," she said, and then, raising it to a biblical level, "a kind of deep-freeze Garden of Eden." She'd been ruminating about her last two choices of subject matter: "Texas . . . and Alaska . . . were as unlike as the moon is unlike the sun. One thing only they had in common. Vastness."

Between bouts of geographical dislocation and physical swings from exhilaration to pain, she was beginning to sum up her life. It seemed the *Giant* experience had a good deal to do with her coming to terms:

> That same psychiatrist whose name escapes me for the moment because he never existed and I never, therefore, have consulted him—if this one actually had been my mentor he possibly could have told me why all the major women of my fourteen full-length novels have been stronger than the major men characters. If this quaint writing conceit had been deeply diagnosed, however, I might have become self-conscious about it and quite possibly would have been unable to write about

either men or women. This would have deprived me of a vast amount of work and pleasure; also, my livelihood.

The reaction to Elizabeth Taylor's performance of Leslie in *Giant* dovetailed with Ferber's intentions. Taylor seemed to intuitively support the original creation, bringing surprising crackle and spine into her delivery. It was a quality more than the lines spoken. Some critics mentioned her well-shaded ambivalence in her marriage, not only to Bick but to all that he held reverent. They also mentioned her makeup: "Miss Taylor gives a fine performance, lilting in youth and sturdy in age, suggesting the latter much better through her own acting ability than through the overdone makeup."

Another critical assessment of Taylor's Leslie is more appreciative of Taylor, her character, and her costumes: "Miss Taylor, whose talent and emotional ranges have usually seemed limited, turns in a surprisingly clever performance that registers up and down the line. She is tender and yet stubborn. Curiously enough, she's better in the second half of the film, when her hair begins to show some gray, than in early sequences. Portraying a woman of maturity, who has learned to adjust to a different social pattern, Miss Taylor is both engaging and beautiful. Her costumes, incidentally, are most attractive throughout."

It was a subtle but no less powerful form of feminism embodied by Taylor that was being lifted from the novel and offered in the movie. Taylor was certainly ready to explore this after being a violet-eyed Aphrodite on the screen since girlhood. And Stevens, to his extreme credit, was leading but also willing to be led through her surprising performance.

Ferber had to have been gratified by Herbert Kupferberg's review in the *New York Herald Tribune,* which acknowledged what she had fought for: "Elizabeth Taylor's portrayal of Leslie Benedict, the high-spirited wife with a mind of her own, is compounded of equal parts of fervor and Ferber, and she grows old with a grace and sweetness that can arouse only admiration and envy."

And then, Kupferberg's salute to Stevens's savvy bound the two of them closely together: "By reserving most of the social implications of Miss Ferber's novel to the very end of the picture, director Stevens manages to keep them in reasonable perspective and yet to set them forth with stunning climactic effect."

There was a tendency to neglect the fact that Stevens wasn't the first here. He is next in line—as is every good director—to the origins that attracted him. It was as if these characters sprung from the head of Zeus, like his daughter Athena did. It was mostly overlooked that these characters were Ferber's creations.

After the three major openings of the movie, in New York, LA, and Houston, George Stevens was all business, and fraught business at that. There was the rest of the country to worry about. In November 1956, he wired Jack Warner to quite literally get his act together:

> I HAVE FOUND IT TOTALLY IMPOSSIBLE TO GET THE INFORMATION WHICH I HAVE NEEDED AS TO DATES OF THE OPENING OF THE FILM "GIANT" IN SITUATIONS AROUND THE COUNTRY TO DATE . . .
>
> REVIEWS FROM THESE CITIES I LOOK UPON AS VERY IMPORTANT PROMOTIONAL MATERIAL. ON ACCOUNT OF BEING UNINFORMED AS TO DATES AND PLACES, I HAVE BEEN ABLE TO OBTAIN ONLY AN INSUFFICIENT SAMPLING . . .
>
> I WOULD NOT BURDEN YOU WITH THIS IF IT HAD NOT DEVELOPED INTO A SITUATION WHICH I CONSIDER AS OF THIS DATE, NOVEMBER 14, INTOLERABLE.

Stevens was doubly displeased with the advertising campaigns that had been launched. A good deal of the copy made *Giant* less of a woman's inroad in a male-dominated frontier and more of a sizzling love triangle. Warner Bros. ran an ad with pictures of the three stars looming large. Rock Hudson is shown giving Taylor a lusty look with a caption that reads: "Bick Benedict, owning so much except the one part of Leslie's life that is no part of his." Then there is Dean with shirt unbuttoned, looking down at Taylor, who is on her knees, gazing up: "Jett Rink, the outsider—and Leslie, wealthy and beautiful." The most over-the-top lurid portion of the ad shows a lascivious-looking Dean with the caption: "Jett Rink's shack. No one has ever set foot in it—and then, suddenly, Leslie."

¡Caramba!

Stevens's worries accelerated along with the box office success of the picture. There had been advance rumbles of a racial backlash among the Hispanic population. Shortly before the actual release of *Giant*, tester cards had been dispensed at a series of previews for California audiences. Many of the older members still felt strongly about the racial disharmony between some Mexican Americans and white Okies during the Great Depression. The cards signaled trouble: "True theme of the picture—Mexicans disliked in Texas, although Texas did belong to Mexico," was one statement, and others objected to "the racial stuff" and "the emphasis on the anti-Mexican part." One relatively young woman wrote about Stevens's focus on the Mexican American theme without attention being paid to Ferber's other issues with Texas: "Not enough ridicule of Texas as in the book—wetback problem became the dominant one."

The studio responded by playing a card that threatened to backfire. They might have been goaded into a bad decision by one particular response, which read, "I don't think this is a picture to be shown abroad." The Warner's executives bypassed George Stevens's production team and edited the version to be released in Mexico and other Latin American countries.

Stevens personally told Ferber about what he considered an insider's betrayal: "I have had no information in regard to this from anybody. It seems from the newspaper that Warners have quite definitely done this. They are doing it, of course, without any legal right."

She reacted strongly and knowledgeably. She also couldn't resist a little one-upmanship:

> As I had read of this months ago, I naturally thought you knew about the picture-cuts for Mexico. I was appalled at the time. Also, I read that these cuts are to be made (or have been made) for all Spanish-speaking countries, including, of course, the South American Spanish-speaking countries whose audience potential is very large. When I read of this the first thought I had was Texas. This, thought was due to Texas pressure because of the Mexican-Texas labor situation. I don't know if you have seen Texas (Mexican labor) work camps. Down around the Brownsville border I visited a ranch which was paying 25 cents an hour for Mexican labor.

Conspiracy theories were not born yesterday, as Ferber had concluded. In this next bit of her letter to Stevens, she cautions, "Texas could bring a lot of pressure to bear on Warner for a cut in the Mexican showing. I don't know what their interest would be in South America."

This was an unproven possibility. Oil could have been another motive. There is an early 1948 document by Carey McWilliams that points out "the oil elites' growing investments in Hollywood." This could have a link to Ferber's portrayal of Jett Rink's rise to oil power, which enabled him to fully express his racism. Subsequently, this could have offended oil companies whose feathers Hollywood executives did not want to ruffle.

Another possible answer to why the film was cut for Mexican and Latin American audiences could have been a clumsy attempt at tact. A review for a Mexican periodical called *Cine Universal* suggested that the scenes from the story reflecting white racial prejudice were cut so as not to offend and garner negative publicity from Mexico. The picture was reduced from twenty-two reels to nineteen, deleting seventeen minutes of screen time. The response from Warner Bros. was one of too-late blues: "Since *Giant* was amputated of all that 'smelled' like racial discrimination, the picture remains 'cut-off,' confusing, very long and without detail in that which refers to the Benedict family. It is a shame that this happened."

Roundup

In a real sense, the death of James Dean drove this picture home in popularity, finances, and artistry. Dean is the one who is remembered, who is in bronze. In fact, his is the name most associated with *Giant*.

Nowhere in the realms of written criticism does there seem to be a negative assessment of Dean's performance in *Giant*—or Taylor's or Hudson's, for that matter. The movie was considered a lucky charm for all three reputations, although Taylor had proved herself on the screen since childhood. Hudson, who was perhaps the most overlooked, reflected on the good luck of being cast at all. He had to be borrowed from Universal, but he had the right age span—at twenty-nine he could dip to the early twenties and stretch to the mid-fifties—and he had a reputation for being easygoing. Moreover, his salary request was not extreme.

Now, in retrospect, we know that Hudson was complicated. Forced to lead a suppressed life at that time, he wore the cloak of amiability—not to be mistaken for being a patsy. He had definite likes and dislikes. He adored Taylor, defining her as an "earth mother," and hotly defending her when she felt too stricken to perform right after Dean died. He voiced his antipathy toward Dean, saying, "Once you got into the habit of Jimmy Dean . . . he had his own style; you could not alter that style; you had to go along with him, had to do things his way."

All in all, Hudson had a transformational time doing *Giant*—as did his agent, Henry Willson, who because of placing Hudson was able to sign on two of his other clients, Jane Withers and Fran Bennett. In the aftermath, Hudson's career had ignited to the point where he wanted a piece of *Giant*. At that time, it was a bold request.

He was taken seriously. He had approached Morris Ernst as well as Henry Ginsberg. In this letter from Ernst to Ginsberg, one can feel the wheels being put into motion. The letter is a trailblazing one for what is now relatively standard for production companies and their stars:

> Margaret and I had dinner a few nights ago with Rock Hudson and his gracious bride. I just want you to know that I congratulated him on hooking up with you. It is about time actors got some sort of an option to buy hunks of pictures. I have not explored the possibilities but have often thought that it might be wise for the Giant Company to allow the stars to buy for cash small pieces of the property, or in the alternative, to give one or two leading actors an option to buy. The option could run for thirty days after the opening. Producing company of the Giant type that takes a step in this direction would find that it has every actor begging for participation in the company's next picture.

Rock Hudson was a trailblazer in more ways than one.

Elizabeth Taylor's life changed radically in the aftermath of *Giant*. Respect for her as an actress seemed greatly enhanced. It was reported that while she was away filming *Giant*, her husband supposedly was busy booking the services of strippers who made house calls. Wilding may have been considered the "forgotten husband" at that time, but earlier he had been thought of as a catch and had been heavily pursued by Taylor. He was one of the most popular stars in England when they met there in 1949; she was only sixteen and filming *Conspirator* with Robert Taylor. Three years later, when she was back in England filming *Ivanhoe*, she fell madly in love with Wilding. Their twenty-year age difference led to an *A Star Is Born* kind of scenario: when she made *Giant*, she was on the upswing, he was on the descent. In a relatively short time she changed partners from Wilding to the producer Mike Todd. In a strange way this pleased Ferber, who thought Todd was smashing and had very much wanted him to realize her novel *Great Son* as a movie.

George Stevens had another project on the docket relatively quickly. *The Diary of Anne Frank* seemingly could not have been farther from the world of *Giant*. However, it also dealt with prejudice—albeit to a horrifying extreme—as well as familial loyalty.

Giant would follow Stevens into 1957, when he won his second Oscar for Best Director. His first had been for *A Place in the Sun*.

One of the most audacious ascents was that of Carroll Baker, twenty-five when *Giant* was released. Ironically, she was nine months older than Elizabeth Taylor, who played her mother. *Giant* had been her first film, and although she had said she was "insecure" and had wanted to "start out with a little less profile" than she would have in a leading role—and supposedly others were offered to her—she made an authentic mark. This made her next performance all the more anticipated. It proved what director Elia Kazan had already known when he had cast her in the title role in *Baby Doll* prior to the filming of *Giant*.

Marfa, Texas, 1955

She had barely finished her work on *Giant* when she found herself in a slip in Benoit, Mississippi, playing the original nymphet in whose footsteps *Lolita* would follow in 1962. Inadvertently, she caused a scandal in Times Square in the fall of 1956 when a 135-foot billboard of her as Baby Doll—part of a publicity campaign—was denounced by Cardinal Francis Spellman of Saint Patrick's Cathedral, and ultimately the film wa condemned by the National Legion of Decency.

And the Winner . . .

The three-hour-and-eighteen-minute movie with no intermission (termed "Lawrence of Marfa") was nominated for Academy Awards in nine categories in 1957. They were Best Picture; Best Director; Best Actor; Best Actress in a Supporting Role; Best Screenplay, Adapted; Best Art Direction/Set Direction, Color; Best Costume Design, Color; Best Film Editing; and Best Music Score of a Dramatic or Comedy Picture. Factually, it clocked in at ten nominations, because it included two for Best Actor—Rock Hudson and James Dean.

George Stevens was up against directors William Wyler for *Friendly Persuasion*, King Vidor for *War and Peace*, Michael Anderson for *Around the World in 80 Days*, and Walter Lang for *The King and I*. Most film pundits have concurred with the choice—save for the renowned French director François Truffaut, who called Stevens's *Giant* "silly, solemn, sly, paternalistic, a demagogic movie without any boldness, rich in all sorts of concessions, pettiness, and contemptible actions." It was one of the biggest hits of that year in France. In US and Canadian rentals during its initial release, it earned $12 million (equivalent to about $140 million today).

Modern watchers of award programs, especially Hollywood's "biggest night," are used to a bit more pomp surrounding the presentation of the coveted Best Director award than what took place on March 27, 1957.

Comedian Jerry Lewis was the host of the evening. He turned the presentation over to Ingrid Bergman, who happened to be in Paris on the roof of her hotel. Somewhat awkwardly she introduced the Arc de Triomphe and the Eiffel Tower. She then ran off the list of nominees, among them George Stevens for "*The Giant*." She then turned the proceedings back to Lewis to announce the winner. He did so quickly. Stevens strode up with an unsmiling face, collected the Oscar, and said, "As the director chosen from this fine group of nominees, let me say that the director's chair is a fine place to see a film." He gave a short half smile and strode off. Almost half a decade devoted to one movie and that was it.

Ferber had watched the ceremony on a small Magnavox television in Molly's room in the back of her apartment. When my mother called with congratulations, she sounded wintry and told her that the whole thing had been "too much trouble." Perhaps Ferber's hopes for *Giant* were never realized. Stevens had accommodated her wishes for Leslie's racial activism and had made Jett more complex as a sympathetic villain, but censorship took the sting out of the novel's main focus on race and gender problems for both national and international releases. Perhaps Ferber felt that ultimately Stevens made a "man's movie" and not Leslie's movie. However, studio publicity and reviews championed Stevens for the racial bravery that was already there in Ferber's novel.

This rationale of Ferber's disappointment seems to resonate in a letter to Ken McCormick shortly after the premiere: "The thing eventually will turn out to be enormously profitable, I suppose, but it never will be worth the annoyance and irritation and time and precious energy it has cost me. I wish I could walk away from the whole thing right now and never hear of it again."

Perhaps Stevens didn't look entirely elated because between the picture's release and the trophy he was handed was an unpleasant year in terms of *Giant*. The triumvirate of himself, Ginsberg, and Ferber was on shaky ground at the start of 1957, as is reflected in a letter Ferber wrote to Ginsberg. It addresses an amendment that was to be made— ironically—because of the success of the picture. It is interesting to note that she goes solo, hammer and tongs, at these seeming infidelities instead of leaving the messy business to her lawyers.

> In our telephone conversation of about ten days ago you said, to my surprise, "The partnership sum of money due at such time as the picture (*Giant*) is fully paid for, has dwindled from $250,000 to $175,000. Did you know that?"
>
> No, I didn't know it. But now, knowing this fact, I think I must request that no further use of the remaining sum be made without the consent and signature of the three partners, prior to the contemplated use of further sums.
>
> I have signed the amendment, and copies, which you sent to the Ernst office, and they are hereby returned. I ask you, when Warner Brothers signature has been affixed, to return a copy for my files, or the Ernst office files.
>
> This amendment was made necessary, your letter said, "because of the extended run of the picture."
>
> It is pleasant to know what *Giant* has achieved; in a number of cities it runs longer than originally planned. If, as this amendment shows, additional hundreds of thousands are to be allocated to advertising in the first two months of the picture's career, this picture will practically never yield a return to the partners.
>
> My contention is that there must now be a curb set on the money spent on the completed picture, *Giant*.
>
> I recollect that you stated in your letter that you and George Stevens were employing a tax expert in the matter of clearing the tax situation on the partnership share of *Giant*. This is all extremely confusing. Is an auditor to be engaged to handle the situation? Where? In New York or in Hollywood? Though I have never commissioned the Ernst office to investigate the tax situation, and you state you have never commissioned them to do this work, Mr. Ernst and Mrs. Pilpel insist that they have investigated this situation, visiting Washington to do so. Is your tax man also working for me?
>
> I have been writing and, in connection with writing, handling business situations for decades. I have never encountered a muddled situation such as this.

The Blackwell School, Marfa, Texas, in 2019, unchanged since it
was built in 1919. It inspired Ferber to investigate the treatment of
Mexican Americans in Texas.

Because she pouched her letter, Henry Ginsberg received it quickly
and two days later pouched back his response: "I find nothing in any
of my letters stating that we intend engaging tax people . . . I am the
one who is confused about the content of your letter . . . which in the
main is repetitious considering the number of letters that I have written, along with the contractual records that exist with respect to all of
these questions."

This head-scratching took place in January 1957. In August, Giant
Productions was officially dissolved. The partnership made up of
Stevens, Ferber, and Ginsberg had done its duty and run its course.
There was a bit of financial altruism involved when the original 1953
contract was signed. The voided contract contained a potent clause—
one that was to be extremely beneficial to my mother, Janet Fox Goldsmith; her sister, Mina Fox Klein; and their mother, Fannie Ferber Fox.
Ferber had stated that she was acting "in their behalf" by becoming
a partner. In dissolving the contract, it would seem that those three
women's benefits would stop. Not so. On May 20, 1957, Ferber had
signed a drafted letter that enabled her to extend the rights granted in
1953 to September 20, 1980. Even though Giant Productions would no
longer exist, payments would continue for Janet, Mina, and Fannie.

The outcome of the dissolution of Giant Productions turned in Ferber's favor. The help, vigilance, and support she received from Harriet Pilpel and Morris Ernst were incalculable. They were devoted in the old-fashioned way, meaning they were always available and would change their personal plans if need be. They worked for—not with—Edna Ferber, which was a vow of sorts. Their sense of professional pride would not let her down. She was part of their reputation.

The postscript is that Ferber went rogue. She was advised to enter into an agreement with Warner Bros., that would pay her $650,000 for her one-third interest in the *Giant* negative upon her exit from Giant Productions. So, she officially became a part of the Warners engine in April 1958, when the studio paid her more than $18,750,000—which was 11 percent of the movie's gross—because she accorded them the television rights. She was able to do this because she held the underlying rights, assured that wherever the film went, so did her name.

The movie and those attached to it continued to trail Ferber. Elizabeth Taylor and her new husband, Mike Todd, became part of her social life when they were in town. In a charmingly kooky note Taylor sent to Ferber, she wrote: "Dearest Edna, don't mind us. We're back and want to give you a buss." James Dean was never far. Harriet Pilpel wrote in a letter about a piece she had seen: "I am sending it along because I know of your keen interest in Mr. Dean." And Morris Ernst, in a letter discussing movie interest in *Ice Palace,* wrote, "At the proper time, however, I will suggest that if you can pick the director of your choice, a duplicate of the form of enterprise set up for *Giant* would appear to be inviting. This, although no one could have prophesied when the deal was first made, the odd complexities of the director of *Giant*."

Giant was a fixture for the rest of Ferber's life. Akin to a benediction is one of her preparatory notes for the novel: "Certainly there were locutions and colloquialisms characteristically Texan. Words and expressions of the region. But they deliberately talked Texan. They assumed a role. It was, or carried with it, an assumption of homily illiteracy. They were playing a character Texan, as though it were expected of them. They knew, 'I'm not going.' They said, 'I ain't a-goin'.'"

Ferber: A Giant in Her Time— Why Not Today?

Edna Ferber's fame and ardent readership lasted for more than half a century. She was not a radio or television personality, nor was she profiled frequently by the press. She was a serious and prolific writer, who happened to be female. However, her novels held substantial appeal to men as well. She was a storyteller, a writer of popular fiction. And herein lies the rub, I think, as she is hardly ever read anymore. Unlike a "classic" writer, forever green on student's reading lists, Ferber's popular novels have all but vanished.

Occasionally, I will come across a blog that exalts Edna Ferber. Usually, it is a woman who has discovered the powerful impact of Ferber's work. The gist of the question asked and comments made is: "Why isn't she read today? She is so contemporary in her depiction of men and women within a prescribed structure. She is great at characterizing the personality and values of various states in our Union. Where has she gone?"

Her books are still here. Readers have gone elsewhere. They want sensation; they want abstraction; they want quirky; they want "outsider" antiheroes with whom to identify. They do not want American dreamers whose reality, when they finally "make it," alters their dream. Ferber exalted all walks of American life. For her, the melting pot never got tired. Her heroes and antiheroes were given equal opportunities. She dealt each of her characters a fair hand. Readers seem to have grown out of caring whether characters have equal opportunities in America. The American dream is precarious, and readers seem more intrigued by and embracing of damaged characters who are thwarted from leading the life they could have or would have carved for themselves.

Edna Ferber understood disappointment but not doom. She believed in hard work and deep hope. I'm not sure that those are the values reflected in the latter half of the twentieth century and the first quarter of the twenty-first.

As Ferber said: "A closed country is a dying country. A closed mind is a dying mind."

America has grown more complicated and more cynical than the country Ferber wrote about. She could write lean and mean, but not cynical. Her liberal patriotism could be perceived as eccentric today. But what is so quaint about upholding the notion of the land of the free? Ferber was able to locate a moral center in her novels. She laid out a clear map of the better and lesser ways to navigate. Her characters fought and forgave; they learned and grew. Reading Ferber today could be a reintroduction to the values this country once represented. What she had to say pertains to us. Everything is prescient and cautionary. The content reveals the way we were, but also the way we can be.

> "What could be more exciting! As long as you're fascinated and as long as you keep on fighting the things you think are wrong, you're living. It isn't the evil people in the world who do the most harm. It's the sweet do-gooders who can destroy us."
> —Edna Ferber

Edna Ferber was alert to injustice and did something about it in her work and in her life. There was always more to do, more to point out.

> "A bully must be met with instant repulse or he multiplies his own violence. A placated bully is a hand-fed bully."
> —Edna Ferber

"There is an interesting resemblance in the speeches of dictators, no matter what country they may hail from or what language they may speak."   —Edna Ferber

Many of her novels begin at the end, work back, and then come around again. That is the way she saw the cycle. At the end, we're back where we started.

"No one in the United States has the right to own millions of acres of American land. I don't care how they came by it."
                                                              —Edna Ferber

"Big doesn't necessarily mean better. Sunflowers aren't better than violets."   —Edna Ferber

And Ferber on living:

"To be alive is a fine thing. It is the finest thing in the world, though hazardous. It is a unique thing. It happens only once in a lifetime. To be alive, to know consciously that you are alive, and to relish that knowledge—this is a kind of magic."
                                                              —Edna Ferber

Epilogue

The year was 1977. I was thirty. Rock Hudson was in his early fifties. I was meeting him on the set of *McMillan & Wife* at Paramount Studios in Hollywood, but I had trouble getting onto the set because someone had neglected to call me in. I was rescued by the actor Barry Newman, who believed my story about having lunch with Rock Hudson, and that I was expected to interview him for a biography I was writing about my great-aunt Edna Ferber.

Once on the set, I was in a rarefied atmosphere. This was where a hit show was put together every week. This was where an older mega movie star made an incredible amount of money, and this was where a young actress named Susan Saint James set a hairstyle for a generation of young women.

An assistant with a clipboard asked me if I was acting in the episode being filmed. I told her I was calling for Rock Hudson in order to interview him for a book, feeling I had just raised my status. She told me he would break for lunch soon and that she'd let him know I was there.

Rock Hudson seemed taller than anyone I had ever stood or walked beside. He was courtly, if somewhat distant.

When we reached the commissary, we were met by Rock's press agent. She was pleasant but brisk, indicating that they had just so much time to give a rookie biographer, and that they pretty much were only doing it because I was a relative of Edna Ferber, whose film-adapted novel had given Rock one of the best starring roles of his career.

After we ordered, I pulled out my clunky 1970s tape recorder from my tote bag. I asked if he would mind my taping our session, to which he shrugged, as if to say why would he mind? It is a slight indication that he was not as one hundred percent involved as I was and that it was simply a pro forma interview, all in a day's work.

But when we started to talk about Ferber, his whole demeanor changed. As he ate two cheeseburgers, he mellowed with the memory of his time shooting on the set of *Giant* as well as his personal friendship with Ferber: "She used to talk about her girlhood and the fight she knew she had in front of her. I remember she said something like, 'I had to learn to fight early because I was too little and too ugly.' Edna had a knack of telling things in the palm of her hand. She was a power—but an older power, which is so much more commanding. Older ladies of authority command much more attention than younger women, middle-aged women, or even men—even older men of authority. Edna *was* authority. She was a giant lady, truly."

Postscript

Ferber died of stomach cancer on April 16, 1968, at the age of eighty-three. The Frank E. Campbell Funeral Chapel on New York City's Upper East Side was filled with family, close friends, and business associates. There was no coffin, as her wish was to be cremated. There were flowers, however, in large vases throughout. They were mostly freesias, her favorite.

The speakers were Dore Schary, George Oppenheimer, Ken McCormick, Howard Teichmann, Kitty Carlisle Hart, and Bennett Cerf, who called her a "gallant, dauntless, irrepressible champion of causes she believed in." All said equally appropriate, stirring, often amusing things.

A tall man came in late and stood in the back. It was Rock Hudson. He had flown from Los Angeles to pay tribute to his "giant lady."

When I think about Ferber's happiness in her later life, I reflect on two men who made a difference. George Stevens and James Dean altered her composure for a brief but meaningful time. Each contributed to a different sense of herself. There are two photographs that reflect this: In the first, Ferber is being given a lesson by Dean on how to twirl a lasso. She looks almost girlish in her cotton shirtwaist, feet planted sturdy and wide, ready for an adventure. In the second, she is standing shoulder to shoulder with Henry Ginsberg, Jack Warner, and Stevens, looking purposeful, as if she is on her way to conquering something. "The eyes of Texas are upon her." And she's staring right back.

Acknowledgments

My professional thanks to these good and smart souls who guided me:

Huge thanks to Gregory T. Smith, director of History Piquette, whose help with attaining archival materials was invaluable. He was always at the ready, cheerful, industrious, resourceful, and very kind.

Mary Huelsbeck, assistant director, Wisconsin Center for Film and Theater Research. She has seen to it that nothing is ever impossible. She is the essence of graciousness.

Joan Cohn, heavenly researcher, who found exactly what I needed—and more.

Dina Rubin, a master formatter; she is knowledgeable, efficient, and perceptive.

And to the people who added such nourishing information:

Karen Bernstein, Dr. Andrea Cousins, Héctor García, Earl Holliman, Dr. Candis Cousins Kerns, Ron Martinetti, Carolyn Pfeiffer, Sarah Cousins Shapiro, and Tino Villanueva; and to the late Fannie Ferber Fox, Henry Goldsmith, Janet Fox Goldsmith, Katharine Hepburn, Rock Hudson, Joseph Linz, Ken McCormick, and Harriet Pilpel.

.   .   .

My personal thanks to my lovely, lively, supportive friends and family to whom Edna Ferber is a household name:

Pat Addiss, SuzAnne and Gabe Barabas, Lynnette Barkley, Susan Cohen, Cliff Goulet, Keena Gumbinner, Foster Hirsch, Mark Kaplan, Helene and Chuck Klein, Kate Klein, J. Barry Lewis, Nia Lourekas, Jerry Majzlin, Leonard Majzlin, Lois Oppenheim, Sheilah Rae, Michele Rubin, Holly Wechsler Schwartztol, Patrick Suraci, Lois Walden, Julie Weinberg, Mary Pleshette Willis, and to the late and very dear Peter Klein.

A special thank-you to Carroll Baker for her open-hearted generosity in allowing me access to her "giant" written memories.

My deepest gratitude to my editor, Victoria Wilson, who encouraged me to do a lot of new thinking.

Thank you to Marc Jaffee for sending me what I needed, and to Ben Shields for getting right into the spirit of things. And my deep and abiding gratitude to Lisa Kwan for carrying the torch into production.

Heartfelt thanks to Deborah Goodsite, a true wizard of attaining photo permissions.

Thank you to Genevieve Maxwell at the Margaret Herrick Library, to Mary Ellen Jensen at Alamy, and to Derek and Todd at Photofest for their consistently cheerful help.

Thank you to my agents on this book: Steve Ross and David Doerrer. And thanks to Charles Kopelman for his invaluable help and support in all things Ferber.

Notes

PREFACE

13 In many ways she was very much like: Stein.

PRECOGNITION

31 "I'm really disappointed to learn": Personal letter to her family, date unknown.

32 "Though you've made the reservation": Ferber, *A Kind of Magic,* pp. 99–100.

44 "The blueprints of the house": Ibid., p. 46.

45 "There was the land under my feet": Ibid., p. 48.

46 "There was another reason for my cozy state": Ibid.

61 "In that summer, I learned": Ferber, *A Peculiar Treasure,* pp. 333–35.

THE VARMINT

68 "Mike was in the middle": Cohn.

89 The Blackwell School of Marfa: Blackwell School Alliance.

91 "The sign on the door said": Butcher.

95 "I knew that the old habit was still with me": Ferber, *A Kind of Magic,* p. 262.

96 Naturally, she loved reading: Ferber and Rebecca West kept in touch over the years with sudden flourishes of intimacy on West's part. It appears that she trusted Ferber enough to discuss the nature of her novelist son, Anthony West: ". . . One of the greatest of analysts, Hans Sachs, analyzed Anthony and gave up, said he was not a case for analysis . . . It just happens that a strain of queerness has come out in him, and in a cousin of his, a girl who is the light and life of the British Communist Party. And there is nothing

to do about it—except to see that it happens as inconspicuously as possible, which I will try to do." She signs off with "Blessings on you, and may we meet soon." (April 3, 1956) As I have said, Ferber was only partial to people of (what she thought of as) character. West was in this category.

96 "We've got minds and souls": Showalter, p. 171.

96 And years later Ferber echoed: Ferber, *A Kind of Magic*, p. 340.

103 ". . . I arranged the meal": Groves, p. 158.

105 "Dan had a way of managing": Smith.

125 "The eyes that were too small": Ferber, *Giant*, p. 141.

145 "Texas overwhelmingly despised": O'Connell.

THE BLAZE

157 Her feud with Moss Hart: Another letter from Ferber went out to Kitty Hart, attempting to explain, but maybe making things worse. This letter is classic Ferber: reasonable, furious, hurt, articulate.

> Kitty, dear, you can, as you wrote me, cease to be my friend. But you can't prevent me from being your friend unless you assume a pattern of behavior which I can't imagine in you.
>
> My letter to you didn't mention Moss because he had made it impossible to think of him in terms of friendship.
>
> Moss had just experienced his first success when I met him more than a quarter of a century ago. I've known him through his mounting successes, through the years of his illness [Hart had suffered from debilitating depression until his later years], and then when he had health and you and the children. It was a thing for rejoicing. In all those years he had from me friendship, understanding, appreciation and respect.
>
> In my long life I never had heard directed at me (or at anyone) such undeserved vindictiveness, such venom, as Moss Hart hurled at my bewildered head. Horrified, I could only say, over and over, as I did—but Moss, I don't know what you're talking about, I don't know what in hell you're talking about! And I didn't know. And I don't to this day.
>
> You must believe me when I say that I didn't resent his decision to discontinue work on *Saratoga*. I never understood why he decided to do it in the first place . . . Naturally, I was delighted. When, after a few days of preparatory work, he found that he didn't want to go on with it, he would have needed only to say so, quietly and definitely. Instead he opened a barrage of the most savage and uncalled-for abuse. Myself, I hadn't particularly relished the idea of working again

on a book I had written, years back. I was rewriting, really. But Moss had said he wouldn't do the musical play's book unless I agreed to collaborate.

In the weeks just preceding this ferocious outbreak Moss had experienced your sudden and shocking illness; the children's mumps; his own virus infection; and his disappointment on the Rodgers-Hammerstein decision on *Saratoga Trunk*. Perhaps he had to vent his pent-up emotions on someone and that unfortunate someone was me. This is the kindest interpretation I can put upon his conduct.

As he shouted (among other courtly statements) that he was sick of looking at my granite face, I told myself that I mustn't take this shocking behavior as a normal manifestation. This was, I thought, a man temporarily ill after prolonged strain. I chose to believe this if I could, rather than to believe that this was a deliberate performance for deliberate reasons. It was, in any case, a saddening spectacle. I was, and am, ashamed for this man who was, I had thought, a friend.

The clobber method may be fine for children. I wouldn't know. I don't meekly permit it to be applied to myself.

160 At the time of *Giant's* publication: Leleux.
161 "Many Texans . . . are calling for": Smyth, p. 199.
162 "Miss Ferber's new novel": Kittrell.
170 "Writing about Texas": Tinkle.

AUTUMN IN NEW YORK

178 The director King Vidor was blatantly: Ferber's personal letters.

MORE WAS MORE

204 "How flat it is!": Ferber, *Giant*, p. 109–11.
206 ". . . Edna Ferber . . . deplored": Gill.
207 "Actually, our picture": Production and script notes from the George Stevens Special Collection.
207 "Reading the novel, it's clear": Lambert, p. 274.
207 profiles of the three main characters: The profiles that follow are in the George Stevens Special Collection at the Margaret Herrick Library of Motion Picture Arts and Sciences; see also Lambert.
214 "I want only to say this": Moss, p. 211.
219 ". . . To produce and direct": George Stevens Special Collection.
224 "I feel that Leslie has to quite a degree": Smyth, p. 203.

234 A Warner Bros. press release: Moss, p. 215.

237 "Leslie glimpsed this Jett": Ferber, *Giant,* p. 107.

238 "This guy was fascinating": Moss, p. 216; Jim Silke, interview by the author, December 12, 2001.

238 "They met, and she fell hard": Ferber, *A Kind of Magic,* p. 266.

239 "She was a little nervous": Gavilanes.

245 "I was offered a starring part": Baker, p. 103.

249 Pilpel wrote to Ginsberg: Letter, June 30, 1955.

FILMING WHERE?

250 Clay Evans was nineteen: NPR, "On Location."

253 In the evenings after dinner: Warnock, "Elizabeth Taylor's Summer."

255 ". . . Everything was of an age": Baker, p. 134.

256 This made the characters seem taller: Moss.

258 ". . . It's a cookbook": Hurlburt.

260 Another "sport" among the character-actor crew: Olsson.

262 "When Jimmy was 11": Sessums.

263 "Elizabeth and Rock took this": Baker, p. 135.

266 "He said, 'You Bob Hinkle?'": from a transcript provided to the author by Ronald Martinetti, "The James Dean I Knew."

FERBER ON THE SET

282 "Stevens now has two hours forty minutes": Moss, p. 219.

283 "Contract provides Giant required": Moss, pp. 219, 220.

287 Ginsberg perhaps more: Interoffice communication from Carl Milliken to R. J. Obringer, January 18, 1954.

292 "The day following the finish": Ferber, *A Kind of Magic,* p. 268.

295 In July of 1981, he signed a contract: Raskin, p. 138.

TRUE GRIEF

299 The mourning for Dean was widespread: Castillo.

301 "furious at Taylor's histrionics": Lord, p. 55.

302 "You are a callous bastard!": Kelly, p. 107.

303 "George Stevens is the greatest director": Martinetti.

304 These included Liz (Dizzy) Sheridan: Sheridan wrote of her romance with Dean in a book called *Dizzy & Jimmy: My Life with James Dean—A Love Story* (New York: HarperEntertainment, 2000).

307 "The preliminary estimate for *Giant*": Jack L. Warner Collection

307 "We have been too busy cutting": Memo to J. L. Warner from George Stevens, March 8, 1955; Jack L. Warner Collection.

309 ". . . Sometimes after we have worked": Moss, p. 221.
309 "I want height": Moss, p. 221.

WAITING FOR GEORGE STEVENS'S *Giant*

315 Her good deed had come full circle: Another good deed that she performed
was to record, for Columbia in 1953, her short story "The Gay Old Dog"
as well as "An Incident from *Show Boat*"—a recording that happened to
prove very popular among US Army officers. She received a most extraordinary letter from a certain major in Fort Campbell, Kentucky, which
she acknowledged by saving and marking certain passages. The letter says
so much about how she affected him; it says so much about the best of
Edna:

> I hope you will excuse this letter, but it is something I feel I
> must write. Tonight sitting in my room at the Officers' Quar-
> ters I heard you read . . . The most amazing thing about it was
> your voice . . . so young, so vibrant. It just wasn't possible that
> this was the voice of the woman who for thirty years has been
> top-ranking American novelist. Or maybe it is; perhaps that
> explains a great many things about you. And it did, after all,
> match the picture on the album cover—the really beautiful
> face, so lightly limned by the marks of living.
>
> But the outstanding moments came during your last selec-
> tion, when you talk about Buchenwald. You mentioned that
> you have always been "stage struck." That isn't quite true, Miss
> Ferber. You are not "Stage Struck" at all. The voice I heard
> was that of a great artist. As you talked, I suddenly found
> myself with tears in my eyes (that hasn't happened within
> my memory). It was not only in the words, but it was some-
> thing behind the words, something so deep that only those
> who have experienced the feeling would recognize it. The only
> comparison I can make is with those wonderful movies that
> Garbo used to make, when, with a single gesture and a word
> or two, she was able to strike right thru the plastic screen and
> the loudspeaker into your insides.

The major goes on, including long, wrenching passages about his experience having to view the Buchenwald camp, some of which Ferber circles as
if to render it indelible. He ends with:

> And all this came back tonight when I heard your plan-
> gent voice talking about Buchenwald. People forget. But you
> haven't forgotten and anyone who has seen these things will
> know that the instant they hear your voice. I am sorry that

your many gifts precluded my ever seeing you where you really belong . . . in the theatre . . . moving people by your voice as well as your typewriter.

FINAL CUT

316   Because Hornbeck had worked so well: Bill Hornbeck had a matter-of-fact ego that directors highly valued, and woe to the one who challenged it. Joseph L. Mankiewicz once tried, as Hornbeck recalled:

> I've heard editors say you couldn't cut while the camera's moving. I've always cut when the camera's moving. I've never let it bother me . . . Joe . . . said, "Well, I made a scene today that you can't handle." So we ran it, and when the scenes were over, I said, "What do you mean, I can't handle it?" And he said, "Well, you cut it and you'll find out." So I cut the scene together, and ran it for him the next night. And he said, "Well, for God's sake, it worked!" And I still didn't know what he was talking about. He said, "You know, I have an editor at Fox, and she told me you never can cut on a moving camera." Well, it isn't so at all. It depends on where you cut. You can't cut anywhere in a moving camera. But he was so delighted; he said, "Well, I learned something now." . . . If you get the right action you can cut. The audience are not watching the camera move, they're watching the players. You can't do it all the time. And Mankiewicz was so sure that he was going to have a retake. (Thompson and Bordwell, p. 38)

316   "the studio was getting very irritated": Thompson and Bordwell, p. 39.
317   "I had organized it": Moss, p. 222.
317   "The film ran about": Moss, p. 222.
318   "Long beforehand, I wanted to see": Cronin, pp. 102–3.

GEORGE STEVENS'S PRODUCTION OF *Giant*

323   The introductions dwindle from there: Dennis Hopper is commandeered next, along with a pretty young blonde. "Is this your wife?" Meadows inquires. "No, no," Hopper laughs, "it's not my wife!" The woman is Joanne Woodward, before her marriage to Paul Newman and before *The Three Faces of Eve*. Next comes Carroll Baker, who announces that *Giant* was her first movie, this is her first opening night, and she's terribly excited, to which Meadows replies, "Of course you must be! Well, I hear that Elia Kazan says that you're going to be a great star, so with Elia Kazan and George Stevens you will be, I'm sure."

324   The movie literally saved the town: See Warnock, "*Giant* and That Texas State of Mind."

325   "It's the sheer magnitude of the operation": *Texas Observer*, July 4, 1955.

327   The viewing of *Giant* must have stayed buried: Villanueva read Ferber's *Giant* at about the time that he wrote the poem. He taught at Wellesley College and Boston University. He might have come late to the novel, but he was very much alive to what he found:

> First of all, I was taken by surprise to see some Spanish sprinkled in certain parts of the text, more than I expected, which, for me, grants Ferber's narrative some linguistic realism. She must have heard an ample amount of Spanish in her travels around Texas, such that she felt it necessary to incorporate some of it into her novel.
>
> The other striking thing is the diner scene . . . It doesn't appear in the novel quite the same way it's depicted in the film . . . The script writers took some liberties here . . . the novel is its own genre, and the scene in chapter 29 where Leslie, Juana and her child are turned away at the roadside diner is dramatic enough, getting across the discriminatory practices of that era in Texas. In her home state of Virginia, this would not have happened to Leslie. It's clear that this scene in the novel has been richly embellished by script writers Fred Guiol and Ivan Moffat for the movie.

I believe Ferber would have admired Villanueva for his combination of truth and tact. While he did not feel that the film was antithetical to the novel, he noted where he thought it went too far in its attempt to introduce a liberal equation:

> I find the final shot overly done, excessively symbolic, hammering home the point that it's 1950, and we've left the old Texas behind . . . we're in a new era now—the latter half of the twentieth century where a new Texas has emerged, with the races a bit closer to each other. After all, we've witnessed the union in marriage of an interracial couple, Jordy (Dennis Hopper), the son of Jordan (Bick) Benedict, get married to the Mexican-American Juana. In this last shot of the baby crib, one observes a brown child and a white child together—the future of Texas, one surmises. Fine. I get it—a more racially unified Texas. My criticism would be that this symbolism need not be duplicated with the black and white sheep inserted in the scene . . .

Ferber concurred about that final shot. At the start of 1957, when many of the returns were coming in from her friends, she wrote to Joe Linz:

". . . You seem to have liked the film *Giant* better than I. Unnecessarily long; scenes (like the Mexican boy's funeral) that went on interminably; lack of pace; that final scene with the dark baby and the light baby, the black lamb and the white lamb . . ."

It is interesting to note how as time went by, she came around to preferring much about her novel to the film. Villanueva was the more impartial of the two: "I would say that the film contains a significant dose of cultural and socio-political commentary, quite in line with what I believe Edna Ferber attempted to highlight about Texas and its new-found wealth, and new position in the world at the beginning of the twentieth century." However, he put forth a personal wish that neither the Caucasian novelist nor the Caucasian director considered for this story: "I, for one, would like to have the 'other side of history' fleshed out. Specifically, I'd like to know a bit more about the Mexican American cowboys who are the ones that really ran the cattle ranch. The Spaniards and Mexicans introduced cattle ranching to that part of what is now the United States, and, with it, a vocabulary migrated into English: bronco, chaps, corral, lariat, lasso, mustang, rodeo, etc."

Ferber's copious notes reflected that she *had* gathered this information, that the Mexican American history *did* compel her—perhaps too much for the story she had in mind to tell. Where she and Villanueva and Stevens— and perhaps Guiol and Moffat—met is ultimately about the character of Leslie. She seemed to come through as the heroine Ferber intended. Villanueva approved of the character: ". . . Leslie, who, for me, comes through as most admirable and whom I relate to. She is the outsider who does what an archetypal outsider does: she distinguished herself for being different, acting counter to custom at times, and, in so doing, brings a set of values absent in her new surroundings."

I think Villanueva was applauding both Leslie and her creator. Ferber fought for the movie's Leslie and won. Mostly.

327   The movie was pronounced an unqualified smash: Crowther.
328   "That same psychiatrist": Ferber, *A Kind of Magic*, p. 283.
329   The reaction to Elizabeth Taylor's performance: Powers.
329   "Miss Taylor, whose talent": *Variety* Staff.
330   Stevens was doubly displeased: Lord, p. 54.
330   "Jett Rink's shack": Ibid.

¡CARAMBA!

331   "Not enough ridicule": *Children of GIANT* was written and directed by Hector Galán, who became interested in making this film when he was researching the notorious Blackwell School in Marfa. "My dad had to go to a segregated Mexican school in West Texas in San Angelo. All of the towns—big towns, little towns—in the Southwest had segregated Mexican

schools. That is what drew me to the story. I started to see the parallels of what George Stevens was doing—trying to tell a story of segregation. It struck me that it was way ahead of its time."

As producer Karen Bernstein told me in an interview:

> There was a bigger story. The story Hector told reflected what happened with Ferber and Stevens—on the same page, and yet, typical of Stevens, in a way that was entertaining.
>
> I got Hector out to Marfa and said, "You have this film to make—this one." He didn't get Marfa. He hated it—didn't understand. Here was this desolate heap. Ferber understood the beauty of the landscape and the indignity of it.

The project came alive for Galán when Bernstein brought him to the town cemetery, where a fence divided Anglo from Latino. Bernstein recalled for Galán a memory from a Blackwell School alumnus who said, "I have relatives on this side of the fence and on the other side. All of these people were related."

Bernstein lamented, "There is this virulent theme of indignity. The question is: what keeps people there, raising families—a bunch of depressed people."

There was a Q&A at the premiere of the documentary where a Caucasian Spanish teacher named John Johnson called for a petition to take the fence down in the cemetery, noting that the community had to give up tearing itself apart. "But the old tensions always reappear," said Bernstein. "It's as recent a story as yesterday."

Bernstein drew a very clear parallel between the two eras. "Hector attracted and responded to the big names at PBS. According to them he was the only filmmaker able to make a profit—similar to Stevens. The Latino Public Broadcasting loved the star quality. They were not looking for the grays and the subtleties. Hector took the simple story aspect. I was hoping that he would focus on Angel's funeral, pointing out the complications dealing with death in the community."

One of the actors who was deeply touched by the documentary was Earl Holliman, who had played Bob Dace, the character who became Bick and Leslie's son-in-law. He and Elsa Cárdenas, who played Juana, Jordy's wife, reunited for Galán's documentary and were interviewed at length. Now a vigorous-voiced nonagenarian, Holliman has two Marfa visits to reflect on, and the moments that made him proud. "There was that whole long funeral for Angel in the movie, and I thought, I was part of that. It was so fascinating to note the difference of me, white boy, being celebrated at the train station for coming home from the war, and then the silent dirge of Angel's funeral. Such a stark contrast. I was proud of being part of that. And then, during the last scene, I turned to Elsa and said, 'Those were our children.' I was surprised in retrospect what a strong division Hector's film points out."

Now making her home in Marfa, Carolyn Pfeiffer, executive producer of *Children of GIANT,* knows the place from the inside. She knows that Marfa is far from a solved habitat. It is 70 percent Latino. The average yearly income today for a Mexican in Marfa is $19,000, even though Mexicans are the backbone of the county. The president of the bank is an Anglo, but the workers are Latino. Inequity is a daily fact, yet a good deal of Marfa's Anglo community is in absolute denial that racism exists. She feels that the film is an honest portrayal of the town, which remains proud of the movie *Giant.* They still project screenings of it on Main Street about once a year.

"In all the positive stories about Marfa and Marfans, there are terrible stories of Mexicans in town and in the movie of *Giant.*" Pfeiffer believes in looking at the bigger picture, as Ferber did. "She was a righteous woman," says Pfeiffer. "She was just, well, righteous."

332 "I have had no information": Letter from Stevens to Ferber, September 18, 1957.

332 Conspiracy theories were not born yesterday: Letter from Ferber to Stevens, September 22, 1957, George Stevens Special Collection.

332 Another possible answer: George Stevens Special Collection.

ROUNDUP

335 "Margaret and I had dinner": Morris L. Ernst, March 12, 1956.

335 Elizabeth Taylor's life changed radically: Taylor's next career move turned out to be unwise. She went into MGM's *Raintree County,* meant to be torrential but which could only be said for its box office, as it turned out to be a turgid, limp variation of *Gone with the Wind.* Taylor's spoiled southern belle is the polar opposite of the racially evolved Leslie Lynnton Benedict. Her new character "goes nuts—babbling, gurgling, and ultimately drowning herself—from fear that she has 'Negro blood'"(Lord, p. 56). Taylor was introduced to Michael Todd in late 1956 through cinematographer Kevin McClory, who had been working on Todd's extravaganza *Around the World in 80 Days.* She filed for divorce from Wilding in November of that year, and with a 24.9-carat diamond engagement ring on her finger, she married Todd in February 1957.

AND THE WINNER . . .

339 Stevens strode up: That evening was stocked with *Giant* alumni as presenters: Carroll Baker for Best Original Song; Rock Hudson (with Eva Marie Saint) for Best Musical Score and Best Dramatic or Comedy Score; Mercedes McCambridge (with Robert Stack) for the documentary awards; and Elizabeth Taylor for the costume-design prizes.

342 The postscript is that Ferber went rogue: See Smyth. It is no surprise that

loving progeny would perpetuate the *Giant* cause. George Cooper Stevens Jr. was Stevens senior's only child. He grew up to be an accomplished pillar of the motion-picture community. He founded the American Film Institute, initiated the AFI Lifetime Achievement Award, produced the Kennedy Center Honors, and co-chairs the President's Committee on the Arts and Humanities.

Having been assistant to his father on *A Place in the Sun, Shane,* and *Giant,* he understood how to honor his pedigree. One of the ways was to make documentaries about his father and his father's filmmaking. He made two of them: *George Stevens: A Filmmaker's Journey* (1984) and *George Stevens: D-Day to Berlin* (1994). The jacket cover on the DVD release of the first shows a photo of George Stevens captured from behind, sitting on a canvas director's chair, seemingly in the middle of nowhere, and gazing straight ahead at the construction that was Reata. Included in the documentary are some generous portions from and about *Giant.* It is clear from the film that Roger Ebert's evaluation of Stevens is right on: "He attracted actors of quality." This documentary is chock-full of them, as was *Giant.*

George Stevens Jr. well understood the labor and ardor that his father put into *Giant.* He understood that the 114-day shoot would run almost two months over schedule and $3 million over budget. He watched as it took a year for his father to edit 875,000 feet of film down to almost three and a half hours of viewing time. He did think his father was more scrupulous about the editing process, suggesting that he stop fixing things after three very positive previews, to which Stevens Sr. replied, "When you think about how many man-hours people will spend watching this picture, don't you think it's worth a little more of our time to make it as good as we can?" (Graham, *Giant*)

"That's kind of a favorite picture," Stevens Jr. has said in reflection. "I worked with my dad on the script and then went in the Air Force for two years and came back and worked with him on the editing. That was the pace he was moving at!"

Stevens Jr. seems to have been more matter-of-fact about James Dean than many others: "He was about what you'd expect for a successful 23-year-old actor. Moody and eccentric and playing a role. I spent a considerable amount of time with him and never really felt any kinship." And weighing in about the whole sports-car issue: "My father had talked to him before the picture. He said, 'Jimmy, you know you can't do that when we're making this picture.' Jimmy resisted and my father said, 'You know, too many people are depending on you, and if you break your arm, you know all these people—that comes to a halt.' And he stopped, put the car away. And then the day he finished, he was leaving the studio and Dad said, 'Where are you going?' He said, 'I'm going up to race the car.' . . . The next night they were in the projection room—Carroll Baker, Rock Hudson and all—and the phone rang. It was the call."

On Ferber's relationship with his father all he had to say was: "They had fun. They kept it light."

Stevens Jr. has never abandoned *Giant.* In 2003, he brought out a newly remastered version in a DVD DigiPak, and then in 2005 he brought out a version that came in a keep case. The transfer is on a two-sided disc and there are bonus features on a separate disc. Although the picture is simultaneously crisp and lush, the "stature" is still and forever a bit squat, compliments of CinemaScope. Stevens Jr. mentions in his commentary how his father desired a sense of height but that CinemaScope was "only useful for the Last Supper."

There are two retrospectives within this version: *Memories of "Giant"* and *Return to "Giant."* Each brings alive various aspects of the filmmaking and the actors' experiences, including their reactions to the death of Dean.

No one could do more for the legacy of the film *Giant* than George Stevens Jr.

Bibliography

Baker, Carroll. *Baby Doll: An Autobiography*. New York: Arbor House, 1983.

Biskind, Peter. *Seeing Is Believing: How Hollywood Taught Us to Stop Worrying and Love the Fifties*. New York: Holt Paperbacks, 2000.

Blackwell School Alliance. "History of the Blackwell School," in "Our Story" (pamphlet). Marfa, TX: Blackwell School Alliance, 2018.

Bordwell, David, Janet Staiger, and Kristin Thompson. *The Classical Hollywood Cinema: Film Style & Mode of Production to 1960*. New York: Routledge & Kegan Paul, 1985.

Brammer, Billy Lee. "A Circus Breaks Down on the Prairie." *Texas Observer*, July 4, 1955.

Bruns, Roger. *Border Towns and Border Crossings: A History of the U.S.-Mexico Divide*. Santa Barbara: Greenwood, 2019.

Butcher, Sterry. "Marfa's Blackwell School Has a Painful Past. That's Why the Town Wants to Save It." *Texas Monthly*, January 2019.

Castillo, Juan. "How '50s James Dean Movie Dared Show Racism Against Mexican Americans." NBC News, April 16, 2015.

Cohn, Art. *The Nine Lives of Mike Todd: The Story of One of the World's Most Fabulous Showmen*. New York: Random House, 1958.

Cronin, Paul, ed. *George Stevens: Interviews*. Jackson, MS: University Press of Mississippi, 2004.

Crowther, Bosley. "Screen: Large Subject; The Cast." *New York Times*, October 11, 1956.

Daugherty, Tracy. *Leaving the Gay Place: Billy Lee Brammer and the Great Society*. Austin: University of Texas Press, 2018.

Ferber, Edna. *A Kind of Magic*. New York: Doubleday, 1963.

———. *A Peculiar Treasure*. New York: Doubleday, 1939.

———. *Fanny Herself*. New York: Grosset and Dunlap, 1917.

———. *Giant*. New York: Doubleday, 1952.

Gavilanes, Grace. "10 Secrets of Rock Hudson's Heartbreaking Final Days." *People*, October 2, 2015.

George Stevens Special Collection at the Margaret Herrick Library, Academy of Motion Picture Arts and Sciences, Beverly Hills, CA.

Gill, Brendan. "Talk of the Town: What Housewives Know." *New Yorker*. July 18, 1953.

Graham, Don. *Cowboys and Cadillacs: How Hollywood Looks at Texas*. Austin: Texas Monthly Press, 1983.

———. *Giant: Elizabeth Taylor, Rock Hudson, James Dean, Edna Ferber, and the Making of a Legendary American Film*. New York: St. Martin's Press, 2018.

Groves, Helen Kleberg. *Bob and Helen Kleberg of King Ranch*. Houston: Bright Sky Press, 2004.

Hall, Carla. "George Stevens: A Life in the Movies." *Washington Post*, April 17, 1984.

Hinkle, Robert. "The James Dean I Knew," in *The Real James Dean: Intimate Memories from Those Who Knew Him Best*, Peter L. Winkler, ed. Chicago: Chicago Review Press, 2016.

Hinkle, Robert, and Mike Farris. *Call Me Lucky: A Texan in Hollywood*. Norman, OK: University of Oklahoma Press, 2009.

Hurlburt, Roger. "Voice from the Past Actress Mercedes McCambridge Has Brought a Special Intensity—and Voice—to Her Roles Since the Days of Live Radio and TV." *Sun Sentinel*, January 23, 1992.

Kelley, Kitty. *The Last Star: The Unauthorized Biography of Elizabeth Taylor*. New York: Simon and Schuster, 1981.

Kittrell, William. "Land of the Boiling Gold." *Saturday Review*, September 27, 1952.

Lambert, Gavin. *The Ivan Moffat File: Life Among the Beautiful and Damned in London, Paris, New York, and Hollywood*. New York: Pantheon, 2004.

Leibson, Art. "The Wetback Invasion." *Common Ground*, Autumn 1949.

Leleux, Robert. "Giant Scandal." *Texas Observer*, August 22, 2011.

Lord, M. G. *The Accidental Feminist: How Elizabeth Taylor Raised Our Consciousness and We Were Too Distracted by Her Beauty to Notice*. New York: Walker Books, 2012.

Martinetti, Ronald. *The James Dean Story: A Myth-Shattering Biography of an Icon*. New York: Birch Lane Press, 1995.

Moss, Marilyn Ann. "Our Town: *Giant*" in *Giant: George Stevens, a Life on Film*. Madison: University of Wisconsin Press, 2004.

O'Connell, Joe. "Book Review: UT Professor on the Making of Texas Film Epic *Giant*," *The Austin Chronicle*, April 13, 2018.

Olsson, Karen. "Besieged by Sophisticates." *Texas Observer*, August 26, 2005.

"On Location: 50 Years of Movie Magic in Marfa, Texas." *All Things Considered*, NPR, July 15, 2011.

Powers, James. "George Stevens' *Giant* an Epic Film in a Class with the All-Time Greats: Giant-Size Drama of Texas Is Big in Scope, Treatment." *Hollywood Reporter*, October 10, 1956.

Raskin, Lee, and Tom Morgan (designer). *James Dean: At Speed*. Phoenix: David Bull, 2005.

Sessums, Kevin. "Elizabeth Taylor Interview About Her AIDS Advocacy." *Daily Beast*, March 23, 2011; updated July 13, 2017.

Showalter, Elaine. *A Jury of Her Peers: Celebrating American Women Writers from Anne Bradstreet to Annie Proulx*. New York: Alfred A. Knopf, 2019.

Smith, Judith Haas. *Larger than Life: The Legacy of Daniel Longwell and Mary Fraser Longwell*. Bloomington, IN: AuthorHouse, 2015.

Smyth, J. E. *Edna Ferber's Hollywood: American Fictions of Gender, Race, and History*. Austin: University of Texas Press, 2010.

Stein, Sadie. "Quivering with Pride." *The Paris Review*, August 15, 2014.

Teichmann, Howard. *George S. Kaufman: An Intimate Portrait*. New York: Atheneum, 1972.

Terry, Marshall. "Texas Classics: For Lon Tinkle, Literature and Texas Were a Perfect Match." *Dallas Morning News*, June 27, 2014.

Thompson, Kristin, and David Bordwell. "From Sennett to Stevens: An Interview with William Hornbeck." *The Velvet Light Trap: Review of Cinema*, no. 20, pp. 38–39.

Tinkle, Lon. "Ferber Goes Both Native and Berserk: Parody, Not Portrait, of Texas Life." *Dallas Morning News*, September 28, 1952.

Variety Staff. "*Giant*." *Variety*, October 10, 1956.

Warnock, Kirby F. "Elizabeth Taylor's Summer in Marfa." *Texas Monthly*, April 2011.

———. "*Giant* and That Texas State of Mind." *D Magazine*, September 1996.

Index

Page numbers in *italics* refer to illustrations.

12 (top) Courtesy of Everett Collection / Alamy

14 (top) Courtesy of Everett Collection

15 TCD/Prod DB / Alamy

64 Entertainment Pictures / Alamy

72 (bottom) Courtesy of cineclassico / Alamy

136 Courtesy of Frank Scherschel / The LIFE Picture Collection / Shutterstock

140 Sophia Smith Collection, Smith College Special Collections, Northampton, Massachusetts

147 With permission of Book of the Month. Courtesy of Julie Gilbert.

153 With permission of Catherine and Christopher Hart. Ferber Family photo collection. Courtesy of Julie Gilbert.

169 Drawing © Jack Markow. *The New York Times Book Review*. With permission of David Fallon.

198 George Stevens papers, Margaret Herrick Library, Academy of Motion Picture Arts and Sciences

231 Core Collection, Margaret Herrick Library, Academy of Motion Picture Arts and Sciences

233 Courtesy of the Everett Collection?

234 mptvimages.com

235 ARCHIVIO GBB / Alamy

236 Photograph by Floyd McCarty. George Stevens papers, Margaret Herrick Library, Academy of Motion Picture Arts and Sciences.

237 Photograph by Bob Beerman. Core Collection, Margaret Herrick Library, Academy of Motion Picture Arts and Sciences

238 Warner Bros. / Photofest

243 mptvimages.com

246 Photograph © Frank Worth / ZUMA Press Wire

247 Warner Bros. / Photofest

248 Photograph by Floyd McCarty. Core Collection, Margaret Herrick Library, Academy of Motion Picture Arts and Sciences

249 Warner Bros. / Photofest

253 Warner Bros. / Photofest

259 Courtesy of Everett Collection

A NOTE ON THE TYPE

This book was set in Adobe Garamond. Designed for the Adobe Corporation by Robert Slimbach, the fonts are based on types first cut by Claude Garamond (ca. 1480–1561). Garamond was a pupil of Geoffroy Tory and is believed to have followed the Venetian models, although he introduced a number of important differences, and it is to him that we owe the letter we now know as "old style." He gave to his letters a certain elegance and feeling of movement that won their creator an immediate reputation and the patronage of Francis I of France.

Composed by North Market Street Graphics,
Lancaster, Pennsylvania

Printed and bound by Berryville Graphics,
Berryville, Virginia